Unhappy Valley

Unhappy Valley

Conflict in
Kenya & Africa

Book One: State & Class
Book Two: Violence & Ethnicity

Bruce Berman
Professor of Political Studies
Queen's University, Ontario

&

John Lonsdale
Fellow of Trinity College, Cambridge

James Currey
LONDON

Heinemann Kenya
NAIROBI

Ohio University Press
ATHENS

James Currey Ltd
54b Thornhill Square
Islington
London N1 1BE, England

Heinemann Kenya
Kijabe Street, PO Box 45314
Nairobi, Kenya

Ohio University Press
Scott Quadrangle
Athens, Ohio 45701 USA

British Library Cataloguing in Publication Data
Berman, Bruce
Unhappy valley : conflict in Kenya & Africa
Book One: State & Class
Book Two: Violence & Ethnicity
1. Kenya. Social conditions
I. Title II. Lonsdale, John *1937*-
967.6203

ISBN 0-85255-021-9
ISBN 0-85255-022-7 (pbk Book One)
ISBN 0-85255-099-5 (pbk Book Two)

Library of Congress Cataloging-in-Publication Data
Berman, Bruce (Bruce J.)
Unhappy valley : conflict in Kenya and Africa / Bruce Berman & John Lonsdale.
p.   cm. —— (Eastern African studies)
Includes bibliographical references and indexes.
Contents: bk. 1. State and class —— bk. 2. Violence and ethnicity.
ISBN 0-8214-1016-4 (Ohio Univ. Press : cloth)
ISBN 0-8214-1017-2 (Ohio Univ. Press : pbk. : bk. 1). ——
ISBN 0-8214-1025-3 (Ohio Univ. Press : pbk. : bk. 2)
1. Kenya——Politics and government——To 1963. 2. Great Britain——
Colonies——Administration. 3. Kenya——Dependency on Great Britain.
4. Kenya——Economic conditions——To 1963. 5. Kenya——History——To
1963. 6. Clans——Kenya. 7. Mau Mau——History. I. Lonsdale, John.
II. Title. III. Series : Eastern African studies (London, England)
JQ2947.A2B47   1992b
325'.341'096762——dc20   91-48091
                                                    CIP

Typeset in 10/11pt Baskerville by Colset Private Limited, Singapore
Printed and bound in Great Britain

iv

Contents

BOOK ONE: *State & Class*

One
Introduction
An Encounter in Unhappy Valley
BRUCE BERMAN & JOHN LONSDALE

Part I
Conquest

Two
The Conquest State of Kenya, 1895–1905
JOHN LONSDALE

Contents

Three

The Politics of Conquest in Western Kenya, 1894–1908

Part II

Contradictions & the Development of the Colonial State

Four

Coping with the Contradictions: The Development of the Colonial State, 1895–1914

BRUCE BERMAN & JOHN LONSDALE

Five

Crises of Accumulation, Coercion & the Colonial State: The Development of the Labour Control System, 1919–29

BRUCE BERMAN & JOHN LONSDALE

Contents

Contents

Maps

Acknowledgements

Some of the chapters in this book were first published in the journals and collections indicated below. We would like to thank the publishers and editors for permission to reproduce them here.

Cambridge University Press
'Bureaucracy and incumbent violence: colonial administration and the origins of the Mau Mau Emergency in Kenya', *British Journal of Political Science* 6(1) (1976).
'The politics of conquest: the British in Western Kenya, 1894–1908', *The Historical Journal* 20(4) (1977).
'Coping with the contradictions: the development of the colonial state in Kenya, 1895–1914', *Journal of African History* 20(4) (1979).

The Canadian Association of African Studies
'Crises of accumulation, coercion and the colonial state: the development of the labour control system in Kenya, 1919–1929', *Canadian Journal of African Studies* 14(1) (1980).
'The concept of articulation and the political economy of colonialism', *Canadian Journal of African Studies* 18(3) (1984).

Sage Publications
'Structure and process in the bureaucratic states of colonial Africa', *Development and Change* 15(2) 1984.

The Leiden Centre for the History of European Expansion
'The conquest state of Kenya', in J.A. de Moor and H.L. Wesseling (eds), *Imperialism and War: Essays on Colonial Wars in Asia and Africa*, E.J. Brill/Universitaire pers Leiden, Leiden, 1989.

The Centre of African Studies, University of Edinburgh
'African pasts in Africa's future', *African Futures*, Seminar Proceedings No. 28, Edinburgh, 1988.

Preface

In writing these papers over a period of some fifteen years, we have incurred many debts to institutions and individuals that have helped our research and sharpened our thoughts, and which we gratefully acknowledge. Kenya has been fortunate in attracting a remarkable body of scholarship since its independence. The calibre of this work has facilitated and inspired our own. Individual authors and works are cited in our footnotes, but we would like to record some special thanks here. This is a more invidious exercise than most; so much good work has been done; and by an unusually generous group of scholars. But we have particularly important debts, both intellectual and personal, to Dave Anderson, David Cohen, Fred Cooper, Michael Cowen, Tabitha Kanogo, Greet Kershaw, Colin Leys, Godfrey Muriuki, Atieno Odhiambo, John Spencer, David Throup, Richard Waller and Luise White.

Our work has been made possible by the remarkable collections and efficient staff of the Public Record Office, London, and, especially, of the Kenya National Archives in Nairobi and its Chief Archivist, Mr M. Musembi. Professor Ahmed Salim, head of the Department of History at the University of Nairobi, offered us the facilities and hospitality of his department during our most recent visit in July and August 1988. He and Professor Henry Mwaniki, head of the Department of History at Kenyatta University, also enabled us to present some of our findings in seminars of their staff and graduate students.

We would also like to thank the Social Science and Humanities Research Council of Canada, the Smuts Memorial Fund of the University of Cambridge, and the School of Graduate Studies and Advisory Research Committee of Queen's University for grants that over the years have made our research possible. The Master and Fellows of Trinity College, Cambridge, have enabled us to work together during the closing stages of this work.

xi

Preface

To James Currey, long-suffering publisher and friend, we owe the idea for this book. His encouragement and his patience through repeated delays were vital in bringing it to fruition. Roger Thomas provided essential editorial assistance; while Dr Jocelyn Murray efficiently compiled the index and glossary.

Finally, we thank our wives, Elaine Berman and Moya Lonsdale, for their patience and understanding in the face of our repeated absences, especially during summer holidays, and our distracted absorption in the problems of Kenya and colonial Africa. We dedicate this volume to them.

Cambridge and Kingston

Glossary

Note: words in this glossary, unless marked, are Kikuyu. Like Swahili, Kikuyu is a Bantu language, and singular and plural nouns are shown by prefixes. For most nouns of the person class, the singular prefix is mu- *or* mw-, *and the plural is* a-.

acenji (mucenji) heathen, savages

ahoi (muhoi) tenant, tenants in friendship

il aigwanak (Maasai) warrior leaders

aimwo good-for-nothings

Akurinu 'growlers', nickname for a sect

anake young men, warriors

anake a forti the unmarried warriors of 1940

andu ago (mundu mugo) medicine man/men; diviners

aramati trustees

arathi prophets

aroti dreamers

aregi 'those who refuse'

athami 'people on the move', migrants

athamaki, (muthamaki) 'those who can speak', 'big men'; Sing. sovereign

athomi readers, = Christian converts

athoni relatives by marriage, in-laws

athoni ahoi friends by marriage

athuuri elders, 'those who choose'

atiriri 'Hear!', 'Listen!'

batuni the 'fighting oath' (from the English 'platoon')

bara (mbaara) fight, battle

buruni country, land

comba (from Sw.) foreigners, Muslims

dini (Sw.) sect, religion

ereriri selfish ones

Gikuyu na Muumbi the Kikuyu 'Adam' and 'Eve'

githaka, (ithaka) land, farms

githukumo waged work

gitonga, (itonga) 'a man of means'; pl. wealth, property

gitungati, (itungati) rearguard

gwika to do

hinya power, strength
hongo (Sw.) road-tolls

ibuku book
ibuku ria Ngai Book of God, =
  Bible
ihii uncircumcised youth
  (insult)
imaramari hooligans
iregi 'those who refuse', a
  generation name
irungu 'straightener', a
  generation name
ithaka na wiathi land and
  freedom; self-mastery through
  land
itonga 'men of means'
ituika generational handover of
  ritual power

kaburu corporal
karing'a true, real
kiama council, society
kiama kia bara war council
Kiama kia Wiathi Freedom
  Council (Mau Mau central
  committee)
kibaata a warriors' dance
kifagio (Sw.) broom, sweeping
kimaramari, imaramari
  hooligan(s)
kipande registration certificate,
  carried by adult African males
kirira silence, secrecy
kiriika destruction
kirore thumbprint, 'those who
  have signed'
komerera bandits
kuna first clearance of land;
  right derived from this
kuuga to say

laibon (Maasai) prophet
'laini' from English 'line':

labour lines, also town
housing

mai ni maruru water is bitter
Maina generation name
mambere those in front,
  forerunners
mangati (Maasai) enemy
mashambaini (Sw.) fields, farms,
  the white highlands
maraya prostitutes
maskini (Sw.) the poor
mbari sub-clan
mikora 'spivs'
miri roots
mitaro trenches, terracing
mkunga mbura rain gatherer,
  rainbow
mucenji heathen, savage
mugumo fig tree, site of sacrifices
Muhimu Nairobi headquarters
  of Mau Mau central
  committee
muhiriga, (mihiriga) clan, clans
muingi community
muiritu circumcised but
  unmarried woman, grown girl
mukuyu fig tree
Mukuruwe wa Gathanga Kikuyu
  'Garden of Eden'
muma oath
mundu, andu man, person; men,
  people
mundu mugo medical
  practitioner, diviner
munene big, chief
muteithia helper
muthamaki one who can speak,
  leader, sovereign
muthami, (athami) one who has
  moved, emigrants
Muthirigu Song of the big uncut
  girl
Mwangi generation name

Nabongo (Luyia) chief, chiefly title

ndamathia mythical Kikuyu rainbow dragon

ndege bird, aeroplane

nduiko (Embu, Meru) generation handover of ritual power

ndungata servant, servants

Ngai God

ng'aragu famine

ngerewani vanguard

ngero evil, crime

ngwatio neighbourhood work party

njaguti serfs, good-for-nothings

njiraini by the roadside

nyimbo hymns, political songs

nyoka snake

nyumba house

orkoiyot (Kalenjin) ritual expert

riigi door

riika generation

ruguru the west

ruraya Europe

safari (Sw.) caravan, journey

tene eternity

tha compassion

thabari Kikuyu equivalent of Sw. *safari*, caravan, journey

thahu ritual uncleanness

thaka 'handsome ones'

thama moving, Exodus

thenge he-goat, ram (used in traditional sacrifices)

thingira men's house or dormitory

tuthuuri anti-elders (contemptuous)

ucenji 'heathendom'

uiguano unity

uhuru (Sw.) freedom

Uiguano wa Tha League of Compassion

ukabi Maasai

ukombo slavery

umaramari (Maasai) depravity, lack of self-control

'wabici' (from English) office

wanyahoro 'man of peace'

Watu wa Mungu (Sw.) People of God (a sect)

weru plains, grassland, wilderness

wiathi moral growth, 'freedom', self-control

wira work

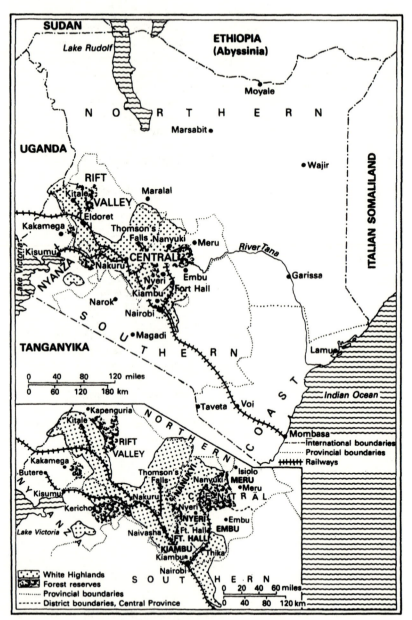

Map 1.1 *General and administrative map of Kenya, 1956–7*

One

♪♪♪♪♪♪♪♪♪♪♪♪♪♪♪♪♪♪♪♪♪♪♪♪

Introduction

An Encounter in Unhappy Valley

BRUCE BERMAN & JOHN LONSDALE

Once upon a time a smart set lived in Kenya's Happy Valley, at the foot of the Nyandarua Mountains. An immigrant clan of British aristocrats, they were good at handling guns, women and a constant flow of champagne. Some of them seasonal refugees from northern winters, their playground had been carved by the colonial state from the dry-season pasturage of the former lords of East Africa, the Maasai. Years later, other white settlers, envious perhaps, wondered if their high jinks, rather dirty business in retrospect, had not brought retribution on the entire colonial enterprise through the Mau Mau rebellion.[1] Drugs, drink and dalliance had perhaps made the natives lose their respect. And scarcely more than ten years after the declaration of the Mau Mau Emergency the lordly vistas of the Wanjohi Valley had vanished entirely, parcelled out in the crabbed little plots of the Million-Acre Settlement Scheme, which underwrote the politics of Kenya's independence. Kikuyu goats now grazed once-English lawns, piles of maize cobs weighed down the springs of dancefloors. On land once more reallocated by the state, the less smart sets of African clans were moving in.

Happy Valley was scarcely responsible for Mau Mau, however; hard-working farmers with mud on their boots had more to do with it, and they were not by any means all white. In the Unhappy Valley of colonial capitalism, class formation among African agriculturalists wrought as much social violence as the imported privileges of white settlement. The smarter sets within the myriad African cultivating clans learnt only too well how to profit by the delegated responsibilities of

1

doing the dirty business of the state. Chiefs and their clients divided the benefits of colonialism for themselves and transferred its costs – principally the coerced export of labour – on to those with weaker claims on their patronage. In self-justification they rewrote (in writing for the first time) the local histories of allegiance and custom, including some Africans within the respectable pales of parochial citizenship of clan and ethnic communities and excluding many others. The fissures of colonial Kenya were manifold. There was the obvious line of racial land apportionment drawn around the White Highlands: the boundary fence that supposedly divided white capital accumulation from the African reserves of subsistence farming and herding, the homelands of migrant labourers. But it was in fact a flimsy fence, full of gaps, and the oppositions of capital and labour sprouted up in an intricate patchwork all over the African lands as well, if at very different times in different places, so that the several African peoples of Kenya faced the moral and political implications of class formation with very divergent degrees of urgency.

Struggling to control the border conflicts of race, class and clan, the colonial state occupied centre stage in Kenya, symbolically and materially standing over colonial society. It was a structure of public power that shaped the conflicts of private interest and yet was also shaped itself by them; the state struggled through its institutional incoherence to enforce, nonetheless, some degree of control and unequal cohesion. Its officials, practical men, were pushed both by the competing and sometimes conflicting demands of metropolitan and settler interests and by the material and political needs of effective control over the African population to take refuge in the useful ideological claim to be the benevolent and disinterested arbiters of opposed interests and thus defenders of the commonweal.

We were drawn together by a shared interest in this contested and ultimately violent history of colonial Kenya, and a desire to find explanations of its institutions and events that probed further and deeper than their descriptive recounting. This book records a collaboration of more than a decade. While only a minority of the following chapters were actually jointly written, they all, after the earliest (Chapters 3 and 6), represent the results of a continuing dialogue on a common series of theoretical and historical issues. There is little doubt that without this dialogue these essays would either have been very different in content or would not have been written at all. The two completed before our collaboration began may give a sense of how we found our way into the issues we have probed together and how our perspectives have changed and developed in its course.

One misconception must be dispelled at the outset. The two papers jointly written in 1979 and 1980, reproduced here as Chapters 4 and 5, have apparently spawned some speculation that they represent the marriage of a historian's knowledge of 'the story' with the conceptual and theoretical interests of a political scientist. This was not and is not the case. The political scientist Berman's theoretical and methodological convictions had long since led him to a rejection of the ahistorical approach of his discipline and to a belief that explanations had to be tested against the detailed and often ambiguous historical record if large-scale processes of social and political change were to be more adequately understood than they were in the liberal 'modernization and political development' theories in which he had been trained. The historian Lonsdale, conversely, had developed an increasing conviction that theoretical and conceptual clarity were essential to make sense of the often apparently unconnected 'facts' provided by historical evidence. We thus share an interest in conceptual and methodological problems, substantial exposure to long periods of interviewing and archival research on the history of colonial Kenya, and a continuing belief that the constant confrontation of the two is essential to writing better theory and better history.

Our most serious difficulties stemmed from the very different stylistic and expository conventions of our cultural and disciplinary backgrounds, Berman being trained in the grey, unemotive, detached and, supposedly, scientific prose of American social science; Lonsdale in the more literary and allusive style of British historical writing. 'Crisis of accumulation' and 'palimpsest of contradictions' are phrases expressing the two poles from which we began. We have hopefully both learnt to be fluently expressive *and* analytically rigorous.

In the course of our collaboration our ideas and interpretations have gone through significant development and modification as part of a continuous process of critical refinement. These essays record how far we have come up to now, not where we think our work, or that of scholars who share our concerns, should come to an end. Indeed, one of our deepest methodological convictions is that there is no true and tested theory of the colonial state or colonial capitalist development that will eventually be 'discovered' and no definitive interpretations of the history of colonialism in Kenya or any other part of Africa. There are only theories more or less adequate to the objectives of particular groups of analysts and the concerns characteristic of the varied contexts in which they function. We have been shaped by the characteristics and concerns of our particular time, just as our predecessors and successors have been and will be by theirs.

We continue to share a belief in the power of Marxist analysis to illuminate the experience of 20th-century colonialism in Africa, as indeed it has clarified the understanding of many other dimensions of the history of capitalist development, provided we remember that Marx was as much concerned with how men and women come to the

3

consciousness of political possibilities as he was sure that productive structures and forces shaped historical probabilities. At the same time, we believe that such theory should not be used as a substitute for writing history, but as its most essential tool. We share Michel Foucault's view of theory as a 'toolkit', as 'an instrument, a logic of the specificity of power relations and the struggles around them'.[2] Good theory should not produce bad history, but such is often the case when it is asserted that something must have happened because it is logically required by the postulates of theory, and when all evidence to the contrary is conveniently dismissed as 'historicist' (in the sense employed by some Marxists) infatuation with mere surface experience. Our initial collaboration, reprinted in Chapter 4, began with our agreement that the facile identification of the colonial state as an instrument of metropolitan capital and the assertion that it was 'overdeveloped', because of its lack of connection to indigenous social forces in a colony, both did violence to the historical record as we had read it and obscured the theoretically significant complexity it seemed to contain. Instead, we wanted to show that the colonial state in Kenya was only the partly intended outcome of the often contested interaction of numerous impersonal structural forces and subjective agents, both metropolitan and local. From our present vantage point, that essay now strikes us as still rather too deferential to the then dominant structuralist theory of the state and is more mechanically functionalist in the model it employs than we would be happy with now. More recent research has increasingly uncovered the fluidity of social structures and identities in Kenya in the late 19th century, and the haphazard and often casual violence with which the institutions of colonial control and production emerged to contain and channel future development.

We have organized the collection into five sections and some comments may be useful to reveal the general themes explored in each and how the individual chapters work together to investigate them. They encompass a number of different types of writing: research papers based on primary and secondary sources, theoretical critiques and reflective essays. However, since they explore a common set of themes and were written initially for different purposes and audiences, there is inevitably some overlap between them, particularly in the exposition of the theoretical concepts on which they are based. We have not tried to eliminate such overlapping, but rather have left the texts largely in their original forms, eliminating only a few instances of obvious repetition, updating notes where they referred to unpublished sources that have subsequently appeared in print, and imposing some consistency in style.

Part One is concerned with the processes through which Kenya was brought into the orbit of British colonialism, how the institutions of colonial political control and economic development emerged, and how their internal contradictions and conflicts shaped further change. Lonsdale's Chapter 2 (1986) connects Kenya to its past and examines how force was used to create effective political power. This chapter introduces a key distinction between *state-building*, as a conscious effort at creating an apparatus of control, and *state-formation*, as an historical process whose outcome is a largely unconscious and contradictory process of conflicts, negotiations and compromises between diverse groups whose self-serving actions and trade-offs constitute the 'vulgarization' of power. Chapter 3 (1976), written by Lonsdale before we began our collaboration, is a more empirically detailed and narratively focused account of the complexities of the process of conquest in western Kenya, and should be read as a complement to Chapter 2. It is also an example of how theory can grow out of empirical problems. Lonsdale had little idea of how to 'make sense' of the complexities of the story until the construction of Table 2.3 showed a distinct pattern of 'political accumulation'.

Part Two consists of the two jointly written articles in which we attempted through an examination of the experience of Kenya to develop an approach to the analysis of the forces that shaped the development of the colonial state. We believe that states are human creations that are too easily treated as abstractions. This approach portrays them as logically necessary structures that meet the needs of dominant classes, whether by impersonal structural imperatives mediating social conflict at a distance or as the purposive instrument of sectarian will. Somehow by contrast, we believe, one has to find the conceptual space between systemic structuralism and wilful instrumentality, and insist that states are storm-tossed relationships of power derived from the productive logic of any given social organization and the conflicts of interest that threaten to disorganize it. In particular, we were interested in identifying the meaning in historical experience of the 'relative autonomy of the state', the most provocative and paradoxical of the concepts of contemporary Marxist theories of the state. Even if this is done, however, a focus on states can still exclude real people. Setting out with however fallible a state, it is still extraordinarily difficult to organize the evidence so as to capture the sense in which even 'knowledgeable social actors'[3] must necessarily find themselves, in their contemporary history, on that 'darkling plain/Swept with confused alarms of struggle and flight,/Where ignorant armies clash by night.'[4]

Chapter 4 (1979) was our initial effort to marry some Marxist theory about the functionality of the state to capitalist accumulation in an 'articulated' situation with empirical data on the conquest and the establishment of white settlement before the First World War. We tried to do away with the bleakly ahistorical opposition between settler capitalism and 'peasant society' by asserting that the productive expansion of both rested on and in so doing brutalized the differentiations within African peasantries, factionalisms that were also the levers of state power. Although rather too schematically structuralist, it remains the only attempt to relate the strategies of settler accumulation, via the politics of administrative control, to the production relations of African society down to the household, if a bit sketchily, and, if you look quite hard, even gender relations. It also stressed the degree to which effective control involved the formation of a group of African intermediaries and the provision of regular material benefits for them, unleashing a process of class formation that quite unintentionally constituted the central contradiction shaping the history of capitalist development in Kenya.[5]

Chapter 5 (1980) is a fairly direct sequel that shows how the post-First World War economic crisis raised in acute form the contradictions between settler accumulation, which required great pressure on the supply of African labour, and the conditions for stable political control over African societies. This was resolved by increasing state intervention in the regulation of the recruitment and treatment of labour, but in a way that revealed the limits of the ability of the state to act as the agent of settler interests and the need, directly felt by officials, to maintain to some degree the apparent and real autonomy of the state if the legitimacy of colonial control over the African population was not to be compromised. This chapter also suggests how the contradictions that were 'built into' Kenya in the very earliest stages of colonial rule continued to shape the patterns of administrative action and the most minute details of the development of the institutions of the colonial state.

Part Three consists of theoretical critique and comparative analysis growing out of our earlier work. Chapter 6 (1984) deals with the concept of articulation, an idea that we continue to find useful, but only in so far as it is considerably modified from its original formulations. This was Berman's first attempt directly to confront the rigidities of structuralist Marxism. It offers a critique of earlier formulations and defines 'articulation' so that it comprehends a complicated historical process of widely varying outcomes rather than making the impossible assumption that whatever happened had to serve the 'needs' of capital as either the necessary result of teleological systems following 'laws' of historical development or through the intentions of improbably omniscient historical actors.[6]

Chapter 7 (1984) is an effort by Berman to relate our general theoretical approach to the actual histories of the state in colonial Africa outside of Kenya. It points out the similarities as well as the differences in French and British colonialism, especially with regard to relations with the metropolitan state and capital, patterns of administrative structure and practice, and the variable paths of political and economic development in different colonies. It suggests that the recognition of difference

6

and the explanation of historical variability do not preclude but, rather, are based on generalization and comparative analysis. Such generalization and comparison rest, however, on the identification of factors both universal and idiosyncratic within the colonial context that interact to produce diverse outcomes.[7]

Part Four consists of two essays that try to pull together the various elements of the theoretical approach we have been developing and to explore the implications of our concerns for African historiography. Berman's Chapter 8 was originally written in 1987 and appears in print here for the first time. It focuses on the colonial state and its relationship to the political economy of colonialism and relies on reflections on the Kenyan experience to show how, in the first instance, empirical evidence undermines both dependency theory and structuralist models of the state, and how, further, it can serve as the basis for elaborating the key processes that constitute the dynamic elements of the colonial experience in Africa. These four interacting processes – articulation, political domination and control (including cooptation and collaboration), regulation of relations of production and class conflict, and class formation – are the principal components of a theoretical perspective on the state that properly treats the diversity of social forces involved as part of a history that is dynamic and open-ended. In so doing we attempt to transcend the closed loop of self-reproducing systems that pervades structuralism and restore the original vision of what Gavin Kitching has recently called Marx's generational theory of history, a vision in which explanation can treat both structural constraint and human agency as fundamental components of experience.[8] The crucial consequence of this approach is that we must again take seriously the subjective cognitive dimensions of colonial and contemporary Africa – the construction of meanings as well as structures – contained in knowledge and belief, ideology and culture among Africans as well as Europeans, as they acted within and against the constraints of their times.

These issues form the basis for Lonsdale's reflections in Chapter 9 (1989), which treats historical analysis as an intrinsic part of the reality it seeks to apprehend. The discourse of historians and social scientists constitute political acts that reflect positively and negatively on contemporary societies and on the meaning of their institutions and practices for their current inhabitants. Politicians seem to understand this power of ideas and knowledge rather better than scholars. To be sensitive and self-aware with regard to this important dimension of the academic enterprise in our own work, as well as that of others, requires that we reassess some of the most basic and taken-for-granted concepts in African studies – such as nationalism and the secular industrial nation-state as the inevitable end of development, and, even more important, African custom and tradition – as socially constructed artefacts that

7

reflect particular social and political interests and continue to shape vital and living African histories.[9]

In Part Five our focus returns to Kenya and the long-term effects of the early colonial conflicts we analysed in our first chapters. The 'Mau Mau' Emergency of 1952–60 had deep roots. In these final chapters we hope we do more than explain material change and political struggle; we also try to understand the African and European cognitive responses which gave events their distinctive character and meaning. These are among the first and the latest of our studies of Kenya. They complement each other in a way that reflects the underlying continuity of our concerns.

Berman's Chapter 10, the earliest piece in the book, first appeared in 1976. It remains unique among Mau Mau studies in its approach to an explanation of the colonial state's growing repression, which was a major stimulus to the growth of Mau Mau. Berman enters the colonial administration's world by means of a perspective more Weberian than Marxist. He shows how the consistent (mis)reading of African politics by the British, particularly the district officials, was shaped by the structural and ideological attributes of the system they served. Berman wrote this piece while developing a critical approach to aspects of mainstream American political science, especially bureaucratic theory and theories of rebellion and revolution; he conceived this essay as a critique of the latter.

This chapter is only marginally concerned with Kenya's political economy. But its argument accords with our other, more Marxist formulations because these latter grant to state structures and practices a larger economic role than more economically determinist Marxisms can allow. The chapter expounds the colonial officials' understanding of and preoccupation with 'order' and 'control'. Ironically, these very British cultural concepts clashed with the strikingly similar Kikuyu ideas of social order that Lonsdale analyses in 'The Moral Economy of Mau Mau', an essay that spans Chapters 11 and 12. The three chapters thus need to be read together; they frame the Emergency with accounts of the internal responses of its chief antagonists. They remind us that social relations are interpreted and acted on in the mind; consciousness is complex and ambiguous rather than simply and structurally determined.

In Chapter 10 Berman remarked that studies of Mau Mau in the 1960s and 1970s had taken out its 'strangeness' – the cultural content that so disturbed Western minds – and emphasised the material causes of Kikuyu discontent. Lonsdale's essay, not previously published, brings the strangeness back, so to speak, by dealing with the moral roots of Mau Mau. It is not a straightforward narrative analysis; its structure needs some prior explanation. In Chapter 11 Lonsdale shows, first, why the Kenyan memory of Mau Mau is so contentious. He then puts this 'problem' of Mau Mau into the context of Western assumptions about what type of nationalism was a proper response to modernizing change. British officials and American theorists constructed a model of a secular, culturally eclectic, African nationalism that was supposedly imitative of the rationalizing response of Europeans, the British especially, to their own earlier industrializations. Mau Mau, 'tribal' and 'magical', seemed to confound these expectations. Whites responded with brutal revulsion and, later, with academic embarrassment. Savage 'mumbo jumbo' was supposed to have been eradicated by modernization. It should certainly not reappear among a people counted as the most ambitious and progressive in Kenya. Even worse, Mau Mau's barbarous tribalism was thought to be led by a man who seemed to be the charismatic national leader expected by modernization theory; Kenyatta had spent long years in Britain, studied at a British university and even visited the most secular of modernizing societies, the Soviet Union.

Subsequent historical research has shown the supposed European model of rational class and national responses to industrialization to be a wish-fulfilling myth. The fault of the 1960s myths – both of the nineteenth-century European nation state and of African freedom – was that they ignored the question of moral economy: the subjective criteria of equity and exploitation, honour and shame, identity and alienation on which people act, if within strong structural constraints. Self-interest was, wrongly, assumed to follow a de-natured standard of rationality that was constructed by the academic observer rather than by historical actors. In Chapter 12, by contrast, Lonsdale explores Kikuyu moral and intellectual reactions to colonialism and its divisive effects on their own society. Mau Mau's cultural forms looked to whites to repudiate the supposed benefits of Western civilization brought by a benevolent colonialism. The internal reality was very different. Mau Mau was the outcome of material struggles between Kikuyu and white settlers and officials. But it was more. It brought to a head an internal debate among Kikuyu that had its roots in precolonial society.

Recent research has dissolved the static and 'functionally integrated' image of African societies, Kikuyu among them; they now appear to have been open to inter-ethnic currents and internally competitive.[10] Colonial change sharpened many such Kikuyu divisions. Bitter debate created the identity of newly emergent classes and, in the process, Kikuyuness itself. Only after reconstructing this contested history did Lonsdale feel able to explain Mau Mau within the moral terms of its major actors. Kikuyu divisions continued within Mau Mau. At the time most whites saw the rising as a symptom of the bewildered failure of Kikuyu society as a whole to face up to social change. Men of power often thus disqualify their political opposition as socially or psychologically deviant. But Mau Mau was not mad. Rather, it was bitterly divided between the needs of moral authority and effective action, between seniors and juniors, rich and poor, men and women. It summed up the debates which constructed Kikuyu identity. Similar debates, differently resolved, are a condition of nationhood. The pasts that we have studied, the violent constructions of states, classes and ethnicity, all speak to issues of the present day, not just in Kenya nor indeed merely in Africa.

Notes

1. James Fox, *White Mischief* (London, 1982), pp. 31-2.
2. Michel Foucault, *Knowledge and Power* (New York, 1980), p. 145.
3. Anthony Giddens, *A Contemporary Critique of Historical Materialism*, Vol. 1: *Power, Property and the State*, (London, Macmillan, 1981).
4. Matthew Arnold, 'Dover Beach'.
5. Sharon Stichter, *Migrant Labour in Kenya: Capitalism and African Response* (London, 1982), especially Chapters 1 and 2. The contradictions of the colonial state have also been subject to an acute analysis in Anne Phillips, *The Enigma of Colonialism: British Policy in West Africa* (London, 1989).
6. Lonsdale has also discussed articulation in relation to the state in his 'States and social processes in Africa', *African Studies Review*, 24 (1981), pp. 180-96.
7. These methodological issues are most usefully discussed in Charles Tilly's 'Introduction' to his edited collection, *The Formation of National States in Western Europe* (Princeton, 1975).
8. Gavin Kitching, *Karl Marx and the Philosophy of Praxis*, (London, 1988), pp. 36-48.
9. This point is more generally and forcefully argued by James Clifford in the introduction to his *The Predicament of Culture* (Cambridge, Mass., 1988) where he notes that Third World peoples 'may be dominated, but they have not been passive' and that we must make room for the possibility of 'multiple pathways to modernity'. (pp. 16-17)
10. See the illuminating and wonderfully told analysis in Charles Ambler, *Kenyan Communities in the Age of Imperialism: The Central Region in the Late Nineteenth Century* (New Haven, 1988).

Part I

Conquest

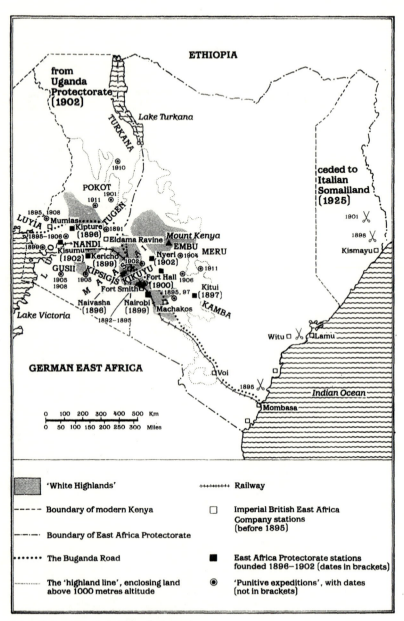

Map 2.1 *The East Africa Protectorate*

Two

The Conquest State of Kenya
1895–1905

JOHN LONSDALE

In the ten years between 1895 and 1905, 'Kenya' – if such a retrospective concept may be permitted – was transformed from a footpath 1000 km (600 miles) long into a colonial administration. Territory that had taken up to three months to traverse could now be crossed in two or three days; and carriage by train cost a tiny fraction of the outlay that had been needed for a caravan of porters. And if one takes 'Kenya' to indicate a social formation rather than a level of power, then in 1895 it was an overlapping patchwork of hunting, cultivating and herding peoples. They exploited varied ecological arenas – forests, hills and plains – that were linked by the exchange of women, goods and trust. A decade later it had been wrenched into one, as yet very disjointed field of competition between Africans to appropriate the power of colonial rule. Their former cultural identities, which had insured them against natural disaster with a non-sectarian elasticity, were being hardened into new 'tribes' by the factional politics of access to the narrow institutions of the young conquest state.

This transformation was the work of force. The British employed violence on a locally unprecedented scale, and with unprecedented singleness of mind. Their external force redefined internal power. Before the colonial conquest African power had been stored in unequal human relations that were underwritten by an ideology of lineage seniority and kinship. Men's future capacity to produce meat, grain and milk was banked in their wives, in cattle loans, trading alliances and in grants of rights in land as payment for labour. Theirs was an intimately political

13

capital, working face to face, not hidden in institutions. It demanded constant attention to its reciprocal undertakings if it was to yield returns. In normal times, therefore, its yields were marginal; Kenya's precolonial societies showed little stratification in their standards of living. Death could be a different matter. In hard times it visited the weak more than the strong. For the inequalities of power were most brutally revealed when, in some areas once in every generation, subsistence was threatened by prolonged drought – when the rains failed for more than just a couple of seasons – or by cattle plague. In such crises a strong man's dependants ceased to be his extra hands; they became extra mouths instead. Their claims for succour in return for service might have to be repudiated, if they failed to make good their patron's losses at the point of the spear. But at such times the weak could also beg for survival by pledging their labour or their children to other protectors less afflicted by drought or pestilence, often among neighbouring peoples with a different language and an alien mode of subsistence. Kenya's peoples were like the American nation, made up of strangers, both adventurers and refugees.

After the conquest Kenya became a more harshly politicized economy. This was partly because power had been centralized in the state, which rested on force and the new imperial ideology of progress. It was also because of the new nature of productive capital. Modern capital has a dual character. It is partly subject to political protection and exclusion, as productive power had previously been. But it is also a commodity in a global circulation that pays little respect to local privilege. It is amenable to political hierarchy and yet subversive of it. So it was in colonial Kenya. Capital seemed fixed in property and racial identity. Both preserves were demarcated and protected by the state. Exclusive property rights and bureaucratic power laid the ground for an acquisitive differentiation rather than a rough parity in the enjoyment of resources. For propertied capital was designed to recruit labour by seizing productive assets from workers rather than by allocating resources to dependants. And taxation, which was levied on all, made it possible for public expenditure to subsidize the few, to make them more attractive to outside investors. At times of economic crisis organized force enabled the strong to squeeze the weak harder, giving an entirely new meaning to the repudiation of their claims. 'From that time,' the Kikuyu elder Kabetu wa Waweru remembered some 30 years later, 'the state of things began to change more and more rapidly, and ceased to be at all like it was in the olden days. The country became like a new country that was unknown to us.'[1]

But, despite appearances, it was not an entirely new country. Conquest enlarged African power as much as it redefined it as European. There was continuity as well as disruption. State-building could not be a wholly destructive process. The British conquerors had to create a new high politics, a hierarchy of self-interest, out of the existing networks of authority. African leaders may have been forced to carry unprecedented burdens, but they had also to be allowed new means to pursue old interests. Without obedient followers they were as useless to their new rulers as to their old communities. And it was not only African notables who found much that was familiar in the unknown. For the embryo state was not only *built*, as a deliberate means to contain and direct power for the benefit of the few. It was also *formed* out of the anonymous actions of many. In evading servitudes ancient and modern the weaker members of African society used novel forms of association to regain old personal freedoms. However unwillingly, the state protected these subversive young ways of common life and labour as much as it fostered fresh privilege. State-formation – the vulgarization of power, and state-building – its cultivation, were contradictory processes that complemented each other.

This was because conquest was not only a political process but also an economic force. It made room for both the oppressive and the corrosive tendencies of propertied capitalism. Colonial rule entrenched power; it also enlarged markets. The African poor could exploit the new demands for their produce and their labour because there was also new competition for the prestige of their protection. They even found a market in land, despite its alienation to Europeans. As workers they were oppressed but as dependants they benefited from the rivalry for their service among a wider range of patrons. Their chiefs were fastened more securely over them with administrative sanctions but, as before, they were not the only masters. The power of the state had made room for others. Missionaries, produce-traders, officials and landlords bid up the price of the productive allegiance of the poor, insisting that the state protect them from the inflationary consequences of their own competition.

The violence of conquest was thus never quite complete. It was to be repeatedly renewed in Kenya's subsequent history. Men of property and power would always demand new forms of protection whenever they discovered, yet again, that they could not appease the resentful ingenuity of the people, except by letting slip some of the existing privileges by which capitalism was sustained locally and made profitable to backers overseas.[2]

Conquest: the investment of force

The story of Britain's imperial interest in the East African interior and the subsequent colonial conquest has been often told and cannot be repeated here in any detail.[3] Until the mid-1880s Britain's position rested on the shaky fiction of the mainland sovereignty of her protected creature the sultan of Zanzibar and, more securely but at unwelcome expense, on the squadron of the Royal Navy that scoured the Indian Ocean coast for Arab slavers. Once the sultan had been pushed aside in the European scramble for Africa, the scarcely more substantial Imperial British East Africa Company was chartered to occupy the British sphere of influence. Then, in late 1889, Britain woke up to the prospect of a prolonged occupation of Egypt. Strategic panic over the control of the Nile headwaters overcame her determination to do nothing in East Africa that would antagonize Germany. But the Company was already sliding into bankruptcy, sunk by its efforts to hold Buganda rather than by improving the route to the interior, the future Kenya. By 1895 Britain had no option but to annex what was then called the East Africa Protectorate, but showed how little she welcomed the Company's legacy by putting it in the care of the British consul-general in Zanzibar.

The conquest of the territory proceeded in three distinct phases. First, an awkward paramountcy was established over the coastline, its sovereignty nominally shared with the sultan. Then, for six years, the British were preoccupied with the defence of the Buganda road, which was gradually strengthened into the line of the Uganda railway. This iron backbone of conquest reached Lake Victoria in 1901. In the following year the railway was brought under one administration by shifting the boundary between the East Africa and Uganda Protectorates 300 km (200 miles) to the west, from the rim of the Rift Valley to the northeastern corner of the lake. The foundation of control had been laid. It had yet to be put to profitable use. The final and most violent phase of conquest followed, occupying the highland core of modern Kenya. In acknowledgement that diplomatic adventure had become administrative responsibility, the Foreign Office relinquished control to the Colonial Office in 1905, and peace, of a sort, came three years later.

Conquest is the proper term to use. The British forces were tiny and their armaments light; until the railway was complete they were less mobile than the forces of African resistance. Their supply was a constant nightmare, their intelligence often a farce. They depended on local African manpower for auxiliary troops and porters. They bought tons of food from African growers at prices that could not be dictated. They owed their political intuition to self-interested African informants. As in the rest of the continent, it was largely an African rather than an imperial conquest. But not entirely. The British were able to control the process and impose their own sense of direction because the disciplined, uniformed core of the violence was unequivocally theirs. They employed strangers, recruited in distant labour markets, men whose home was a regiment rather than a district, who could be rewarded with pay instead of power. Many of these were Africans from elsewhere, but whenever the going got rough the British looked first to their Indians.[4]

Control over the coast did not mean storming the gates of Kenya but defending the ramshackle outposts of Zanzibar. The British feared that the abolition of coastal slavery might mean war with the Arab slave-masters. In the event, their extreme caution over this social revolution,[5] together with the openings provided by Arab dynastic rivalry and disputed successions, allowed the British to retain the alliance of Zanzibar's notables even while supplanting them. The decisive events came in the early 1890s. Two Arab dynasties were crushed, the Nabahani of Witu[6] and the Mazrui, formerly of Mombasa, both of whom contested the overlordship of the Al Bu Sai'di sultans of Zanzibar. These were the only campaigns of the conquest in which British units and heavy guns were employed, both loaned by the Royal Navy. The two further engagements at the coast, against the Somali, were also to protect the old Arab trade network rather than to establish a distinctively British presence. The expeditionary forces, again, reflected British supremacy in the Indian Ocean rather than over the mainland; they were composed of Zanzibaris, Sudanese, the Aden Camel Corps and, crucially, the foreign legionaries of the empire, Punjabis and Baluchis from India.

The two subsequent phases of conquest were quite different in character. The Protectorate government inherited, it is true, the rag-tag troops of the Company, both the Sudanese of the upper Nile with their wives and children, and the sultan's guardsmen, the *viroboto* or dancing fleas, of whom some were Swahili coastmen, others Baluchi soldiers of fortune. They were renamed the East African Rifles, but the regiment was scarcely native to the protectorate. It recruited in India and in Egypt, where former Sudanese soldiers, some of them ex-Mahdists, could be picked up on the streets of Cairo. It also signed up men who had been the porters of the Zanzibari ivory and slave trades, Nyamwezi from what was now the German mainland to the south, and Manyema, ex-slaves from the still farther interior, now King Leopold's Congo. The disruptions of the African hunting frontier, which had expanded in advance of the European scramble, had cast up many such homeless adventurers, ready to be enlisted in an imperial service that did not greatly differ from the employment they had already known.[7] By 1897 they numbered about 1,100 men, all strangers to the people they were ordered to fight. But they were products of African, not Indian Ocean history, and they would have been both blind and immobile without the assistance of barefoot warriors more local still.

The East African Rifles was not an impressive force. One of its companies bolted when charged by Somalis. Its white officers were said to be rejects from their home regiments; they kept their African mistresses in their quarters. As late as 1902 the troops were armed with single-shot rifles; these were rusted up for lack of a rifle range on which to fire.[8] But then the regiment's adversaries, the people of Kenya, were not very warlike either. They were stateless peoples, without standing armies. Having only recently met Zanzibari traders, few of them had learnt the use of guns. Their young men, certainly, saw raiding as a legitimate means to acquire cattle, but most of Kenya's peoples valued livestock principally as the working capital of family formation, farming and trade. And household heads, the men of property and power, had good reason to curb the aggression of the young. War became destruction only in response to natural disaster, when social control crumbled and survival was at stake. Even then, war had a self-limiting quality. Land, cattle and manpower had to be kept in a rough equilibrium in societies with such simple working tools. There was no point in having more cows than one could herd, more land than one's wives could hoe or one's young men defend. Accumulation of resources was impossible without the accumulation of people. People could not be controlled without giving them a share in resources and in esteem. Defeated peoples could not be kept in strict subjection. It would have entailed a literally unimaginable expense.[9]

This is where colonial warfare differed. In comparison with 'civilized warfare' it was ridiculously cheap, but its costs could still be calculated. It is estimated that Britain's 70 million new African subjects cost about 15 pence each; most of that paltry sum was spent not on armies but on the railways that followed them.[10] Even those who reject the concept of economic imperialism must concede that it had to be economical, and to the men who made this investment in European law and order the outlay was ruinous. It bankrupted the Imperial British East Africa Company, which found that export duties on ivory – the only local export that could bear the cost of porterage – were quite inadequate to sustain even its feeble pretence at control. The successor East Africa Protectorate did no better. In 1905 its treasurer was appalled to find that a decade of military effort had cost more than £600,000, very nearly one-third of all public expenditure and rather more than total domestic revenues.[11] This was nothing when set beside the £5.5 million spent on the railway, itself a military necessity. It would have put another company out of business, and was not what the British taxpayer expected from Empire.

The British urgently needed to convert the external, costly and destructive force of conquest into internal, negotiable and productive power. They had to emulate their own Roman governor, Agricola, of whom the admiring Tacitus had said that 'when he had done enough to inspire fear, he returned to mercy and proffered the allurements of peace'.¹² Was Sir Arthur Hardinge, the protectorate's first commissioner, recalling his own schooldays in his echoed premise that: 'These people must learn submission by bullets – it's the only school; after that you may begin more modern and humane methods of education'?¹³ But if Africans had to learn the European lesson of submission, the British had to learn the local African lesson, how to pacify their mastery.¹⁴ 'Pacification', rightly, is no longer used to describe colonial conquest. What needed subjugation was not so much the disorder of Africa as the irruption of Europe. But pacification is still a proper term to describe what the British had to do *to* their conquest rather than *with* it. They had used African power in order to undermine it; now they had to make it profitable. They had to capitalize on the politics of conquest.

The highlanders of Kenya

Kenya is about as large as France, with an area of about 582,600 square kilometres (225,000 square miles).¹⁵ Most of it is arid steppe, in some places virtual desert, usable only for extensive pastoralism by sparse populations. Not more than about 14 per cent, or 80,000 square kilometres (31,000 square miles), is suitable for agriculture or more intensive grazing. This high-potential land is concentrated in the southwestern corner of the country, 400 km (250 miles) and more from the coast. It is enclosed by the 1000 m (3,250 feet) contour, above which rainfall of over 500 mm (20 inches) can be expected for at least seven years in every ten. This is the area of the Kenya highlands, split down the middle by the Rift Valley. It was the scene of the second and third phases of the colonial conquest.

The population of what became Kenya may have amounted to 3 million in 1890, of whom some three-quarters would have lived in the highlands. Three main groups of people were involved in the conquest. Inland from the coast the first to be met were the highland Bantu, primarily the Kamba and the Kikuyu, but also the Embu and Meru of Mount Kenya. They were peoples, not tribes, potential nations rather than actual dispersions of related lineages. There were boundaries between them, and they gave their neighbours different names, but these served to demarcate different environments and the different cultures that had grown up in their management, not absolute breaks in political allegiance and economic self-sufficiency. Trade, marriage and patronage knew no confines. The men of power within each group had dealings with their opposite numbers up in the hills or down in the plains.

All the highland Bantu were neighbours to the Maasai, the lords of the Rift. As the one purely pastoral people of the highlands, the Maasai could survive only in close connection with the 'mixed farming' peoples who lived beyond their escarpments. They were the bankers of the highlands. Their capital, and their currency, was livestock.[16] The cultivators who surrounded them needed to invest any surplus harvest in stock, and much livestock in women. They had no other long-term means to store grain; vermin and humidity saw to that. So they traded grain for cattle and goats, using them to speculate in the future reproduction of manpower. Conversely, the Maasai had to reinsure their cattle. They fostered exchange friendships with their neighbours, married their daughters and took in the apprentice stockherd labour of their sons. When their livestock was next decimated by drought or disease they might then hope to reach accommodations that were not too unequal with near relatives across the agricultural border. At best, they might get by simply by selling off stock at famine prices. It was only on those rare occasions of real disaster, the famines that killed large numbers, that unequal exchange gave way to large movements of starving populations and desperate raids.

Westwards still, beyond the Rift, lay the peoples who looked out on the Victoria Nyanza. The Kalenjin-speaking peoples, principally the Nandi, the Kipsigis and the Tugen, lived up on the watershed. Each controlled hill and plateau, farmland and pasture. It may be because they encompassed this marked dual economy within one culture that they seem to have had less intense relations with their neighbours than was typical of the highland peoples. Yet the more lowland peoples of the Nyanza basin, the Bantu-speaking Luyia and Gusii and the Nilotic Luo-speakers, had equally mixed economies and pursued trading strategies that linked them all, and the Maasai, in a regional system as busy as the one that also joined the Maasai and the highland Bantu.[17]

In order to understand the politics of their British conquest one must first grasp some idea of their own. They were all colonizing peoples, for whom the control of scarce labour was paramount. Their basic unit of production and consumption was the extended family. But no family could survive in isolation. Each needed the cooperation of others in the seasonal chores of agriculture and in herding. The idiom of cooperation was patrilineal descent through the generations and the kinship of contemporaries. But the organization of work was less egalitarian than its ideology. It was focused on big men with large families who could exploit more than their families alone – impoverished dependent workers, immigrant families grateful for protection, marriage alliances with neighbouring settlements or herding sections, and mutual defence agreements with other big men. Small settlements could not prosper without wide networks.

This way of life had thrown up four different forms of authority, based on seniority, ambition, inspiration and organization. The pervading source of power was seniority. Age conferred superior knowledge of the environment, control over women and therefore control over young men. Its supportive ideology of lineage descent differentiated full citizens with prior entitlement to local resources from client outsiders who were most at risk when subsistence was squeezed by disaster, but whose descendants might earn full incorporation. Lineage was a court of claims rather than a family tree.

Lineage was matched by generation, both as a perceived division of society, and as a source of social control. Most highlanders dramatized in civic ritual the successive stages of life, from gallant youth to mature family headship and awesome old age. Youth was the time of ambition, an unruly phase that many peoples, the more pastoral especially, sought to discipline within the institution of the warrior age-group. But warriorhood was the moment to evade the elders' control by investing stolen stock in marriage. Youthful leadership paid off in later life in the ability to marry more wives, to enlist male dependants and to tend the alliances that protected trade in the products of home, pasture and field. The impatience of ambition was often relieved by the colonization of a fresh settlement, not so much by the single 'lineage founder' of oral tradition as by the families associated with him and their followers.

The inspiration that could divine and manipulate supernatural forces was the gift of few. It was inherited in prophetic lineages and fostered by apprenticeship. Its oracular power was most strongly developed among the Maasai as the sanction for internal alliance and external raids, but there was a wide regional market in the arcane knowledge believed necessary to cope with the unpredictable cruelties of climate, disease and personal misfortune.

All authorities were subject to the frailties of personality and chance. Their mutual competition was but rarely suppressed by organized hierarchies of precedence, consultation and control. The nearest approach to a power stable enough to be termed chiefship was found in the far west, over some of the Luo and Luyia settlements. Everywhere else chiefship was a figment of the ethnographic imagination of the early British officials.

These fragile powers had grown up to exploit and control the divisions of age, gender and natural environment. Never secure, their holders were always on the alert to buy fresh insurances against new threats. In the later 19th century they were faced with two challenges, one that could be turned to profit, the other that threatened disaster.

State-building 1: The politics of conquest

The Swahili trading frontier offered the challenge of profit. Backed by the Indian financiers of Zanzibar, it first advanced into the highlands in mid-century. The Swahili came for ivory; they captured or bought people only where they could most easily exploit social division or distress. Their caravans were well armed because they were also well capitalized. They traded rather than raided. They imported fashion items rather than productive goods, cloth, beads and iron and copper wire. Their external market intensified the regional highland traffic, linking more closely the domestic production of forest and plain, each with their elephant herds, and cultivated hills. Local circuits of influence and exchange opened out, making alliance with the coastal strangers a more reliable investment in power than anything previously available.

Internal leaders reinforced their role as external brokers. They could be elders, war-leaders or chiefs. Prophets flourished too, as successful men fretted over the rising stakes of power. Spirals of local accumulation developed. The caravan food market coupled the hire of outside fire-power in local conflicts to the acquisition of the livestock needed to command more domestic labour, whether by increased polygyny or by funding young male clients.[18] There were new opportunities for conspicuous consumption, especially in dress. One or two gatekeepers with the wider world diversified their ideological standing with some outward show of Islam.

Much of the subsequent politics of conquest turned on the historical accident of whether the British advent reinforced or threatened these new commercial interests. The caravans of the British East Africa Company resembled the Swahili parties in every way save for their avowed hostility to slaving. They employed the same leaders, recruited the same porters and guards, acted as wholesalers for some of the Swahili traders,[19] and had no stronger bargaining position with the local African food and ivory brokers. But while the Company men kept to the main track to Uganda, the Swahili fanned out more widely, as elephant were shot out nearer to hand and the Company tried to impose ivory duties at the established markets. By the early 1890s a series of concentric trading systems had begun to emerge, centred on the main food-buying areas on the Buganda road, in the southern Kamba and Kikuyu countries, at Baringo in the Rift valley, and in the Wanga chiefdom among the Luyia people.[20] The inner circle of contacts in each region traded with both the Swahili and the Company, the outer circle with the Swahili alone. In these frontier zones the guns that were used to shoot elephants seem to have been put more freely to political use. Swahili traders and ambitious young men joined in exploiting a new means of destruction over which there was no social control. Beyond the Company's reach a military revolution was stirring. In some places it overlaid a previous such revolution manned by hired Maasai spearmen.

It has been said that, in the context of the conquest, the Maasai were the hinge of Kenya.[21] If so, by the 1890s they were distinctly rusty. In the middle years of the century they had been engaged in recurring civil conflict, the Iloikop wars. These left the victorious sections, at the centre of the Rift's seasonal grazing system, with pastures too vast to defend. Conversely, the strong men of agricultural colonization on its margins rearmed themselves with the client warriors of defeated sections. Most notably, refugee prophets started to build a clannish ritual ascendancy among the Nandi. The Maasai world looked to be falling in on them.

As if these man-made troubles were not enough, in the 1890s the Maasai were assailed by natural disasters that affected them more severely than the mixed farming peoples (Table 2.1). The catastrophes were partly cyclical and predictable. There were droughts and locust infestations at the beginning of the decade and again, more viciously, at its end. As usual, famine gave rise to epidemic smallpox, as non-immune pastoralists searched for food among agriculturalists with whom the disease was endemic. The epidemic then raged among herders and farmers alike.[22] But these old scourges were reinforced by two calamities apparently new to Africa. The first was rinderpest or cattle plague. This also visited twice, in 1890–1 and in 1898. On the first occasion it swept down from the north, apparently imported in Russian cattle, the meat ration for the Italian invasion of Eritrea. The second rinderpest advanced from the coast along the line of railway construction, brought in by draught oxen from India.[23] Jiggers were the other newcomer, sandfleas from Brazil that arrived by ship on the Congo coast and spread across Africa. Burrowing into toes, they crippled cultivators or killed them off with gangrene.

It is difficult to quantify these disasters. European travellers penned pictures quite as harrowing as those seen by television audiences a century later. But it is not clear how widely the horror spread. Rinderpest can kill up to 90 per cent of affected herds, but it travels only along the lines of trade, raids and transhumant grazing, and Kenya's peoples knew the value of quarantine. Maasai herds were devastated, but not all of them. The same patchwork fate seems to have befallen virtually all their neighbours. The hill-dwelling Kalenjin, the Nandi included, were most able to preserve their herds from danger.[24] The scale of human suffering is just as uncertain. Death was best reported among the Maasai, the southern Kikuyu and the Kamba. Among some of their settlements anything up to 40 per cent may have perished; the mortality was heaviest among the very old and the very young. Death did not similarly ravage the populations of the Victoria lakeshore until the century's turn, when a sleeping-sickness epidemic advanced in parallel with the tsetse-infested bush that well-stocked pastures had previously kept at bay.[25]

The social consequences of demographic collapse were just as varied at both the societal and the individual levels. Among the Maasai civil strife was renewed in the Morijo war. Their pastoral sections regrouped and raided each other under the rival leadership of the brothers Olonana

The Conquest State of Kenya 1895–1905

	Nyanza Basin	Kalenjin	Turkana Basin	Maasai	Kikuyu Embu	Kamba	Coast
1870				Iloikop		famine	
		pleuro					
				civil			
1875							
				wars			
		pleuro					
1880							
	pleuro-pneumonia			pleuro			
						famine	
1885			smallpox				famine
	pleuro				✗ Teleki		
1890	r i n d e r p e s t						✗ Witu
	smallpox	locusts		s m a l l p o x			
	jiggers				jiggers & locusts		✗ Witu
					✗ Kabete		
1895	✗ Bukusu	✗ Nandi	smallpox	✗ Kedong	✗ Githunguri	✗ Mwala	✗ Mazrui
		✗ Tugen			locusts		
	pleuro	✗ Nandi		✗ Morijo war	jiggers	Kilungu	famine
				r i n d e r p e s t			✗ Somali
	✗ Luo			famine — smallpox — locusts			
1900	smallpox	✗ Nandi	drought				✗ Somali
	sleeping —	✗ Pokot			✗ Maruka		
	sickness	✗ Nandi			✗ Tetu		
				1st move	✗ Mathira		
1905	✗ Gusii	✗ Sotik					
	drought	✗ Nandi			✗ Embu		
	✗ Gusii						
	smallpox		rinderpest				
1910	rinderpest	✗ Turkana	drought	pleuro			
	rinderpest	✗ Marakwet	drought	2nd move	✗ Tharaka		

Note: smallpox (etc.) = natural disaster (pleuro = pleuro-pneumonia in cattle)
     ✗ Nandi (etc.) = official military action or government pressure, with the exceptions of
     (a) ✗ Teleki, which represents the fighting passage of Count Teleki's private expedition through Kikuyuland, and
     (b) ✗ Kedong, which represents the massacre of 650 Kikuyu and Swahili porters by the Maasai, followed by the massacre of 100 Maasai by a private British trader.

Table 2.1 The disasters

and Senteu, who competed for the prophetic mantle of their father, the great *laibon* Mbatiany. Thousands of Maasai also sought refuge with their neighbours, principally the southern Kikuyu. The Kikuyu and Kamba mixed farmers profited from Maasai distress. They raided the shattered herdsmen, bought up their surviving stock at bargain prices, and used their refugee labour to expand their own cultivation, ready for the next rains. But the frontier of Kikuyu agriculture also receded northward, as colonist settlements fled from drought and smallpox to the better-watered homes of the lineages they had left behind in central Kikuyuland.

Within these broad demographic struggles individual social differentiation seems to have become more marked. Big men were expected to organize the means of survival, offence and defence. Their large herds would have been prudentially scattered among dependants and allies, less vulnerable than concentrated small herds to the caprice of calamity. Their warrior sons could enforce the repayment of livestock loans. They could protect their closest followers by rejecting those with lesser claims. With their famished refugee workers they could exploit soaring food demand with increased production. Between 1890 and 1899 grain prices on the Kikuyu caravan market rose at least thirty-fold. It is no wonder that elderly Kikuyu 60 years later, when asked who died in the famine, answered simply, 'the poor'.[26] How much of the price inflation should be blamed on the increased food purchases of the British, now feeding railway navvies as well as troops and porters, is a matter for dispute.[27] But it is scarcely open to doubt that many more of the poor would have died had they not been able to find a new refuge in the civil and military labour markets of conquest.

The politics of conquest was an integral part of the crisis. The conquest itself, not of Kenya alone but of the rest of Africa, bore a heavy responsibility for the disasters. Rinderpest, jiggers and the tsetse fly would not otherwise have wreaked their havoc. But conquest also provided outdoor famine relief. Many Africans reconstructed their resources, if often at the expense of their fellows, by drawing in an auxiliary role on the British investment in force. The politics of conquest was 'intensely local'.[28] But one can discern four broad patterns, each related to the double trading frontier and to the disasters.

Until 1901 the chief British interests remained the security and supply of the Buganda road. By the mid-1890s there were three main food-buying stations, each with a small garrison: Machakos in southern Kamba country, Fort Smith at the southern end of Kikuyu, just above the swamp that became Nairobi, and Mumias, a village named after its Luyia Wanga chief.[29] These became the forward bases of conquest. In each area the British attracted market brokers from the nearest settlements. There was nothing new in their mutual confidences. But in each of the three areas a rift developed between an inner circle of those whom the British saw as 'friendlies' and an outer circle of recalcitrants. These rifts became the fault-lines of violence.

Local economic differences became the frontiers of British security. Among the Kamba, John Ainsworth, a Company man who became the senior Protectorate official in the interior, trained firearmed militias from among his food-suppliers, so that they could defend themselves against the Maasai. But they soon became his tactical reserve against the more pastoral northern Kamba settlements, amongst whom the displaced Swahili found auxiliaries for ivory and slave hunting farther afield.[30] A similar patchwork of alliances and hostility evolved among the southern Kikuyu. Their cultivation may have expanded as early as the 1860s, in response to the caravan market.[31] And although the evidence is slender, it appears that senior members of Kikuyu settlements, who controlled the core arable land, became increasingly incensed with their junior members who were more interested in cattle, and with the warrior age-grades. Both the latter pursued ambitions that disrupted trade. The Fort Smith 'punitive expeditions' of the middle 1890s can well be interpreted as defending Kikuyu grain suppliers against their more pastoral relations, impoverished by rinderpest, lower down the hills. Swahili adventurers do not seem to have provided an additional irritant here. Indeed, the Kikuyu leaders on whom the British most relied, Waiyaki and, after him, Kinyanjui in the south, Karuri in the centre and Wang'ombe to the north, had all risen to prominence as brokers for the Swahili trade, the last three by virtue of their close ties with the Athi forest people, the elephant hunters.[32]

The politics of conquest among the Luyia, finally, combined elements of both the Kamba and the Kikuyu patterns. Until 1902 this arena of conquest came under the Uganda Protectorate, a sideshow to the drama of royal resistance and rebellion in the kingdoms of Bunyoro and Buganda. Mumias was like Machakos, its storekeeper Charles Hobley not unlike Ainsworth. He too armed a local militia, struggling to survive in a fragmented regional economy set on edge by rinderpest and famine. Its conflicts profited long-established Maasai military colonies and Swahili traders, who tried to retain their local alliances while evading British censure. Hobley's forces gradually supplanted both. Mumia, at the centre of the British supply network, had the same interest as the Kikuyu grain sellers in shuffling off his pastoral spearmen, in this case his Maasai. And the Swahili cut their losses by shifting their attentions to the Luyia periphery, as their colleagues had done among the Kamba. It was not until 1908 that the Bukusu, the northernmost Luyia people, were forced to give up their Swahili-supplied guns.[33]

That was the first pattern of conquest. It enlarged the power of the agricultural authorities along the road, at the expense of their more pastoral interests. But the British would have been unable to engineer these accommodations with such comparative ease had they not enjoyed the alliance of the Rift Valley Maasai, the former victors of the Iloikop wars as distinct from the losers who had settled among the Luyia. So the second pattern of conquest entailed the reconstruction of the pastoral system at the heart of the highlands. The Maasai found the British military labour market more rewarding and culturally more congenial than farm work for the Kikuyu.

In virtually all the minor campaigns that stitched together the defence agreements of the Buganda road, a company or two of the East African Rifles was supported by Maasai auxiliaries, often many hundreds of them. These volunteered to raid people they may now have been too weak to attack without British help, often in support of British 'friendlies' with whom the Maasai had previous understandings. The conduct of warfare did not change greatly in the 1890s; enemy African casualties were not so large as they later became. The British aimed to destroy huts and crops, and to capture livestock, so as to enforce submission. And their peace terms were not, at first, particularly onerous – the surrender both of guns and the deserter Swahili porters who knew how to use them, promises to give free passage to official caravans and readiness to sell food.[34]

On the early expeditions the Maasai were awarded most of the stock, which they themselves had looted. British power was still questionable enough to need sharing out. Indeed the Maasai were only doubtfully under British control. Their misinformation was distrusted, especially with respect to their old rivals the Nandi. In one early skirmish the Maasai word for 'enemy', *mangati*, was taken to be the proper name of a Luyia settlement.[35] But to the Maasai the significance of their British alliance lay in its domestic ramifications. The patronage of providing opportunities for military adventure accrued to Olonana and helped his clientele to win the Morijo civil war. But the threads of patronage then slipped through Olonana's fingers into the hands of the separate warrior leaders, the *il aigwanak*. As the political capital of cattle accumulated once more, providing fresh breeding stock for family herds, so Olonana's prophetic assets declined. The chief support of the British, he became the main loser in the final reckoning of conquest. Maasai herdsmen were well on the way to recovery from the disasters and could afford to disengage from the British connection. Nor did the British stand in such need of the Maasai. Without bargains to negotiate, Olonana was no longer broker but broken. The politics of conquest had certainly enlarged pastoral power, but it was not clear how it could be used in the new dispensation.[36]

The Maasai lever of conquest lay ready to hand because of the disasters. And openings for its insertion along the road were available

Table 2.2 British military operations in the Kenya highlands 1893–1911

Date	Enemy	Auxiliaries		Numbers killed		Livestock confiscated	
				'British'	'enemy'	cattle	small-stock
Nov 1893	Kabete Kikuyu	87	Maasai	?	many	6	922
June 1894	Githunguri	124	Maasai	{2	{90	10	847
July 1894	Kikuyu	220	Maasai	{	{	—	1,100
Nov 1894	Bakusu Luyia	—		70	—	—	—
Jan 1895	Bukusu Luyia		{ Maasai / Luyia	2	?	450	?
Aug 1895	Bukusu and other Luyia	900	{ Ganda / Maasai / Luyia	70	420	1,900	?
Nov 1895	1st Nandi	25	Ganda	28	190	230	2,400
Dec 1895	Mwala Kamba	800	Maasai	?	?	560	1,300
Mar 1896	northern Kamba	{300 / 900	Kikuyu Maasai	?	many	many	
Aug 1896	southern Luyia		{ Luyia / Maasai	2	?	273	?
Feb 1897	Kilungu Kamba		{ Maasai / Kamba	3	100	700	1,000
May 1897	Tugen (Kamasia)	200	Maasai	?	100	300	8,000
June 1897	2nd Nandi	400	Maasai	6	few	140	1,500
Nov 1899	Kamelilo Nandi	75	Maasai	?	?	58	1,072
Dec 1899	central Luo		{ Luo / Luyia / Maasai	1	250	2,620	many
July 1900	3rd Nandi	1,000	{ Maasai / Tugen / Luo	127	350	3,470	29,370
Jan 1901	Pokot (Ribo Post)	500 / 100	{ Maasai / Il Chamus	43	300	520	10,000
Sept and Dec 1902	Maruka & Tetu Kikuyu	300	Maasai	12	310	1,300	10,000
Mar 1903	4th Nandi	700	Nandi	4	40	300	4,500
Feb 1904	Mathira Kikuyu	450	Maasai	?	1,500	1,087	8,150
Apr 1905	Sotik (Kipsigis)	900	Maasai	2	92	2,000	3,000
Sept 1905	Gusii	150	Maasai	—	120	3,000	?
Nov 1905- Jan 1906	5th Nandi	1,500	{ Maasai / Somali / Tugen	97	1,117	16,210	36,200

28

Table 2.2 *cont'd.*

June 1906	Embu	—	2	407	3,180	7,150
Jan 1908	Gusii	Nandi	—	240	7,000	?
Dec 1911	Marakwet (Kalenjin)	—	—	22	8	350

Note: Operations are grouped together where they were directed against the same or closely related peoples, or where they comprised part of a regional campaign.

Only the larger operations are listed. There were at least as many more smaller skirmishes. But those listed probably accounted for 90 per cent of all casualties and livestock confiscations.

All forces included regular Company or Protectorate forces, as well as the local African auxiliaries. 'British' casualties numbered less than half-a-dozen Englishmen.

Sources are to be found in the references cited in the footnotes, save for the Appendix in A.T. Matson, *The Nandi campaign against the British 1895–1906* (Nairobi, 1974).

in the divisions of self-interest between those settlements that were involved in the caravan market and those that were not. It was the people who had suffered least in the disasters who offered most resistance to conquest. These were the Kalenjin highlanders, with the Nandi at their centre. They furnished the third pattern of conquest. The Nandi had lost many cattle from pleuropneumonia in the 1880s, and their people did not escape the drought of the early 1890s. In 1890 some Nandi groups killed their ritual expert, the *orkoiyot* Kimnyolei, for his self-evident failings, the last of which was an abortive Nandi raid that may or may not have introduced rinderpest from elsewhere. The evidence on this point is conflicting, but it does seem that the Nandi avoided the second rinderpest later in the decade.[37] Not only did the Nandi suffer less grievously than others but, despite their central position, they also lay beyond the outer circle of contacts discerned in the first pattern of conquest. For the Swahili avoided them after some pioneer traders had been roughly handled, giving them the nickname that everybody else adopted, *mnandi*, the greedy cormorant. So there was no external trading alliance for the British to pick up, nor any political intelligence to use. Nor were Nandi cultivators and pastoralists at odds over their external relations.

British ignorance was as much a cause of conflict as Nandi obduracy. The British turned more readily to violence for want of any known broker with whom to remonstrate, nor could they find any guarantor of peace. The two expeditions of the 1890s, both in revenge for Nandi attacks on caravans or food suppliers, achieved nothing. The three campaigns of the new century marked a turn in the tide of conquest. They were still in defence of the route, but by this time it was the railway, which was not only a means of swift transport for large bodies of troops but also the start line for concerted attacks. And it was at this point, when conquest started to hurt, that the Nandi began to split in similar fashion to those peoples who had had longer experience of the trading frontier. Some of the men of their core agricultural settlements were persuaded to take the field in support of the British against the younger, more pastoral sections.

Time had caught up with the Nandi, and it is time that provides the fourth and final pattern of conquest. As the 1890s came to their wretched end, so peoples whose previous experience had differed now underwent ordeals that were much the same. The common factor was labour. Many African men were anxious to sell their labour in return for survival, but in some areas the British needed more labour than Africans were ready to sell. In either case, the established Anglo-African alliances were brought to the point of collapse. In the early 1890s African brokers had profited from their control over the fruits of agricultural and military labour, but had provided little of what has been called 'tribute labour' for porterage, path-clearing or fort-building.[38] But any discretion they may have had to negotiate the terms of the labour market was now over-whelmed by the desperation of both parties, in the double crisis of African famine and British military collapse in Uganda.

There were three patterns in the dissolution of authority over labour among, respectively, the Kamba, the Kikuyu and the peoples of the Nyanza basin. Famine was the press gang among the Kamba. They were thrown into a turmoil that was reduced to order less by their own patrons than by the railway contractors who employed them in large numbers.[39] In southern Kikuyuland, by contrast, young men took collective responsibility for their own survival. With a violence that some Kikuyu have compared with the behaviour of both sides in the Mau Mau war 50 years later, warrior bands 'terrorized all and sundry'; they were called *thabari*, after the Swahili caravan *safari*, a term also applied to British raiding parties.[40] The Nyanza story was different again. In 1898 its British officials became little more than recruiting sergeants for the hundreds of porters needed to support the Indian battalion that was rushed across the sea to put down the Sudanese mutiny, away in Uganda. Hobley faced a crisis of collaboration. His broker allies were unable to meet his demands; they could channel food but could not drag out men. So he cast aside these 'tribal chiefs' and dealt directly with the myriad 'clan heads' beneath them. A refusal to turn out labour became, for the first time, a reason for punishment, and its supply a condition of peace.[41] Conquest had begun by building up African power; now it was breaking it down.

The crucial work of recovery from famine must have sprung from the productive and reproductive labour of women, yet for this vital period we know little about them.[42] We know that in some places bridewealth was reduced or even suspended for lack of livestock, which might suggest that marriage was made easier for all men, including the poor. But we can also guess, from studies of comparable periods of disruption elsewhere, that many men abandoned their women to fend for themselves, and that women therefore swelled the followings of any strong man who could protect them.[43] It may also be, but one cannot be certain, that young men went out to work in obedience to the same patrons, performing what was in effect the poor man's traditional labour service for his father-in-law, in place of bridewealth. It is significant that the three men of the 1890s best known for mobilizing large numbers of porters despite the general collapse of authority, Kinyanjui and Karuri among the Kikuyu and Odera Ulalo among the Luo of Nyanza, were shortly afterwards recognized as 'paramount chiefs' over their areas. The British would have granted such a status only to big men with large numbers of settled dependants, families whose formation they had perhaps sponsored. The political economy of conquest, even at its most oppressive, could apparently still provide for the customary enlargement of African power.[44] This was to be the central paradox of the politics of control.

State-building 2: The politics of control

In the politics of conquest, before 1901, public power (an innocuous term for British force) was shared in private African hands. It was the only way in which external force could become socially engaged. Officials had to come to terms with the local contractors of military intelligence, manpower and supply. The initial phase of state-building required alliances that were not too unequal. But usable state power was a different matter. The labour crisis in the late 1890s had already shown that. Somehow, public power had to be concentrated in official hands, above society and yet socially influential rather than merely forceful. Allies had to be made agents, wielding a locally legitimate authority that was nonetheless, in the last instance, delegated from the centre. The British never mastered this alchemy of rule, as rulers never do, but it was not for want of trying.

The official monopoly on public power had begun to emerge in the process of conquest. Backed by the ever present threat, and frequent use, of external force, the British multiplied their allies along the Buganda road. As they grew in number, so each African broker became less indispensable, and more vulnerable therefore to British displeasure. As individually they declined in value, so too the British lowered the collective price of their support. This can clearly be seen in the conquest of Nyanza. On the first sally against the Luyia in 1895, the hundreds of African levies were rewarded with nearly three-quarters of the captured cattle. On the last, in 1908, there were no auxiliaries, and

31

local African friendlies were fobbed off with 3 per cent of the loot. This example makes a second vital point, that force became bureaucratized. There were no spearmen on this last expedition, and thus no African power-brokers. Instead, the African troops and policemen were under direct British command, were paid in cash rather than endowed with livestock, and were beginning to be locally recruited.[45] The two processes together, the accumulation of allies and the bureaucratization of force, were the necessary second stage of state-building. Together they obliged any pretender to power to pay close heed to his standing in the high politics of the state, if he were to enhance his local patronage.

The British increasingly imposed on their allies a discipline more appropriate to agents. By 1900 Olonana was no longer allowed to act as if his enemies were also the enemies of the British.[46] And while some 'punitive expeditions' in the 1890s marched out to avenge rapacious African soldiery killed by a justifiably angry local population, in 1904 a British officer shot five of his own men, both soldiers and auxiliaries, for killing women and children once the battle was done.[47] But British officials found themselves under new disciplines too, especially after the Colonial Office took over in 1905.

British self-discipline became the more necessary as they freed themselves from their prudential dependence on Africans. The third phase of conquest, between the completion of the railway and 1908, was the most ruthless. All African peoples who were not yet submissive were treated like the Nandi. As more obedience was expected of those under control, in particular the payment of hut tax, so African freedom beyond the administrative frontier became less tolerable. Besides the Nandi themselves, the Gusii of Nyanza, the most northerly Kikuyu, and the Embu beyond them were subjected to an organized ferocity quite beyond any British capacity a decade earlier. 'Enemy' mortality rose from scores into hundreds, livestock confiscations from hundreds to thousands. An official sense of shame began to stir. Early in 1904 the report on the expedition against the Mathira (or Iraini) Kikuyu suppressed the true casualty list. Some 1,500 had been killed; the governor admitted to 400 only.[48]

More was at stake than the conscience of local officials. At home, the Treasury was increasingly impatient of African military adventure. The Foreign Office feared embarrassment at a time when international outrage was growing over the savagery of King Leopold's Congo. The Colonial Office was torn between faith in the imperial civilizing mission and donnish pessimism – might not the Empire be destroyed by local conflicts between pushy white capitalists and resentful natives? Punitive expeditions were doubtless a painful necessity, but their conduct ought to foster grateful prosperity rather than rebellion.[49]

The Protectorate government was similarly divided. It closed frontier areas to white and Indian traders, lest African anger at private extortion cause more public expense and endanger new public income.[50] At London's request, district officials were also deprived of their armies, the African levies, who could in future be used only on the orders of the governor.[51] An army officer, the same who had shot his own men for murder, was sent home for overzealously killing the Nandi *orkoiyot*.[52] Officials were forbidden their common practice of keeping African mistresses; it was thought bad for prestige, the social distance that was the cheapest form of security.[53] Above all, the Colonial Office centralized recruitment and improved service conditions, to attract graduate officials in place of footloose adventurers. It selected governors thought to be sympathetic to African interests, and sacked or demoted those who nonetheless put private white interests first.[54] The Oxford classicists of Whitehall were again following Agricola, who had earlier learned 'that arms can effect little if injustice follows in their train. He resolved to root out the causes of war. Beginning with himself and his household, he enforced discipline. He preferred to appoint to official positions and duties those whom he could trust not to transgress, rather than punish the transgressor.'[55]

But all this was a necessary curb on the engine of rule rather than a source of productive energy. If the spoils of war were no longer permissible, how were the Africans to be pacified? On the other side of the continent, in Northern Nigeria, High Commissioner Lugard put his finger on the problem. The British needed a 'class who in a crisis can be relied on to stand by us, and whose interests are wholly identified with ours'.[56] And the British knew what they meant by 'class'. Winston Churchill, Under-Secretary of State for the Colonies, devoted a chapter to the question when recounting his visit in 1907 to East Africa.[57] He could imagine no development without the ambitions of capitalists, employers and professional men who, with discipline, education and justice, would stir 'the African aboriginal' out of his 'contented degradation' into 'peaceful industry'.[58]

The local prospects for such a class were not promising. The Commissioner of the East African Protectorate, Sir Arthur Hardinge, had had ideas of enlisting 'the rising generation of Arabs and Swahilis (of the better class) in the service of Government, and whose interests with theirs would thus become identified',[59] but that was before the focus of British interest shifted inland to the highlands. The foot soldiers and porters of conquest had been the polyglot Zanzibari, 'not a tribe but a class'[60] (and not of the better sort), whose services were civilianized as messengers, hut-counters and policemen, and whose campfire lingua franca, Swahili, became the universal language of command. But, like the Sierra Leoneans of West Africa, they did not long survive as the executive agents of colonial rule. They were kin neither to rulers nor to subjects and jarred on the sensitivities of both. Yet the British had little confidence that the local 'native chiefs' had any of the qualities of a productive ruling class. How could they organize increased production and yet remain socially legitimate?

The British seemed to meet in Africa the two conflicting mirrors of their own mythical past, the Norman yoke of conquest kingdoms, and the Anglo-Saxon democracy of tribes.[61] They did not scruple to use African aristocrats, whom they assumed must be immigrant rulers like themselves, as the agents of economic change. But they did not see how tribal leaders could be similarly used without tearing apart the consensual fabric of 'tribal control', throwing the common people into potentially dangerous disorder.[62] If free tribesmen did not have the habit of obedience, neither could their chiefs be trusted to possess the self-discipline of command. This was the dilemma the early officials believed themselves to face in Kenya. They needed tax, labour and exportable produce from people whom they had just seen die in thousands from famine and disease. London doubted whether any resources could, or should, be derived from a 'poverty stricken peasantry with a backward agriculture.'[63] And when production did nonetheless increase, district commissioners complained that their officially recognized chiefs used their authority 'to enrich themselves at the expense of their people'. They ignored their 'tribal elders', enforced public and private demands with armed retainers whom officials were now debarred from using themselves, and then trusted to the state to rescue them from popular anger.[64] Without established class differences in the relative enjoyment of wealth, increased prosperity, in any case doubtful, seemed to presage not peace but uproar.

The government never resolved this contradiction between legitimate authority and the labour of increased production. It first attempted to do so by the complete separation of export production from authority over Africans. It looked for Punjabi peasants, Finnish homesteaders, even Zionist pioneers; all small farmers, reliant on their own labour. Only the first of these experiments in productive classlessness took any root. And Indian settlement was soon fettered by white immigration. Kenya's white settlement was almost an accident, a private bargain between the second commissioner, Sir Charles Eliot, and the first white frontiersmen who took Lord Delamere for their leader. But it turned Kenya into a proper conquest state, with alien barons impatient of legal discipline and contemptuous of the native population.[65]

White settlement was both the baronial consolidation of conquest and the chief threat to the politics of control. If it could not have politically dependent but independently productive small farmers, the Colonial Office came round to the view that it must have big capitalists instead. Big capital would provide the state with a different but equally controllable answer to the nervous 'rhinoceros questions' of African rights in expanded production. It was 'no good trying to lay hold of Tropical Africa with naked fingers'. What was wanted was 'tireless engines, not weary men; cheap power, not cheap labour'. Capital was the axe with which to cut a path through political jungles as well as nature's. If only it could be given room to exploit African land, then the state could 'regulate in full and intricate detail' the relations between capitalists and the few skilled workers they would need. And the colonial state was indeed a cartographer; maps were its images of order. They showed strategic bases and frontier zones, they marked property and the absence of it.[66] White settlement filled in dangerous spaces with roads, fields and boundary beacons. The imagery should not be underestimated, and the reality hoped for, contented black labour on quiet farms with mortgages, producing payloads for a railway with a sinking fund, was itself the image of the civilizing mission, the self-justifying myth of the state as well as its mirage of calm.

White settlement marked and maintained boundaries, the very essence of state-building, in three distinct dimensions. Settlers, first, were marcher lords; they held 'buffer zones' between warring tribes. They would curb the Kalenjin and divide the Maasai from their neighbours. The final phase of highland conquest owed some of its violence to a government desire so to crush resistance that white settlers on the border would be safe.[67] Second, land alienation would separate the thorny opposites of export production and African authority, capital and classlessness. There was a vital proviso. It must be effected by state confiscation and reallocation, not by private sales between Africans and Europeans. The first few settlers had bought privately, at prices much higher than their successors bought from government.[68] But to the state, if not to settlers, the price of land was secondary to its politics. The land frontier must be 'closed', not 'open'.[69] A free market would invite conflicting claims between the races. It would also raise storms of internal African controversy over whether their rights in land were such as to allow private sale. Official alienation, on the other hand, would literally fence capital into a European preserve. Inside the fence a productive class would form. From outside it, classless Africans would be controlled and temporary immigrant workers. Tribal seigniories would be defended against subversion by possessive individualism.[70]

Finally, white settlement would pin down pastoralism, the way of life that kept Africans idle, unnervingly on the move, and impervious to the benefits and constraints of civilization.[71] The politics of conquest was brought symbolically to an end with the Maasai moves of 1904 and 1911. These fenced pastoralism out of the best grazing in the Rift while fencing capitalist ranching in. Three-quarters of the 'White Highlands' was once Maasailand. Conquest had earlier helped to replenish the highlands' livestock banking system. But from 1905 government started to sell looted stock to settlers, having withheld it from African auxiliaries. Maasai were even banned from bidding against settlers in auctions of imported breeding stock.[72] Allies of conquest were never more fully discarded.

State formation: the vulgarization of power

None of these strategic hopes was fulfilled. The building of power was subverted by the power of markets, in capital, labour and commodities. The white barons were the first to slip the leash of state control. They had to. The state tried to tie their rights in land to strict conditions of improvement, so as to force them to invest in intensifying production rather than rest content with the extensive use of cheap labour or, worse still, idle speculation on the rising land values that could be expected from the state's own continuing investments in roads and peace. But the capital market was nervous of untried land in tropical climes. No settler, large or small, could borrow much without first winning a free market, and secure tenure, in the government's stolen lands. By 1915 they had got it.[73]

This first defeat of state control confirmed a second. Settlers who could not afford to put more than a few acres under the plough could neither afford to let their square miles lie empty. They had to keep the hostile bush at bay. Both their small labour wants and their large land-cleansing needs were met by the South African remedy of 'kaffir farming': inviting in African tenants where these were not already in prior residence on what had been their own land. The buffer zones of white settlement became frontiers of opportunity for African mixed farmers, the 'squatters'. Africans had not been allowed to sell land but, in effect, they were allowed to buy in return for labour service. By the Second World War more than one in ten Kikuyu had colonized Maasailand as dependants of big men who happened to be white. The Kalenjin similarly reconquered their confiscated frontiers. Capitalist production and authority over Africans became inextricably mixed. The strategic white marches on the Land Office's maps were riddled with black lines of cultivation, grazing, trade and cattle theft. Pastoralism was not pinned down, it merely became subversive.[74]

It was the same with labour and authority in the African reserves, beyond the broken boundary fence of capital. By 1910 up to one-third of all adult men in the Kikuyu districts and in lowland Nyanza were out of work at any given time, generally for only a few months. Perhaps half of these were employed on public works and in porterage for government officials. They were recruited through an intensification of state-building, an implosion of raiding. Officials and chiefs colluded in the methods of the 1890s, providing tribute labour, whether public or private. Chiefs were chosen for their ability to get things done without questions asked. Ritual authority was useless for the task; the story of Olonana and the *il aigwanak* was a parable for the times. The ambitious young entrepreneurs of the conquest remained to the fore, men with followers and well-tried connections. The expansion of state power and state demand allowed them to widen the gap between the factional benefits of patronage and the penalties of exclusion from favour. Their armed retainers were press gangs and tax collectors, bullying some and exempting others. White officials could scarcely complain at this flouting of 'tribal control', this enrichment of chiefs at their people's expense. It was the consequence of their own demands. Social division and the corruption of authority were the essential foundations of state power.[75]

But power over people was always slipping from chiefs, just as power over capital escaped the state. Peace drew cultivators out of their defended villages, out of chiefs' sight and close to their crops.[76] Indian traders went everywhere with their ox-carts and donkeys. Thousands of African households sold them penny-packets of grain and vegetables, so much so that by 1912 the white settlers, undersold in the domestic market for workers' rations, were forced to take steps to export their maize.[77] African women toiled harder with their hoes.[78] And large numbers of unmarried young men voluntarily earned the means to invest in marriage, the essential starting capital for market production. To the disgust of their seniors they were reshaping old warrior freedoms.[79]

They protected them with novel forms of association. Squatters and migrant workers pioneered the land and labour markets in chain migrations of friends and neighbours. Squatter families rebuffed unwelcome competitors for white settler land by excluding them from community rituals.[80] Migrants increasingly went out without waiting for their chief's compulsion, not singly but in groups, to bargain as a team with known employers rather than face assignment to unknown ones. In this way they broke the employers' hold on market intelligence, gained the initiative in wage-bargaining and softened the rigours of travel.[81] Mission schools and congregations provided the most noticeable new bonds of allegiance. The numbers of professing Christians increased rapidly from about 1912.[82] Missionaries attracted two very different streams of clients, both the young relatives of chiefs who had an eye to another source of advantage and the poor, including a striking number of orphans, who had no other protector.[83] 'Mission boys' soon became an essential evil for district officials. They were useful as hut-counters and clerks, but they highlighted the factional ills of state-building. Some added intellectual arrogance to a canny chief's retinue; others opposed chiefs who did not befriend them, secure in the support of missionary patrons who could be very naive about the inescapable harshness of chiefs' rule.[84]

Government tried to rescue state control from these vulgarizations of power, conceding representation where no sterner discipline was feasible and bringing oppression under the law. It continually rebuilt institutional power to bridge the social rifts and regulate the oppositions that opened up as people formed the state for themselves, using its public power for their private ends. It was an unending task. The settlers were represented in a Legislative Council in 1907, but refused to be tamed by it. A Native Affairs Department was created at the same time, to meet settler demands to discipline labour. Its officials suggested a greater self-discipline in employers and the settlers marched in a mob on Government House. 'Tribal elders' were then represented in local councils in 1911, but they too could do nothing to tame the demands that the state imposed on chiefs. African evangelists were compelled to get preaching permits from chiefs under the Native Catechists Regulations, but the potentially subversive skill of typing was encouraged by the state and even certified by the governor in person.[85]

African society increasingly conformed to the rules of power. The conquest state appeared to be bending African ambition to its own needs. Africans adopted ethnic identities as novel as any missionary denomination. As early as 1910 some joined themselves together in 'clans' out of previously scattered allegiances, the better to claim or repudiate the rights of chiefship. At a wider level, district boundaries, lines on the map rather than shifting margins of subsistence and trade, began in the same way to mark out 'tribes' that claimed the ethnographic purity that the British expected of them, quite unlike the hospitable eclecticism that had existed before.[86] On a still larger scale, agriculturalists and pastoralists began to specialize in one form of production or the other, and lost their previous understandings. Their trade became channelled within ethnic diaspora. Somali stock traders and Indian produce dealers used the peace of the state in place of the narrower peace of the market, which had nonetheless brought direct producers of different livelihoods face to face. People and goods had once crossed cultural boundaries, now the traffic was increasingly in goods alone.[87]

But boundary-building, whether in pursuit of government policy or in response to anonymous African action, was a two-edged weapon of security. As settlers separated African herdsmen and cultivators so also the state replaced the Maasai as the highland bank, a depository of forced savings rather than calculating investment. It was easier to tax settled cultivators than wandering herdsmen. In 1907 the Maasai paid less than 2 per cent of African direct taxation, the Kikuyu and the Nyanza lowlanders more than 30 per cent each.[88] The Maasai did not have to recoup their capital from the state, the agriculturalists did. These invested their earnings from employment and produce sales in education, winning a footing in the skilled labour markets of government, the railway and business. Pastoralism became conservative, agriculture progressive. Where once there had been ecological arenas of exchange, regional inequalities of wealth and power were on the way. These divisions of interest were a form of political control, but they also became ethnic constituencies for political mobilization. The Maasai replied to their second move not with spears but with a lawsuit, a decade before the Luo and Kikuyu, with men who could type, created their political associations. Tacitus seems to have despised those Roman Britons who described, and in Latin, their temples, togas, baths and banquets as civilization, 'when really they were only a feature of enslavement'.[89] But if conquest shapes societies, even conquered peoples can force changes in the forms that states take, so leading, to some extent, their captors captive.

Notes

1. L.S.B. Leakey, *The Southern Kikuyu before 1903* (3 vols, London and New York, 1977), i, p. 33.
2. The arguments of this chapter have been developed in close consultation with my colleagues David Anderson, Bruce Berman and, especially, Greet Kershaw and Richard Waller. None is responsible for its conclusions. Some of its ideas were first developed in J. Lonsdale and B. Berman, 'Coping with the contradictions: the development of the colonial state in Kenya 1895-1914', *Journal of African History* 20 (1979), pp. 487-505 (Chapter 4, below); others have been more widely deployed in my two essays, 'The European scramble and conquest in African history', Ch. 12 in R. Oliver and G.N. Sanderson (eds), *The Cambridge History of Africa*, Vol. VI (Cambridge, 1895), and 'Political accountability in African history', in P. Chabal (ed.), *Political Domination in Africa* (Cambridge, 1986). The present chapter is concerned with the social rather than the military history of the conquest of Kenya. Its main thesis, that there was much African continuity within the European disruption, represents a revision of the standard accounts listed below in n. 3. This revision took its point of origin in R.D. Waller, 'The Maasai and the British 1895-1905: the origins of an alliance', *Journal of African History* 17 (1976), pp. 529-53.
3. See, especially, R. Robinson and J. Gallagher, with A. Denny, *Africa and the Victorians* (London, 1961); J.S. Galbraith, *Mackinnon and East Africa 1878-1895* (Cambridge, 1972); G.H. Mungeam, *British Rule in Kenya 1895-1912* (Oxford, 1966); D.A. Low, 'British East Africa: the establishment of British rule 1895-1912', Ch. 1 in V. Harlow and E.M. Chilver, with A. Smith, *History of East Africa*, Vol. II (Oxford, 1965).
4. See Sir Harry Johnston's appreciation of his Indian troops in Uganda, 1900, quoted in J.S. Mangat, *A History of the Asians in East Africa c. 1886 to 1945* (Oxford, 1969), p. 43n; and, for labour markets, Winston Churchill, *My African Journey* (London, 1908), pp. 33-5, and S. Stichter, *Migrant Labour in Kenya* (Harlow, 1982), pp. 3-5.
5. R.W. Beachey, *The Slave Trade of Eastern Africa* (London, 1976), Ch. 10; F. Cooper, *From Slaves to Squatters* (New Haven and London, 1980).

The Conquest State of Kenya 1895-1905

6. M. Ylvisaker, *Lamu in the Nineteenth Century* (Boston, 1979).
7. For military recruitment, see H. Moyse-Bartlett, *The King's African Rifles* (Aldershot, 1956), Chs. 4 and 6. For porters, J.W. Gregory, *The Great Rift Valley* (London, 1896), Ch. 16; R. Cummings, 'A note on the history of caravan porters in East Africa', *Kenya Historical Review* 1(2) (1973), pp. 109–38; J. Iliffe, *A Modern History of Tanganyika* (Cambridge, 1979), pp. 44–6.
8. R. Meinertzhagen, *Kenya Diary 1902–1906* (Edinburgh, 1957), pp. 9–11. The EAR was not armed with repeating rifles until 1905.
9. J. Fadiman, *Mountain Warriors: The Pre-colonial Meru of Mt Kenya* (Athens, Ohio, 1976); R.D. Waller, ' "The Lords of East Africa": the Maasai in the mid-nineteenth century', Ph.D. dissertation, Cambridge University, 1978; *idem.*, 'Ecology, migration and expansion in East Africa' (University of Malawi seminar paper, May 1984). R.R. Kuczynski (*Demographic Survey of the British Empire*, Vol. II (London 1949), p. 194) was one of the first scholars to doubt that indigenous warfare was responsible for heavy mortality. And see M. Perham and M. Bull (eds) *The Diaries of Lord Lugard* (3 vols, London, 1959), Vol. I, p. 344 (31 Oct. 1890). When some Kikuyu asked Lugard to help them against Kikuyu cattle-thieves he asked 'what had happened in the scrimmage, and was told one of their men had been badly hit in the foot with a knob-kerry. "Just so," I said. "When Wakikuyu fight, a man gets his skull cracked perhaps at worst. If the British fight, and bring guns, many many men *die*" ' (original emphasis). But local war was not always a game. The British commander of an expedition against the Tetu Kikuyu in 1902, himself 'surprised at the ease with which a bayonet goes into a man's body', observed the killing methods of his Maasai auxiliaries: 'Once their man is down they use their short sword, inserting it on the shoulder near the collar bone and thrusting it down . . . through the heart and down to the bladder': Meinertzhagen, *Kenya Diary*, p. 74.
10. T. Lloyd, 'Africa and Hobson's Imperialism', *Past and Present* 55 (1972), p. 143.
11. Mungeam, *British Rule*, p. 132.
12. *Tacitus on Britain and Germany*, trans. by H. Mattingly (West Drayton, 1948), p. 71.
13. Mungeam, *British Rule*, p. 30.
14. The *'local* African lesson' because, unlike stateless societies, African kingdoms elsewhere were not very good at organizing productive peace.
15. This is the area within Kenya's present boundaries, after the inclusion of eastern Uganda in 1902, and after the cession of Jubaland to Italian Somaliland in 1925.
16. This stage of the argument is heavily indebted to Richard Waller, see n. 9 above.
17. My main sources for 19th-century social history are, for the highland Bantu: Godfrey Muriuki, *A History of the Kikuyu 1500–1900* (Nairobi, 1974); Leakey, *Southern Kikuyu;* G. Kershaw, 'The land is the people', Ph.D. dissertation, Chicago University, 1972; J.F. Munro, *Colonial Rule and the Kamba* (Oxford, 1975). For the Maasai and other pastoralists: Waller (above, n. 9); D.M. Anderson, 'Herder, settler, and colonial rule: a history of the peoples of the Baringo plains, Kenya, *c.* 1890–1940', Ph.D. dissertation, Cambridge University, 1983; N.W. Sobania, 'The historical tradition of the peoples of the eastern Lake Turkana basin *c.* 1840–1925, Ph.D. dissertation, London University, 1980. For the Nandi: A.T. Matson, *Nandi Resistance to British Rule 1890–1906* (Nairobi, 1972); A. Gold, 'The Nandi in transition: background to the Nandi resistance to the British 1895–1906', *Kenya Historical Review* 6 (1978), pp. 84–104. For the Nyanza peoples: G.S. Were, *A History of the Abaluyia of Western Kenya c. 1500–1930* (London, 1967); J. Dealing, 'Politics in Wanga, Kenya, *c.* 1650–1914', Ph.D. dissertation, Northwestern University, 1974; B.A. Ogot, *History of the Southern Luo* (Nairobi, 1967); J.M. Butterman, 'Luo social formations in change: Karachuonyo and Kanyamkago *c.* 1800–1945', Ph.D. dissertation, Syracuse University, 1979; W.R. Ochieng', *A Pre-colonial History of the Gusii of Western Kenya* (Nairobi, 1974); D.W. Cohen, 'Food production and food exchange in the precolonial lakes plateau region',

The Conquest State of Kenya 1895–1905

Ch. 1 in R.I. Rotberg, (ed.), *Imperialism, Colonialism and Hunger: East and Central Africa* (Lexington, 1983). See also note 86, p. 473, below.

18. M.P. Cowen, 'Differentiation in a Kenya location' (University of East Africa Social Sciences Council annual conference paper, Nairobi, 1972).
19. *Lugard Diaries,* Vol. I, pp. 369–10 (14 Nov. 1890).
20. P. Rogers, 'The British and the Kikuyu 1890–1905: a reassessment', *Journal of African History* 20 (1979), pp. 255–69; D. Anderson, 'Expansion and expediency on the colonial frontier: the British in Baringo before 1914' (Institute of Commonwealth Studies seminar paper, London, 1982); Dealing, 'Politics in Wanga'.
21. By Low, 'British East Africa', p. 1.
22. M.H. Dawson, 'Smallpox in Kenya 1880–1920', *Social Science and Medicine* 13B(4) (1979), pp. 245–50; the best summary of the disasters is in *idem*, 'Disease and population decline of the Kikuyu of Kenya 1895–1920', pp. 121–38 in *African Historical Demography* 2 (Centre of African Studies, Edinburgh, 1981).
23. J. Ford (*The Role of the Trypanosomiases in African Ecology: A Study of the Tsetse-fly Problem* (Oxford, 1971)) was the first to emphasize the historical importance of rinderpest. For a summary of its continental effects during the late 19th century see Lonsdale, 'European scramble', pp. 689–11.
24. There appears to be a conflict of evidence on this point between relatively optimistic contemporary accounts and gloomy oral tradition. Compare Matson, *Nandi Resistance,* pp. 68, 313, and R.J. Stordy's observations in *Kenya Land Commission Evidence* (3 vols, Nairobi, 1934), Vol. III, pp. 3338, 3341, with Nandi traditions in Gold, 'Nandi in transition'.
25. Kuczynski, *Demographic Survey*, Vol. II, pp. 190–9; Dawson, 'Disease and population decline'; H.G. Soff, 'Sleeping sickness in the Lake Victoria region of British East Africa 1900–15', *African Historical Studies* 2 (1969), pp. 255–68.
26. From the field notes of Professor G. Kershaw, generously shared.
27. British responsibility was first suggested by Kuczynski, *Demographic Survey*, Vol. II, p. 199; he is followed by Muriuki, *History of the Kikuyu*, p. 155; but Rogers, 'British and Kikuyu', pp. 263–4 questions this thesis.
28. Munro, *Kamba*, p. 49.
29. By this time the Baringo food market had been by-passed by a shorter route. The new halfway house between Kikuyu and Nyanza was Eldama Ravine, in an area where the British could not buy food locally. It was rationed by headload from Kikuyu and Mumias, about 160 km (100 miles) distant in each direction.
30. Munro, *Kamba*, pp. 38, 41. These early militia perhaps gave the Kamba their taste for service in the police and army, for which they supplied a disproportionate number of recruits throughout the colonial period.
31. Kershaw, 'Land is people', p. 148n.
32. Muriuki, *History of the Kikuyu, passim*; Rogers, 'British and Kikuyu'.
33. For a detailed study of the conquest of western Kenya, see below, Chapter 3; R.D. Waller, 'Interaction and identity on the periphery: the Trans-Mara Maasai', *International Journal of African Historical Studies* 17 (1984), esp. pp. 258–9.
34. See below, Chapter 3.
35. The European involved was in fact the German traveller, Karl Peters, but that does not alter the point. See his *New Light on Dark Africa* (London, 1891), pp. 301–10.
36. Waller, 'Maasai and British'; Waller, 'Interaction and identity'.
37. For differing accounts of Kimnyolei's death see A.T. Matson, 'Nandi traditions on raiding', in B.A. Ogot (ed.), *Hadith* 2, (Nairobi, 1970), p. 78; S.K. arap Ng'eny, 'Nandi resistance to the establishment of British administration 1893–1906', pp. 106f in *ibid.*; Gold, 'Nandi in transition', pp. 94f.
38. Stichter, *Migrant Labour*, pp. 5–14.
39. Munro, *Kamba*, pp. 47–8.

40. Muriuki, *History of Kikuyu*, pp. 94f; for central Kikuyu, D.M. Feldman, 'Christians and politics: the origins of the Kikuyu Central Association in northern Murang'a 1890-1930', Ph.D. dissertation, Cambridge University, 1978, pp. 45-6.

41 See below, Chapter 3; Stichter, *Migrant Labour*, pp. 12-14.

42. M.J. Hay, 'Economic change in Luoland: Kowe 1890-1945', Ph.D. dissertation, University of Wisconsin, 1972, Ch. 4 and Hay, 'Luo women and economic change during the colonial period', pp. 87-109 in N.J. Hafkin and E.G. Bay (eds), *Women in Africa* (Stanford, 1976) are the most helpful for this period, but deal with an area much less disrupted than central Kenya. For the Kikuyu two otherwise valuable studies have nothing to say specifically about the 1890s: G. Kershaw, 'The changing roles of men and women in the Kikuyu family by socioeconomic strata', *Rural Africana* 29 (1975-6), pp. 173-93, and C.M. Clark, 'Land and food, women and power, in nineteenth century Kikuyu', *Africa* 50 (1980), pp. 357-70. Neither Leakey, *Southern Kikuyu*, nor W.S. and K. Routledge, *With a Prehistoric People* (London, 1910) are helpful. L. White 'Women in the changing African family', Ch. 4 in M.J. Hay and S. Stichter (eds), *African Women South of the Sahara*, (London, 1984) makes some interesting suggestions that could serve as research hypotheses.

43. For example, M. Wright, *Women in Peril: Life Stories of Four Captives* (University of Zambia, Lusaka, 1984); Wright, 'Bwanikwa: consciousness and protest among slave women in Central Africa 1886-1911', Ch. 13 in C.C. Robertson and M.A. Klein (eds), *Women and Slavery in Africa* (Madison, 1983); E.A. Alpers, 'The story of Swena: female vulnerability in nineteenth-century East Africa', Ch. 11 in *ibid*; M. Vaughan, 'Famine analysis and family relations: 1949 in Nyasaland', paper presented to the African Studies Association annual meeting, Boston, 1983. For an overall thesis, see A. Sen, *Poverty and Famines: An Essay on Entitlement and Deprivation* (Oxford, 1981).

44. Rogers, 'British and Kikuyu', pp. 264-5; Feldman, 'Christians and politics', pp. 49-50; Chapter 3, below; Stichter, *Migrant Labour*, pp. 9-17. The inclusion of Kinyanjui in this list revises the received view, before 1976, that he was merely an upstart camp follower of conquest.

45. See further, Chapter 3, below. The first highlanders, Maasai, were recruited into the East African rifles in 1901; but the Maasai company was disbanded in 1907, as incorrigibly undisciplined. In 1908 a Nandi company was recruited into what was now the 3rd King's African Rifles, but it remained a largely Sudanese force until 1914. The Protectorate's police force, on the other hand, was 40 per cent 'highlander' in composition by 1912 (mainly Luo, Kamba, Maasai and Kikuyu): T.H.R. Cashmore, 'Studies in district administration in the East Africa Protectorate 1895-1918', Ph.D. dissertation, Cambridge University, 1965, pp. 128-9.

46. Waller, 'Maasai and British', p. 544.

47. Meinertzhagen, *Kenya Diary*, p. 144 (29 Feb. 1904).

48. Mungeam, *British Rule*, p. 84; Muriuki, *History of Kikuyu*, p. 165.

49. R. Hyam, *Elgin and Churchill at the Colonial Office 1905-1908* (London, 1968), pp. 207-17; *idem.*, 'The Colonial Office mind 1900-1914', *Journal of Imperial and Commonwealth History* 8 (1979), pp. 30-55.

50. Meinertzhagen, *Kenya Diary*, pp. 119-22 (Nov. 1903) tells how one white freebooter was brought to book.

51. Mungeam, *British Rule*, pp. 171-80, 238-9; Governor Sir Percy Girouard, *Memoranda for Provincial and District Commissioners* (Nairobi, 1910), 'Instructions for the control of expeditions and patrols'.

52. Meinertzhagen, *Kenya Diary*, p. 327 (5 May 1906).

53. Cashmore, 'District administration', p. 40; Ronald Hyam, 'Concubinage and the colonial service: the Crewe circular (1909)', *Jl. Imperial & Commonwealth History* 14 (1986), pp. 26-42.

54. Cashmore, 'District administration', pp. 24-6. The two governors sacked were Eliot

in 1904 and Girouard in 1912 (although both were in fact allowed to resign), both in relation to the Maasai moves (below). Hayes Sadler was demoted to the governorship of the Windward Islands in 1909 for being too weak both with white settlers and the military.

55. *Tacitus*, p. 70.
56. Writing to the Secretary of State, Jan. 1904. Quoted in R. Robinson, 'European imperialism and indigenous reactions in British West Africa 1880-1914', Ch. 8 in H.L. Wesseling, (ed.), *Expansion and Reaction: Essays on European Expansion and Reactions in Asia and Africa* (Leiden, 1978), pp. 159-60.
57. Churchill, *My African Journey*, Ch. 3.
58. *Ibid.*, pp. 42-3.
59. April 1896; quoted in Mungeam, *British Rule*, p. 26.
60. Gregory, *Rift Valley*, p. 304.
61. Henrika Kuklick, 'Tribal exemplars: images of political authority in British anthropology 1885-1945', pp. 59-82 in George W. Stocking (ed.), *Functionalism Historicized: Essays in British Social Anthropology* (Madison, 1984).
62. Girouard, *Memoranda*, 'Native policy'.
63. Lord Lansdowne to Commissioner Eliot, June 1901, quoted in Rogers, 'British and Kikuyu', p. 266. See also, C.C. Wrigley, 'Kenya: the patterns of economic life, 1902-1945', Ch. 5 in V. Harlow and E.M. Chilver (eds), *History of East Africa*, Vol. II, esp. pp. 211-14.
64. R.W. Hemsted, *South Kavirondo Annual Report 1910-11*, Kenya National Archives, Nairobi.
65. M.P.K. Sorrenson, *Origins of European Settlement in Kenya* (Nairobi, 1968) is still the essential authority.
66. Churchill, *My African Journey*; pp. 41,53,36; J.D. Overton, 'Spatial differentiation in the colonial economy of Kenya: Africans, settlers and the state 1900-1920', Ph.D. dissertation, Cambridge University, 1983.
67. For the relationship between expeditions and alienation: *ibid.*, p. 23; and Mungeam, *British Rule*, pp. 141-5, 155-60, 161-4. The later rationalizations for buffer zones are summarized in E.W. Soja, *The Geography of Modernization in Kenya* (Syracuse, NY, 1968), pp. 20-1.
68. P. Mosley, *The Settler Economies: Studies in the Economic History of Kenya and Southern Rhodesia 1900-1963* (Cambridge, 1983), pp. 15-16.
69. For the distinction, see H. Giliomee, 'Processes in development of the Southern African frontier', Ch. 4 in H. Lamar and L. Thompson, (eds)., *The Frontier in History: North America and Southern Africa Compared* (New Haven, 1981).
70. *Report of Commission on Native Land Tenure in the Kikuyu Province* (Nairobi, 1929) is the best early source for official thinking on the matter. For an official view on the contradiction between what I have called state-building and state-formation with reference to land tenure, see J. Ainsworth's memorandum to the Kenya Land Commission (*Evidence* iii, p. 3451): 'I think that the introduction of individual tenure to land through title issued by the Government will tend to break down tribal authority but it should help in time in building up the native state . . . (By the term "native state" I mean each individual adult being responsible to the authorities as opposed to the custom of tribal responsibility.)'
71. The most pungent early official opinions on 'pernicious pastoral proclivities' are conveniently reproduced in *ibid.*, pp. 3438-49, memorandum by C.M. Dobbs. For good studies of official pastoral policy: I.R.G. Spencer, 'Pastoralism and colonial policy in Kenya 1895-1929', Ch. 5 in Rotberg (ed.), *Imperialism, Colonialism and Hunger*; and R.L. Tignor, *The Colonial Transformation of Kenya: the Kamba, Kikuyu and Maasai from 1900 to 1939* (Princeton, 1976), Ch. 14.
72. For the auction ban, R.J. Stordy in Land Commission *Evidence*, iii, p. 3342; for the

moves, Mungeam, *British Rule*, pp. 119–23, 259–69; Sorrenson, *European Settlement*, Ch. 12.

73. *Ibid.*, Chs 2–9 for land policy and its changes.
74. There is a growing literature on squatters. See, especially, R.M.A. van Zwanenberg, *Colonial Capitalism and Labour in Kenya 1919–1939* (Nairobi, 1975), Ch. 8 – which has much on stock theft too; T. Kanogo, *Squatters and the Roots of Mau Mau* (London, 1987); Frank Furedi, *The Mau Mau War in Perspective* (London, 1989).
75. The best published source for all this is *Native Labour Commission 1912–13: Evidence and Report* (Nairobi, 1913). For discussions of early colonial chiefs, see: B.A. Ogot, 'British administration in the Central Nyanza district of Kenya 1900–60', *Journal of African History* 4 (1963), esp. pp. 252–4; E. Atieno-Odhiambo, 'Some reflections on African initiative in early colonial Kenya', *East Africa Journal* 8 (1971), pp. 30–6; W.R. Ochieng', 'Colonial African chiefs: were they primarily self-seeking scoundrels?', Ch. 3 in B.A. Ogot (ed.), *Hadith 4: Politics and Nationalism in Colonial Kenya* (Nairobi, 1972); Tignor, *Colonial Transformation*, Ch. 3
76. Low, 'British East Africa', pp. 33f; Hay, 'Economic change', p. 99.
77. E. Huxley, *No Easy Way: A History of the Kenya Farmers' Association and Unga Ltd.* (Nairobi, 1957), p. 4.
78. For women's labour, see works referred to in n. 42 above; also, importantly, G. Kitching, *Class and Economic Change in Kenya* (New Haven and London, 1980).
79. M. Beech, 'The Kikuyu point of view', Dec. 1912, repr. in G.H. Mungeam (ed.), *Kenya: Select Historical Documents 1884–1923* (Nairobi, 1979), pp. 477–9. For a pioneering discussion of how African seniors and colonial officials together disciplined juniors, both men and women, through the construction of 'customary law', see M. Chanock, *Law, Custom and Social Order: The Colonial Experience in Malawi and Zambia* (Cambridge, 1985); the same exercises in social control were undoubtedly attempted in Kenya, but the research that would confirm this impression has yet to be done.
80. Information from Professor Kershaw, who has unrivalled data on Kikuyu social history.
81. *Native Labour Commission*, pp. 150, 159, 162, 203, 234f (evidence from chiefs and workers).
82. D.B. Barrett *et al.* (eds), *Kenya Churches Handbook* (Kisumu, 1973), p. 158, fig. 1.
83. K. Ward, 'The development of protestant Christianity in Kenya 1910–40', Ph.D. dissertation, Cambridge University, 1976, Ch. 4; Feldman, 'Christians and politics', Ch. 3; R.W. Strayer, *The Making of Mission Communities in East Africa* (London, 1978).
84. J.M. Lonsdale, 'A political history of Nyanza 1883–1945', Ph.D. dissertation, Cambridge University, 1964, Chs 4 and 5.
85. A. Clayton and D.C. Savage, *Government and Labour in Kenya 1895–1963* (London, 1974), pp. 31–40 for Native Affairs Department; Cashmore, 'District administration', pp. 97–100 for elders' councils; J. Spencer, *James Beauttah: Freedom Fighter* (Nairobi, 1983), p. 10 for the typist and the Governor.
86. J.M. Lonsdale, 'When did the Gusii (or any other group) become a tribe?' *Kenya Historical Review* 5 (1977), pp. 123–33; Waller, 'Interaction and identity'; compare Iliffe, *Tanganyika*, Ch. 10. See further, Chapters 9 and 12 below.
87. M.J. Hay, 'Local trade and ethnicity in western Kenya', *African Economic History Review* 2(1) (1975), pp. 7–12; I.R.G. Spencer, 'The first assault on Indian ascendancy: Indian traders in the Kenyan reserves 1895–1929', *African Affairs* 80 (1981), pp. 327–44.
88. Calculated from taxation figures in Cashmore, 'District administration', p. 136 n.
89. *Tacitus*, p. 72.

Three

𝔇𝔇𝔇𝔇𝔇𝔇𝔇𝔇𝔇𝔇𝔇𝔇𝔇𝔇𝔇𝔇𝔇𝔇𝔇𝔇𝔇𝔇

The Politics of Conquest in Western Kenya
1894-1908

JOHN LONSDALE

This chapter studies the making of the conquest state in one of its regions, at ground level.[1] It offers an analysis of a forcible process of political accumulation, the means whereby their British conquerors came to terms with the peoples of western Kenya,[2] and a prerequisite for the pursuit of capital accumulation, the appropriation of economic resources from the native peoples of Kenya to the benefit of its British colonists. The case of western Kenya offers no paradigm for the European occupation of the rest of the African continent. Nor can any other case. The relative weights of subjugation and accommodation, of rupture and continuity within conquest – of such great influence on the structure and texture of the colonial era that followed – were governed by too many variables. Brief mention of only four of them will be enough to indicate some of the pitfalls of generalization, even generalization about difference.[3]

If one takes, first, the advance of the traders' frontier, it is plain that there were great differences in the degree to which production for external markets had impinged upon African societies by the late 19th century and redistributed their economic inequalities or political power. At one extreme the informal empire of the cotton trade had wrought a gross simplification in Egypt, as it declared redundant so many functions of an intermediate status between those of landlord-official and increasingly landless peasant. At the opposite end of the scale there were many areas of inland Africa, of which western Kenya was one, where the distant pulse of the overseas market had barely, if at all, diverted the

45

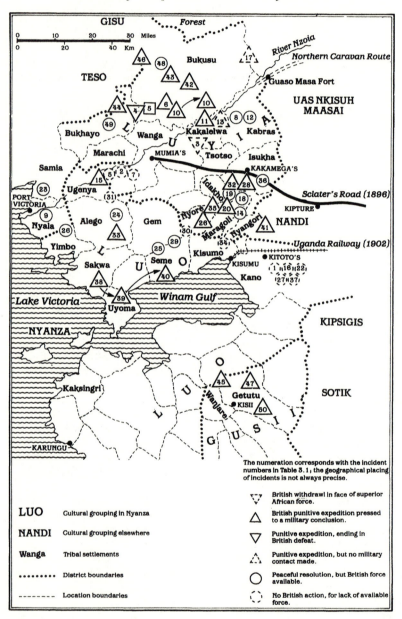

Map 3.1 *The British conquest of western Kenya*

allocation of household labour or opened out the regional circuits of exchange. Between these extremes lay a middling zone of conflict, where old forms of authority struggled to control new sources of wealth and power. To instance but two examples out of many, in the East African interior, what is now Tanzania, authorities over crops and climates were under challenge from protectors of the coastmen's caravans. In West Africa, the military entrepreneurs of Yorubaland failed to redraw the sacred geography that upheld the decaying overlordship of Oyo or the antique shrines of Ife, in favour of the shiny new firepower of Ibadan.

In the first situation, conquest was of little consequence. Egypt was already a colonial economy; the violence had been done to its society. Where, on the other hand, the parochial reciprocities of subsistence, prestation and local exchange had not yet been ferreted out by merchant capital, the connotations of conquest might be expected to be particularly brutal, as the domestic mode of production was forced to yield up a surplus, to its conquerors' profit.[4] The case study that follows, however, suggests that at least in initial colonial situations of this type, historical accident still differentiated those whom economic determinism would herd together. In the undecided areas of Africa, where power or wealth was in unresolved conflict with authority, the course and impact of conquest was just as varied. At its least disruptive, as in Yorubaland, the imperial power was accorded sufficient discretion by Africans to bring to an end, without force, their internal war – but not enough to eliminate the fundamental issues over which the Yoruba continued to be divided. To take the opposite case, the Germans in East Africa encountered effective military resistance as well from peoples who had studiedly isolated themselves from the subversive effects of long-distance trade, as from those who had pioneered it and whose leaderships in consequence straddled conflicting bases of authority.

Another general variable must be the advance of the settlers' frontier. This had an equally complex relationship with conquest. It might reasonably be expected that conquest on behalf of European settlement would be a particularly deliberate affair, since to its native owners land was a more concrete commodity than sovereignty, especially for those many African societies that scarcely differentiated political from kin relations. But it is wrong to suppose that early colonial administrations actively preferred white settler export production to that by African peasants.[5] And the African polity that conceded the highest proportion of its land, Swaziland, did so without obliging a single white man to fire a shot.[6] Where the frontiers of white colonization did crackle into flame, the violence was generally resorted to either by Africans, in despair at privateering land grabs by settlers and their labour demands, or by imperial governments – in Algeria or South Africa – attempting to stamp an order on the racial boundary, precisely to forestall such eruptions. The prospect of mineral wealth, however, introduced an altogether sterner imperial commitment, in Southern Africa against settler sub-imperialism, further north in alliance with it.

The conquest of much of western Kenya had been completed before the arrival of the first settlers, scarcely any land was alienated from the peoples under examination, and rumours of mineral deposits were not proven until many years later. There is no evidence that the distant presence of the first settlers was directly responsible for the increasingly brusque official actions of the later phases of the area's pacification. The process of conquest provides explanation enough. The indirect influence of the growth of a more self-sufficient white society must however have been considerable. The conduct of one of the last military expeditions in the area, against the Gusii in 1908, stirred to anger both Winston Churchill at the Colonial Office – because of its brutality; and the local political officer – because of its stupidity.[7] A military establishment was growing, separate from the civil administration and lacking its local intelligence. But a new social blindness to their common humanity with Africans was inevitable in men whose relaxation – unlike the pioneer administrators' – excluded Africans in any role save that of servant. The young officers who were shooting up the Gusii ought, after all, to have been attending the Railway Institute dance in Nairobi, to which more European ladies had been invited than at any previous function in the history of the young Protectorate.[8]

If one turns to the African perceptions of conquest, it was clearly of some moment whether African polities were sufficiently specialized in function to support principled divisions of opinion over domestic and foreign policy.[9] Where this was so, the sting of conquest might be drawn, in so far as it represented the external afforcement of a domestic group. East Africa furnishes classic examples in the kingdoms of what became Uganda, close neighbours to western Kenya.[10] Where, however, as in the present case, there were small-scale societies with only rudimentary political apparatus, sustained political division and compromise were naturally rare. Political tension was generally relieved by fission along the fault lines of lineage affiliation, often followed by secession and migration. Domestic rivals were always potential outsiders. The seizure of lineage-based societies from outside cannot normally therefore be effected by alignment with an internal faction; where in a complex society that might shift the scales of political influence, in a segmented lineage society it might simply add one more to the number of social-political segments. Two implications follow, both of importance for the experience of western Kenya. First, political advantage accrued to the conqueror more often by arranging external peace between segments than by manipulating division within them. Conversely, the experiences of defeat, accommodation or alliance must have been very

much more total for individual segments of society – at any of the
various segmentary levels of tribe, clan or lineage – than for a more
complex society taken as a whole. Whether these differentiating experiences were also more indelible in lineage society is open to doubt. As,
say, in the kingdom of Buganda, the factional underpinnings of conquest
might later be complicated by the class relations of export production,
so in western Kenya, a tribe's early advantages in official employment
or mission education – the rewards of collaboration – could be nullified
by the subsequent depletion of soil fertility or by distance from markets.

Finally, a variable to which perhaps too little attention is given is the
apparently simple matter of time, the relative timing of an African
society's confrontation with European political ambitions, within a given
regional network of African relations. In some areas of Africa, particularly beyond the moving settler frontier in the south, it could be
argued that the longer an African polity was aware of European aims
and military capacity, the more it observed the consequences of, and lost
the strategic room needed for military resistance, so much the more
would it strive to reach a peaceful accommodation. That must be a large
part of the explanation why the Swazi did not follow the belligerent
example of their neighbours the Zulu. But chronology is also complex
in this matter, for the European appetite for dominion was inclined to
grow with eating. Where an earlier proconsul might be content with
African guarantees of peace and open roads, a successor would demand
tax payments and perhaps a labour tribute. As colonial time proceeded
therefore, there was often greater cause for African resistance. And it
is striking, in West Africa, how often those largely coastal societies that
earliest reached an understanding with the British were able to preserve
right through the colonial era the conventions under which they were
scarcely subject to formal overrule at all.

There are examples of both these implications of chronology in
the conquest of western Kenya. As time went on and British punitive
expeditions multiplied, so the Luo people of southern Nyanza drew
appropriate conclusions from the fate of their kinsmen to the north and
made their peace without ever having occasioned war. On the other hand
the Bukusu and Gusii peoples, on the northern and southern confines
of Nyanza respectively, continued to attract severe retribution from an
administration increasingly well equipped to deal it out.

The western Kenya area is commonly known as Nyanza from its
geographical position, the northeastern segment of the Victoria Nyanza
basin. Eight hundred kilometres (500 miles) inland from the Indian
Ocean, it covers an area of 1950 square kilometres (7500 square miles),
almost exactly astride the Equator, and is divided into three fairly well
defined ecological zones. The altitude ranges from about 1150 m (3700

49

feet) at the Lake shore, to over 2150 m (7000 feet) at several points inland, north and south of the Gulf of Winam. The first ecological zone runs along the Lake margin, its width varying from 15 to 45 km (10 to 30 miles). Its landward limits lie approximately along the 1400 m (4500 feet) contour. Its soils are rather poor and often badly drained; the rainfall is normally adequate but can be most unreliable; it is excellent cattle country and in its pockets of fertility good cereal crops can be grown. The other two zones lie to the north and the southeast of the Gulf, and are alike in their characteristics. They enjoy heavy, reliable rainfall and easily worked, fertile soils; together they contain about a quarter of modern Kenya's best agricultural land.

As is so often the case in Africa, cultural and ecological boundaries more or less coincide. Along the Lake shores live the Luo peoples, Nilotic in language, cattle herders and fishermen according to their own self-image, but also successful cultivators. To the north and south of them, in areas of higher rainfall, live Bantu-speaking groups, people now known as the Luyia and Gusii respectively. Their agricultural crop combinations can be more complex than those of the Luo, their scope for accumulating cattle rather less marked. In precolonial times cultural identities were flexible. The strategies of survival for small colonizing groups in the face of uncertain climatic and epizootic environments, no less than the tactics of trade across ecological boundaries, required an easy acceptance of clientage and adoption, sometimes along lines suggested by previous cross-cultural marriage.[11] The fundamentals of life were guaranteed by communities very much smaller than these cultural confederations. The people of Nyanza lived in groups at once large enough to ensure their own reproduction within an ideology of unilineal descent, and yet compact or homogeneous enough to organize the exploitation and defence of their area of settlement without the overheads of government. There was never an exact match between these requirements; the second demanded a size of community that was unattainable under the former. Prone to segmentation and fission, descent groups could not control their environment save in association with others. All settlements were therefore occupied by associations of clans, linked by descent, marriage or clientage. There was a certain fixity to settlement areas, which were defined by a ridge, or drainage basin, or tsetse fly-free grazing ground. They could be separated from neighbouring settlements by a zone of empty bush, up to half a day's march in width. There was no such fixity in the clans that exploited these lands. Colonization of the area – still far from complete by the late 19th century – filled out by a kind of capillary attraction, by which segments of descent groups were threaded between a number of settlements, providing a dominant clan or group of clans in one area, juniors or clients in others. If by no means all settlements had developed the political institution of chiefship, each nevertheless had a sense of selfhood. They were the largest areas in which the rule of law operated, compensation for homicide being required between their member clans. The term 'tribe', which has come to be applied to these settlements, is therefore not too misleading a shorthand.

At the turn of the century there were nearly 20 of these tribal settlements among the Luo, about 15 Luyia ones, and half a dozen among the Gusii. The total population of Nyanza could barely have reached a million, in a distribution that ranged from the very sparse in the southern Luo and northern Luyia zones to the closely settled, especially along the Luo–Luyia border, where there was increasing competition for land. None of the tribal settlements can have numbered more than about 20,000 people, the largest probably being the Alego tribe among the Luo and the dispersed Bukusu among the Luyia.

The politics of British conquest was hammered out between a few major protagonists. The local British base was at Mumia's or Mumias, named after the then *nabongo* of the Luyia Wanga tribe. The *nabongo* was the nearest approach to an institutionalized chiefship in Nyanza, but was ritual and mediatory in nature, being allowed no executive authority by the Wanga clans. The village had been the centre of operations for Swahili ivory hunters and slave raiders from the Indian Ocean coast for little more than 20 years before the British arrival; the impact of their trade and firepower had not yet been very profound, for Nyanza was at the uttermost limit of their commercial frontier. But for the Wanga, the coastmen's guns had possibly been crucial in turning the encroaching frontier of Luo colonization to their south, of which the cutting edge was the Ugenya group of clans. To the north of the Wanga, beyond an empty zone across the turbulent Nzoia river, was spread the loose confederation of Bukusu clans, the main cattlemen of the Luyia group. Some clans had come from the west of Mount Elgon, an ancient Bantu dispersal centre; others were of quite different cultural origin from the northeast, the home of the Nilotic-speaking pastoralists now called Kalenjin. By the late 19th century it appears that all the Bukusu were, or had become, Bantu-speakers. Under some pressure from the Teso peoples, they were beginning to encroach on the neutral zone that separated them from the Wanga.

Settled at a number of points down the Nzoia basin were groups of Uas Nkishu (Uasin Gishu) Maasai, a section of the most powerful and extensive pastoral people of the East African highlands. Until the late 19th century they seem to have been transhumant visitors only, with the Luyia area providing dry-season pasturage. But then, after a series of internal Maasai wars, Uas Nkishu groups established themselves as refugees among the more northerly of the Luyia agriculturalists, strategically placed therefore to reconstitute their cattle herds by raiding both across the Nzoia into the Bukusu grasslands, and south into the Gem and Ugenya Luo areas. It is difficult to judge how far they were the reliable allies of the people among whom they settled; it seems likely that their own interest in cattle raids more often than not disrupted what defensive understandings were reached among the northern Luyia and that they therefore facilitated rather than hindered the northward spread of the Luo.[12]

While the Luo Ugenya were an expansive group, athwart what was to become the British line of communication to Uganda, another Luo clan cluster, the Kano tribe on the open, swampy plains at the head of the Winam Gulf, were vulnerable to marauders from the surrounding hills. To the north, atop an imposing escarpment, were the Nandi people, members of the Kalenjin branch of Nilotic-speakers, who had recently acquired a refugee Maasai prophet and, with him, a new verve and coordination in cattle lifting. On the highland rim of Nyanza, the Nandi were the key to its conquest.[13] Their age-graded cohesion, their reivers' arts of surprise and concealment, made them the most formidable opponents the British were to encounter in the Kenya interior. Until they were apparently contained in 1900, by the third in a series of British expeditions, there was little that Protectorate officials could do to protect the Kano and their 'chief' Kitoto who, perhaps even more than Mumia, relied for his authority on ritual competence. Kitoto, the British well knew, was a potential ally; if his protection was impossible until the elimination of the Nandi threat, so too was the conquest of the Gusii farther to the south, who looked very much like enemies.

Until 1901, the Nyanza area represented to the British little more than a section of the caravan route, and a most important refreshment station, on the way to Uganda. The main line of communication shifted twice during the period of conquest. The Swahili trade route, used initially by the British, came into Nyanza from the northeast after skirting well to the north of the Nandi grazing grounds. It followed the Nzoia, crossing at the ford that was largely responsible for Mumias' importance. At Port Victoria – imperious name for shed and jetty – government loads were transferred to canoes for the final stage of the journey to Buganda. Late in 1896 a cart track, the Sclater's Road, was run through Nandi. With it the British position became a little less insecure, but it was not until the arrival of the railway (which, with quinine, was the real conqueror of tropical Africa) at the new lake-port of Kisumu in 1901, that the British could feel safe against all local shocks. With the railway their numbers and purposes enlarged. Until then there had rarely been more than three or four white officials in Nyanza, and their chief duties concerned the safe passage of the mails, buying food for passing caravans, the collection of the ivory duty.[14] They were storekeepers, not suzerains. One was stationed at Port Victoria. Sixty-five kilometres (40 miles), or four caravan days inland was the headquarters of Mumias, first established in 1894 under the care of the Commissioner to Uganda's valet. His successor, Charles Hobley, who had come out as geologist to the Imperial British East Africa Company, did not receive an assistant until late in 1895. The only additions to the local white establishment before 1900 were military transients, or private traders under contract to transport government loads. The Mumias station garrison of regular Sudanese troops under a Sudanese warrant officer never numbered more than 60 men.

For its first six years, then, the process of British conquest in Nyanza offers an unusually pure example of the tactical, day-to-day determinants of political accumulation. The peoples of the area presented no major threats to the British position in eastern Africa; their lands were not coveted for white settlement, at least until 1903, nor were they thought to contain any minerals of immediate interest. Yet in these same six years the British had been prompted to thoughts of military action on 40 separate occasions. And in 30 instances they had undertaken coercive steps – if only a minatory promenade – against no less than 18 of Nyanza's tribal settlements. Since in these circumstances to describe would merely be to confuse, a rather austerely abstract analysis is all that will be offered. It may in that form have something to say to other initial colonial situations. On the other hand, remembering the cautionary attempts at generalization with which we opened, it may not.

The dour business of British conquest and African alliance or submission was only one of three concurrent agencies of integration that joined western Kenya by unequal ties to the wider world. In the economic sphere, the market for local products expanded rapidly; labour began to be detached from the matrix of household and clan. Ideological change was less continuous. Islam touched only a tiny minority of people, those – especially at Mumias – who became the commercial partners of the men from the coast. Christian missions made only a false start in Nyanza in the 1890s, not to reappear until 1902. There is perhaps some slight indication that the indigenous cosmologies of the area were themselves being adapted to explain and therefore give a measure of control over the changes of the times, especially the enlargement of the social field of action. Several diviners or prophets among the Bukusu, the Luo and the Gusii – as among other peoples of Kenya – appear to have been anxious to cooperate with the forces of change, at least to the extent of advising their people against military resistance.[15] Finally, conquest itself was part of a continuing political process. The Swahili traders had introduced to Nyanza a source of external alliance. The British were to appropriate and then convert this into a new level of authority, the 'territorial' or 'Protectorate' level, above what may be called the 'parochial' level of the tribal settlements of Nyanza. Intermediate between these two levels there soon developed a 'local' or

'Nyanza' arena, in which British and Africans pursued what appeared to be their common interests as much as they fought out their conflicts.

The core of conquest was the accumulation by the British of local political resources. Its converse, about which one would wish to know a great deal more, was the Africans' attempts to deny resources to the British, to mitigate the effects of expropriation or to acquire fresh resources themselves by joining the bandwagon of ascendancy. Four component processes of political accumulation must be isolated and examined before any periodization of the conquest is possible. It has to be insisted, first, that the precondition for accumulation was British force, unhindered in its application by any parochial ties. At critical junctures in the conquest of Nyanza the British were normally able to use military forces posted from or in transit to other areas of the Uganda Protectorate. This availability of external aid also underwrote the pre-suppositions with which Hobley and the other officials reacted to each new challenge to their local position. The appointment of the first British official to Nyanza had coincided with the declaration of a provisional protectorate over Buganda. This declaration was itself only a stage in a process of increasingly forcible British participation in the affairs of that kingdom and its neighbours that had started in 1890. Nyanza had not been included within the protectorate – it was not legally incorporated until 1896 – but it was unquestionably British territory in the minds of officials. That had been decided by the Anglo-German treaty of 1890. The first British officers in Nyanza might therefore be political striplings, but they were well connected and had great expectations.[16]

What transpired on the battlefield then, when the Hotchkiss or Maxim was assembled or the bayonet charge went in; when the thatch was fired or the cattle captured – all this was of fundamental importance in establishing a sense of mastery or subordination. But force was not power. Power comes not by a single act of confrontation but by repeated transactions within some ordered set of social relations; its costs and benefits must at least carry the possibility of calculation and prediction.[17] Force had manageable consequences, therefore, only when it was associated with the second component of conquest, a complementary process of appropriation from and enlargement of the local Nyanza African political resources. Together these allowed the British possession of force, a power base, to be transformed into a power relationship in which Africans also shared.

The dual nature of the appropriation of African resources can be seen most clearly in the conduct of what the British called, in a term so revealing of their own perceptions, punitive expeditions. In these the resources of African allies were deployed by the loan of warriors, the 'native auxiliaries'. The British needed these to assist – mainly as guides and lifters of livestock – in forcing other Africans to terms. The British were careful, however, to reserve to themselves the identification of the enemy, the negotiation of peace and the redistribution of looted cattle. Ostensibly therefore those who provided the auxiliaries did not earn the political increment of victory, and their material gains in livestock were not a British expense. It is vital to appreciate that the local African political resources were being enlarged nevertheless, and in two ways.

The first was a measure of the mutual misunderstanding between the British and their local allies. It is striking how far the punitive expeditions based on Mumias are locally remembered as the British agencies of Mumia's will. Some descendants of the defeated similarly explain the largest expedition against the Luo, in December 1899: it was the British rejoinder to slanderous reports by their main Luo ally, Odera Ulalo the war leader of Gem, who saw in the British the means to pay off old scores.[18] The British understood punitive expeditions to be a necessary education in submission. Those who 'came in' to accept terms were thereafter treated as 'friendlies'. But where the British perceived submission, their chief allies – *nabongo* Mumia among the Luyia, Odera Ulalo among the northern Luo – were receiving clients. British conquest began the creation of what had hitherto been latent in the exchanges of marriage, barter and ritual – an African political system, with its sources of patronage backed by the terrifying sanctions of British force. These African leaders, and there were others like them at a further remove from the British, lived in a system of social relations that translated the outward manifestations of military victory and cattle redistribution into the latent idiom of clan growth and affiliation. The British could never enter this system of relations, with its alien codes of understanding; and their own need to preserve their social distance did not allow them to try. All they could do was to enlarge both its rewards and reverses, the widening gap between these providing the measure of local African power. Those Africans who furnished native auxiliaries did therefore earn a political increment in British victory; their rewards in looted livestock, to the extent to which they were loaned out to reinforce parochial-level clients of their own, were indeed a British expense. Much of the edifice of British control rested on mutually incompatible calculations of self-interest. These contradictions within the politics of conquest and subsequent rule were periodically exposed by the weight of new British demands; they were resolved by the cooptation of new allies, the creation of new pivots of patronage at different levels of the social system. There will be an opportunity to instance the first example of this in Nyanza, in 1898. The remainder of the colonial era would rarely be free from similar crises in the politics of collaboration.[19]

The second means whereby African political resources were increased by British conquest was through the extension of the *pax*. The officials at Mumias were soon looked to as the external arbiters of disputes between tribal settlements; with their station garrison they were also well equipped to suppress conflict. No less than three-fifths of the incidents recorded, in response to which the British took or wished to take military action during the conquest of Nyanza, were occasioned by disputes between tribal settlements.[20] Clan elders in Nyanza, as among other lineage societies in Africa, emerged as persons of authority by proving themselves able to maintain peace within the clan and repair relations with neighbours. Peacemaking was a valued attribute. Nevertheless, and in this way they were also similar to segmentary societies elsewhere, the Nyanza peoples were not very successful in keeping their peace. There is much evidence to suggest that the spread of chiefship or political authority elsewhere in Africa has been associated with the search by members of small societies for a neutral, external source of justice.[21] To some extent it is permissible to see the growing British state of 'Nyanza', like doubtless many other African conquest states, as a peaceable and peace-making conquest from within. Whether the African parties to the inter-tribal treaties won an unmixed gain in political stature thereby is however debatable. Hobley's diary records a number of instances where local barter markets reopened immediately on the conclusion of peace; and in later years the establishment of the *pax* was remembered with gratitude by Africans who were not in other respects ingratiating.[22] Nevertheless, while the middle-aged household heads of lineage society whose property was subject to rapine may be expected to have supported peace, there were certainly others who did not. The only consistent division of opinion over the issues of war and peace that the British observed in Nyanza societies was between the generations. Elders were prone to pin the blame for conflict on the impetuosity of their warriors.[23] These may have been no more than lame excuses. Equally, they may have reflected the division of interest between those who controlled property in women, grain and cattle and those whose only property came from plundering the same. Colonial peace-making seems therefore to mark an early stage in that growing bitterness between the generations that was one of the most fundamental consequences of alien rule, as the access of the young to wages and education made futile the wisdom of the old.[24] Even the most benign face of conquest masked an inward strain.

The obverse side of this creation of an African political system, and the third component process of conquest, was African conflict with British aims. Process is a proper term; the sources of conflict changed quite markedly over time. This can be the more readily appreciated by reference to the summary of British operations in Nyanza in Table 3.1. The earliest conflicts were over the control of military resources (columns 1 and 2 of Table 3.1). Some of the northern Luyia tribes had already acquired the dubious advantage of refugee Maasai settlements. A few Nyanza tribes, certainly Mumia's Wanga and Kitoto's Kano, had benefited from the transient firepower of trading caravans. By the 1890s these two leaders and other tribes along the northern caravan route – the Kabras, Kakelelwa and Bukusu – were attempting to gain greater control over firepower, by buying guns and bribing desertions from among the caravan guards.[25] The British also controlled resources that were central to this incipient military revolution: guns, Swahili personnel practised in their use, and the trade goods with which to pay them. Defence of British communications thus imposed on Africans a ban on the further accumulation of power. To these conflicting perspectives the Swahili, the objects of competition, added the volatility of their own self-interest. At the very outset of the British presence, more than three years before the establishment of the Mumias government station, the British were determined to deny to African friend and foe alike independent access to guns.[26] But the legitimacy of gun ownership soon differentiated the major British allies from all others. At a time when the recovery of guns was an obsession with him, Hobley spent three days not in impounding but registering guns in Wanga possession. Whereas only 35 Wanga auxiliaries possessed guns in mid-1896, over a hundred were so armed by 1900 and, were, moreover, organized in what appears to have been a standing company or warband.[27]

The second category of conflict was political, over the allocation of power within the local Nyanza arena. It concerned therefore not the enemies of the British but their allies, the Wanga. On a number of occasions these challenged the two monopolies by which the British sought, with increasing deliberation, to reserve to themselves the channels of political accumulation. These were the monopolies of treaty-making and the legitimate use of force. Wanga marriage ties with one particular Bukusu clan seem to have prejudiced any British hopes of reaching an accommodation with the Bukusu as a whole (after incident 10). Wanga fears of the Luo foiled British attempts to make peace with the Ugenya tribe.[28] Twice the Wanga raided the Ugenya on their own account (incidents 7 and 31), and on six other occasions the British felt that the Wanga offers of help against different opponents were so pressing as to jeopardize British control over the punitive expedition (columns 13, 14, 15; incidents 5, 19 to 21, 28, 29).

The third category of conflict was economic, as demands were increasingly made upon African resources by the exercise of British dominance. The first such British demands were for porter labour, in connection with the supply of military operations elsewhere in Uganda. African resistance on this score began in late 1898 (column 8; incident 33). A few years later came the first refusals to pay tax. In this area too there was some differentiation between the experience of the first allies of the British and those who 'came in' later. Labour demands on allies were periodically relieved by the rewards of auxiliary military service;

and the first hut-tax demands in the areas neighbouring Wanga were sometimes enforced by Mumia's armed retainers.[29]

This categorization of the sources of conflict can go some way to show how the scope of conquest widened and its intensity deepened over time, but it is not at all clear that it helps to assess the determinants of African decisions on the other side of the hill, within each parochial settlement. Very little of the necessary oral research has been done, settlement by settlement, clan by clan; and the methodological difficulties in discovering, at this distance, clues to rapid decisions taken in the face of complex events would seem to be insuperable. The evidence simply does not exist over a sample wide enough to permit any correlation between the parochial standing of African leaders and their choice between the courses of action presented by British demands. There are some cases where one can suggest that leaders used compliance with British wishes as a means to seize or consolidate a position of domestic advantage. It remains quite unknown, perhaps unknowable, how many more were prevented from making such peaceful accommodation by the fear of losing their following. It does seem permissible, however, to conclude that long-established settlements under the leadership of an acknowledged head of their dominant clan were more likely to avoid conflict than peoples who were involved in internal dissension themselves. Under the first category one would include the Wanga and the two Luyia settlements to their west, Marachi and Bukhayo. The internal dissensions of Nyanza took various forms. Among the Bukusu, military leadership seems to have been contested between three or four clans. In the southeastern Luyia area, second only to Bukusu in the weight of its British displeasure, there was an unusually intricate and fragmented competition for land on this forested and fertile frontier of expansion. In the Nandi case, external resistance was in all probability the tool used by the refugee Maasai oracular authority, the *orkoiyot*, in trying to build for himself a domestic ascendancy.[30] Similar considerations were present in the case of the Gusii, but here internal conflict was between the component tribes, with Getutu pretending to a local dominance, rather than between different modes of authority. In all these cases, an important cause of persistence in the Anglo-African conflict was a failure of military intelligence, certainly on the part of the British, perhaps on the African side as well. Where parochial leadership was in contention, the British could find neither reliable channels of communication nor effective guarantors of the terms of peace. Disputes could erupt into conflict as much through drift as by design; and conflict once begun was less easily mended. The British experience with the Gusii and Bukusu, as contrasted with many of the Luyia settlements and most of the Luo, well corroborates the hypothesis that in political relationships there exists an inverse proportion of force and information.[31]

The Politics of Conquest in Western Kenya 1894–1908

Not all military intelligence was defective, however, even if it was often subject to the filter of Wanga interpretation. Informed calculations of self-interest could be made on each side, and for the Africans at the centre of the embryo conquest state of Nyanza there was decreasing cause to misapprehend the power, if not the intentions, of the British. Even if, therefore, it is not possible to assess all the considerations behind individual African decisions, one can still make the general point that an increasing distance developed between the defiance of those who resisted British domination and the submission of those who acquiesced in its purposes. This presents a problem of differentiation, like all such problems perhaps the most interesting of its time.

The extent of this differentiation is the more easily outlined by reference to Table 3.1. This purports to measure not merely British action but British intention as well. Its validity is therefore open to challenge on two grounds, that intentions can be hidden in a way that actions cannot, and that it implies that the assumptions of the official mind and the techniques of control remained much the same. It can be said, in answer to the first query, that more than 170 reports from the men on the spot were consulted for the period from mid-1894 to mid-1900,[32] and that thereafter the sources declined markedly in quantity and often in quality. In reply to the second, it is clear that the official mind was by no means a constant, and that, especially after 1900, it presumed much more upon African compliance than it had done before. The first collections of hut tax in that year marked a fundamental shift in the premises of rule. On both grounds then, Table 3.1 should be seen as divided into two parts at 1900, after incident 41. One can compare situations that are comparable before that point and again thereafter, but not both before and after. The concluding discussion on the periodization of conquest should make this proposition clearer.[33]

Three indices in particular mark the divergence in the experience of conquest between the Nyanza tribes. The first is what appears to be a decreasing British willingness to negotiate a peaceful resolution of disputes (column 19), even before the turning point of 1900. By the middle of 1898 (incidents 1 to 31) the British had been moved to action on 22 occasions. They had tried to press matters home to a military conclusion on only 10 of these expeditions, and on two of these they had failed to find an enemy. The character of British behaviour thereafter was quite different. No less than seven of the eight interventions between July 1898 and April 1900 ended with a fight. Figures of African casualties and captured livestock, however, do not, before 1900, reveal a sequence of growing losses so much as two peaks (incidents 10 and 38 to 40) in which the British saw themselves as giving salutary lessons, first to the Luyia and then, as their communications shifted southward with the approach of the railway, to the Luo.[34] It was not until after 1900 that the contrast

Table 3.1 British operations against Luiya, Luo and Gusii, 1894–1914

Incident number	'Period' of the Conquest	People against whom the British employed or contemplated the use of force	Date	1 Threat to communications	2 Retention of guns &/or deserters	3 Attack on British allies	4 Inter-tribal dispute suppression	5 African govt. agent's malpractice	6 Murder of African govt. agent	7 Attack on British official	8 Refusal of labour or supplies	9 Attack on government property	10 Refusal of tax payment	11 Local garrison (police from 1900)	12 Regular troops from elsewhere	13 Ganda auxiliaries	14 Maasai auxiliaries	15 Wanga auxiliaries	16 Other Luyia auxiliaries	17 Luo auxiliaries	18 Nandi auxiliaries	19 British response	20 Numbers killed: govt. forces & Allies	21 Numbers killed: opponents	22 Cattle captured (number if known)	23 Cattle fined (number if known)	24 Surrender of guns/deserters	25 Non-aggression against caravans, etc.	26 'Blood brotherhood' with British	27 Non-aggression against neighbours	28 Provision of labour	29 Payment of tax	30 Cost of British allies, expressed as % of cattle captured/fined
1	'COEXIST-ENCE'	Kitoto's foes	Aug. 1894			x																○	0	0									
2		Mumia's foes (Ugenya)	Nov. 1894			x																◌	0	0									
3		Kakalelwa	Nov. 1894	x	x									x								▷	0	0	o								
4		Bukusu	Nov. 1894	x	x									x								◌	20	0	o								
5		Ugenya & Bukusu	Dec. 1894	x																		◁	0	x									
6		Bukusu	Jan. 1895	x	x									x								○	2	0									
7		Wanga (raid Ugenya)	Mar. 1895	x														x	x			○	0	0	450								72
8		Kabras	July 1895											x								○	0	0									
9		Banyala	July 1895	x		x								x								◁	0	0									
10	'A	Bukusu	Aug. 1895	x	x					x				x	x	x	x	x				▷	0	480	1700	20		x	x	x			
11	S	Kakalelwa	Sept. 1895	x	x	x								x	x	x		x				◁	24	x	200		x	x					67
12	C	Kabras	Sept. 1895	x	x									x	x	x		x				◁	46	0	o								
13	E	Kakalelwa	Nov. 1895	x	x									x	x							○	0	0	30+		x	x	x	x			
14	N	Maragoli	Dec. 1895	x			x								x							◌	0	0									
15	D	Ugenya	Jan. 1896	x																		○	0	0		50							
16	'A	Kitoto's foes (Nandi)	Apr. 1896			x	x								x		x	x				◁	0	0	o		x	x	x	x			
17	N	Maasai (raid Bukusu)	Mar. 1896												x							◌	0	0									
18	C	Maragoli & Idakho	May 1896	x			x					x			x							○	0	?200									
19	Y'	Idakho	Aug. 1896				x							x	x							◌	0	0	o								
20		Maragoli (Kisungu)	Sept. 1896				x	?	x	x				x	x							○	2	0						x			
21		Nyore (Mangali clan)	Sept. 1896				x		x					x	x							○	?1	0					x	x			
22		Kitoto's foes (Nandi)	Sept. 1896	x		x	x							x	x		ix	ix				◁	1	x	273				x	x			24
23		Samia	Oct. 1896			x	x							x			ix	ix				◌		0	x				x	?			
24		Alego	Oct. 1896	x			x							x	x		ix	ix				○	0	0					x	x			
25		Seme & Gem	Nov. 1896				x							x	x			x				○	0	0		x			x	x			

60

Table (rotated), incidents 26–50

	Incident	Date
'COEXISTENCE'	26 Yimbo & Busonga	Jan. 1897
	27 Kitoto's foes	Mar. 1897
	28 Isukha (Mironge clan)	Mar. 1897
	29 Seme	Mar. 1897
	30 Gem's neighbours	Apr. 1898
'D'	31 Wanga (raid Luo)	May 1898
O	32 Isukha & Idakho	July 1898
M	33 Alego	Sept. 1898
I	34 Luo (?Kisumo)	Dec. 1898
N	35 Idakho, Maragoli, Nyore	Dec. 1898
A	36 Isukha (Mironge clan)	June 1899
T	37 Kitoto's foes (Nandi)	Aug. 1899
I	38 Sakwa	
O	39 Uyoma	Dec. 1899
N'	40 Seme	
	41 Nyang'ori	Apr. 1900
	42 Bukusu (chief Mabero)	1901
	43 Bukusu	1903
	44 Marachi & Teso	Mar. 1905
	45 Gusii (Wanjare, Getutu)	Sept. 1905
'CONTROL'	46 Bukusu & Teso	May 1907
	47 Gusii (Getutu)	Jan. 1908
	48 Bukusu	Aug. 1908
	49 Bukhayo	Nov. 1908
	50 Gusii	Sept. 1914

Symbols

(i) British response (column 19): △, Punitive expedition, pressed to a military conclusion (20 cases); ▽, punitive expedition, ending in British defeat (1 case); ∴, British withdrawal from superior African force (1 case); ∴, punitive expedition, but no military contact made (2 cases); O, peaceful resolution, but British force available (13 cases); ∴, no British action, for lack of available force (11 cases).

(ii) *Brackets* join two or more incidents dealt with by the same British expedition.

(iii) x, certain presence of the factor named at the top of the vertical column.

(iv) ?, almost certain presence of that factor, and is included in the column totals.

(v) —, British refusal of African help (columns 14–16); African refusal of/non-compliance with a British peace term (columns 24 and 25).

(vi) x̄, participation of African auxiliaries, against British wishes.

Column headings

Columns 3, 4. Both refer to inter-tribal disputes. Column 3 shows cases of British allies under attack from a tribe not so allied. Column 4 lists disputes between parties of whom either, neither or both were British allies (the only example of the latter was Incident 30).

Column 22. Does not list small stock (sheep and goats) whose numbers were frequently very large indeed.

Column 27. African spokesmen must often have been required to submit disputes to British arbitration, as the alternative to force; but this requirement was recorded only after Incidents 10, 32 and 33.

Column 28. The British required the provision of food as well as labour after Incidents 28 and 24.

Column 39. Tax payment was mentioned as a forthcoming rather than immediate demand after Incidents 32–35.

61

between negligible British casualties and heavy mortality among their enemies became a matter of routine, as the African forces under British command acquired a more rigorous discipline. After 1898 then, and more especially after 1900, African opposition to conquest evidently invited more certain and more costly retribution than before.

The second index of differentiation is provided by the number of cases in which the British needed to take action more than once against the same tribal settlement and the reasons why. In some of these cases the subsequent expedition will have been directed against different clans within the settlement. Nevertheless, these second and subsequent offenders cannot have been ignorant of the fate of their fellow tribesmen; settlements were too small and transactions between clans too intense for that. There were, then, three periods in which Africans provoked more than one act of British retaliation. The first was at the outset of the British occupation, when the Bukusu were mainly responsible for the repeated threats to Uganda's supply line. But then, at their first encounter (incident 4), and just after the Kakalelwa had forced the Mumias garrison to withdraw from its search for missing mailbags (incident 3), the Bukusu had imposed a crushing defeat on the British forces. They virtually annihilated a party of Swahili and Sudanese troops. Such an excuse for African military conceit would not occur again. The second period came in the two years after 1896, when the eastern Luyia were subjected to a series of British attacks. But the major cause was, again, a British weakness, if of a different order to the one that had allowed the Bukusu their early triumph. This time it was due to the classic debility of administrative overextension, the failure to discipline subordinates. In provoking British retaliation by the murder of African soldiers or porters who were brutal or dishonest, often while on food-buying forays (incidents 28, 31, 35, 36; columns 5 and 6) the eastern Luyia were guilty only of elementary self-defence. The third period, after 1900, was one of palpable British strength; African opposition was altogether more wilful, especially in the case of the Bukusu. For the Gusii the evidence also suggests some wilful aggression by the British. Nevertheless, members of both groups attacked a British official, a rare enough occurrence (column 7), as well as refusing a number of British demands.

The increasing intensity and scope of British demands upon Africans furnishes the third index of differentiation. From 1898 the British required porter service from all as the proof of friendship and from 1900 tax, if selectively at first. This growing cost of accommodation serves equally with the rising price of conflict to mark off the generality of tribes that acquiesced in British rule from those that most defiantly did not, the Bukusu and the Gusii.

How is one to explain this difference? Existing studies of African responses to the colonial impact offer a wide range of explanatory variables. The degree of cohesion in a ruling class or social structure; their political fortunes, whether on the upswing or downturn; the availability of a religious tradition for which and by which to fight; the nature of the local economy, especially its responsiveness to market expansion or technical innovation; military capacity; the nature and intensity of initial European demands – these are the factors most commonly deployed in analysis. Taken as a whole, however, they have a rather limited application to the problem of African accommodation and resistance in its western Kenya form. The Nyanza societies are too small, their precolonial histories too imperfectly known, to convincingly test general hypotheses on the relations between their political or social cohesion, their cycles of political fortune, or their organization of religious belief and their early responses to the British. All the local societies had mixed economies and all were to varying degrees seeking to reconstruct their herds after the rinderpest epizootic of 1890; it does not appear therefore that the African response was determined by the relative importance of pastoralism to the Nyanza societies – any more than it was in Kenya as a whole. It is true that the main British allies in Nyanza, the Wanga, were under grave external threat and that the earliest would-be ally among the Luo, Kitoto, was also. But, again, not enough is known about all the other settlements in Nyanza to enable one to determine the relative gravity of their external position. One has the distinct impression that very few Luo or Luyia tribes felt themselves at all secure at this time; there was no local system of alliance – marriage ties secured not so much reinforcements as places of refuge, and passing Swahili caravans were scarcely a system – to assure such security even for the strong.

A weightier and more general objection to the existing explanatory variables than difficulty in their application to Nyanza is their lack of an explicitly chronological element. As they stand they all too easily invite the assumptions both that conquest was an historical moment rather than movement, and that African actions at the point of the European impact in some way expressed the timeless essence of their society, especially if that action was one of 'primary resistance'. The historical limitations of these assumptions are twofold. They allow insufficient room for changes within precolonial societies as they sought adaptation to or better management of their natural and political environments; and they imply too large a degree of political and economic autonomy for each African society. All eastern Africans, not excluding the hunters and gatherers, participated in a network of exchange relations that had some bearing, however slight in some cases, on domestic relations. Resistance to Europeans was therefore never 'primary' in the sense of an instinctual response of a previously closed society to a sudden opening on to the wider world. It was a reaction to adverse changes, actual or anticipated, in the existing terms of contact.

The Politics of Conquest in Western Kenya 1894–1908

In Africa generally those most capable of resistance were the rulers of locally dominant polities for whom the external network was indeed a system of relations, a sphere of influence at risk from the white interloper.[35] Of these the Nyanza case provides only rather dubious examples. The nearest would probably be the Getutu tribe, with its elaborate patronage relations with other Gusii tribes; neither Mumia nor Kitoto dominated their external environments, even if Mumia could inflict damage on his neighbours through the agency of Maasai or Swahili. More typical of Nyanza, as more generally, were those lesser authorities for whom some degree of control over access to external resources by, for example, negotiating marriage, leading a cattle raid or invoking a neighbouring rainmaker, was an important attribute of their parochial authority. Resistance on their part might be prompted either in opposition to European attempts to centralize the locus of force, that is, to create a system out of the capillary network (columns 1 to 5), or by a deteriorating balance between external demands and supports, as European power wrenched the new system round to serve its own purposes (columns 8 to 10). Their resistance might well be, and among the Bukusu almost certainly was, sharpened by fear of displacement by internal rivals who had proved more canny in turning the terms of European contact to their own advantage. Contributory to all these decisions to resist there seems to have been a reassessment of attempts at accommodation, now discovered to be ineffective or dangerous.[36]

To bring this general discussion to bear upon the problem of increasing differentiation between accommodation and resistance in Nyanza it is necessary to ascribe some chronologically specific content to the local network of external relations. Its most relevant attribute was to facilitate both the exchange of goods like grain, livestock, fish, more specialized items such as salt and iron, and the provision of services like marriage, rainmaking and access to land. Before British rule, the most concrete sense in which 'Nyanza' existed was as a regional market. Its exchanges in specialized goods and across ecological boundaries were constrained as much by such technical factors as high-cost communications and a low level of demand as by the pattern of social relations.[37] The likelihood was, therefore, that the market would grow quantitatively and spatially when its technical limitations were alleviated, as they were in the late 19th century. The subsequent extension of the market furnishes the fourth and perhaps decisive component process of conquest.

Commercial costs were reduced both directly, by the importation of coastal trade goods as more wieldy currency, by the development of pack-animal and ox-cart transport in the 1890s,[38] by the opening of the Uganda Railway to Kisumu in 1902 and its associated lake steamer services, by the commercial revolution effected thereafter by Indian traders and the rapid monetization of exchange; and indirectly, by the

spread of the British *pax* outwards from its centre at Mumias. The growth
of market demand was most conspicuously a regional phenomenon.
For its African inhabitants the Nyanza market region's most valuable
function in these years was probably the rapid reconstruction of herds
decimated in the rinderpest epizootic of 1890–2; agricultural productivity rose to meet the scarcity values of cattle bartered from areas that
escaped the worst ravages of the cattle plague. More intensive agricultural production and exchange almost certainly encouraged experimentation with new varieties of seed grains, of which Nyanza, with
its complex diversities of rainfall and soil conditions, had a large
number.[39] The Swahili traders from the coast had stimulated these
regional flows by tapping them. Some parochial authorities, of whom
Mumia was the prime example, were able to enjoy new standards of
consumption, patronage and coercion through brokerage between the
regional and external markets. British needs stimulated the regional
market still further. Their overriding requirement was food. The
Mumias station estimates for 1896/97 calculated that the garrison and
passing caravans would consume over 220 tons of flour in the year; by
1899 the five Nyanza food-buying stations could produce nearly half that
amount within a month and at the beginning of the traditionally hungry
season, to provision a passing Indian battalion and its porters. Food
prices rose with demand, especially at Mumias, despite British attempts
at control. Local manufacture was also encouraged at this early stage
of the colonial impact. The Mumias station bought hoes and rope; Port
Victoria placed a monthly order with the salt-boilers of Kaksingri, to be
delivered by canoe. Even the demand for porters, that most onerous of
British requisites, could be tempered by commercial advantage; some
men were known to volunteer for service, in order to invest in the local
goat and hoe trades the cloth they received as wages. The handful of
Nyanza entrepreneurs adventurous enough to go to the coast seem to
have found it as easy to travel in company with British caravans as earlier
they had done with Swahili.[40] The Nyanza evidence provides support
for the hypothesis that initial colonial situations – whatever may have
been the more adverse structural effects of later colonialism – gave the
kiss of life to hitherto sluggish African economies, by greatly expanding
the market for the products of domestic labour power.

There was more at stake here than the mere expansion of the local
produce market. The pioneer official who best knew Nyanza, Charles
Hobley, elevated the elasticity of the peasant supply response to the
status of political theory. His own success in threading alliances along
the network of food supply led him to commend the creation of a food
market to his neighbour among the unaccommodating Nandi, arguing
that a 'sufficient supply would be forthcoming very shortly for the needs
of that station, and . . . that the close relationship induced by this

development [of the market] would be of incalculable service to that district'.[41] Sir Harry Johnston a few years later similarly agreed that a food-buying station among the northern Kipsigis, a Kalenjin group related to the Nandi, would be the best means of contacting the as yet unknown Gusii. It was unfortunate for the Gusii that they did not respond as Johnston hoped; their external relations to the east were not with the northern so much as the southern or Sotik Kipsigis, and these had tended to be hostile in their rare encounters with the British.[42] The Nyanza peoples were participating unequally in the market expansion.

There were two forms of inequality. To begin with, there was inequality of access. Despite extensive barter trade with the Luo, the Gusii entered neither the new market that serviced the British communications system nor, save to a very limited extent and often through Kipsigis intermediaries, the ivory export trade controlled by the Swahili. The Bukusu, on the other hand, increased their market activity by virtually ignoring the British sector and supplying instead those whom the British had displaced, the Swahili traders who were forced north by the exhaustion of ivory supplies about Mumias.[43] While the Anglo–Bukusu confrontation was fuelled by Anglo–Swahili market rivalry, the mutual ignorance that so catastrophically marked the conduct of government expeditions against the Gusii was the measure of that people's commercial isolation. In 1904 the Gusii were prepared for the same sort of warfare as the Bukusu in 1895, but the British meanwhile had changed utterly in the premises, speed and weight of their reaction. Cultural boundaries must not however be forgotten. The southernmost Luo were as distant as the Gusii from the British sphere of operations before 1900, but did not fight thereafter. They seem therefore to have been as profoundly impressed with British military power in 1899 (incidents 38 to 40) as those against whom it was directly employed, Luo settlements many of whose clans had put out cadet lines across the Winam Gulf. With this one proviso therefore, increasingly unequal market connections over the period of conquest seem best to account for the growing divergence between African accommodation and resistance to the British. They also explain the paradox that of the two peoples that resisted the British longest in Nyanza, one was the region's leader in military technology, the other the laggard. The Bukusu had the largest armoury of guns in the area, perhaps four times as many as the Wanga; the Gusii, by contrast, had none.

There was also an unequal distribution of costs and benefits within the British-controlled sector of the Nyanza market. British punitive expeditions generally involved comparatively little loss of life. They were directed primarily against African property, standing crops, huts and, above all, livestock. Starvation might well ensue from military defeat. Early in 1896 the Mumias food market was thronged with the famished inhabitants of the Bukusu, Kakalelwa and Ugenya settlements, all recent sufferers at the hands of the British.[44] In economic terms punitive expeditions were instruments of wealth distribution. The losers and beneficiaries of this process changed in character over the period of conquest. The identity of the losers changed as the sphere of British operations expanded; they charted the outer edge of conquest. They also began to lose much more, in cattle looted or crops destroyed as improvements in British logistics and the extension of their control made them less sensitive to the need to preserve an enemy economy as a future source of food supply. If the increasing losses of the recalcitrants thus traced the course of political accumulation, they were in this matched by the decreasing gains of the African 'friendlies', as the British lowered the cost of the local native auxiliaries.

On the first punitive expeditions, the African auxiliaries not only captured most of the livestock, they were allowed to keep it (column 30). Of the 2150 cattle captured on the two Bukusu expeditions in 1895 the British retained for their own use only 683, less than one-third. The rest, 69 per cent of the total, was divided between their Ganda, Luyia and Maasai auxiliaries. British standing seems therefore to have been weaker than that of the Wanga, who were accustomed to giving only 50 per cent of looted cattle to their Maasai allies.[45] At this early stage of political accumulation the British could attract allies only by redistributing a very substantial proportion of the patrimony that they had appropriated from others. Only a year later Hobley felt sufficiently sure of his position to keep for government use three-quarters of the cattle taken from the Maragoli (incident 20). This was a very small expedition, but the trend continued even on large ones, with large spoils of war. The 1899 expedition against the lakeside Luo of Sakwa, Seme and Uyoma brought in 2590 cattle. Of these only 335, or 13 per cent, were allotted to allies.[46] The British, dominant now in the local system of external relations, could, without much risk of its withdrawal, depress the supply price of African assistance. By 1908, with official opinion increasingly hostile to the use of native levies, government loot was kept almost entirely in government hands, and African labour suppliers had declined in status from contractors to tributaries.

This growing British confidence is in large measure explained by examination of the wide range of allies who received the captured Luo stock in 1899. Mumia, the Luyia prop of the British position, had by now been joined by Odera Ulalo, the Luo support; they received 200 cows between them, as well as an unknown but very much larger number of small stock. One hundred cows were allotted to Apolo Kaggwa, leader of the Protestant interest in Buganda which had carried the British through the recent crises of Sudanese mutiny and royal rebellion, and who was now, as one of the three regents of Buganda, in negotiation with the Special Commissioner, Sir Harry Johnston, over the Uganda Agreement. Thirty-five were sent to the Maasai *laibon* Olonana (Lenana), whose alliance underwrote the British position in the neighbouring East Africa Protectorate. The British had diversified their allies locally; they numbered them among the Luo as much as among the Luyia. But they also dominated a much wider system of alliances that, if always liable to local shocks, furnished a sufficient diversity of political resources to insure against the possibility of any general collapse.[47] This was a danger that was now past. Some cattle and smallstock were, appropriately therefore, returned to their owners, to show that the British were not simply successful war-leaders. Finally, the destination of many of the Luo cattle retained by government foreshadowed a changing idiom of accumulation in the future. They were driven down to the Nairobi auction ring, there to be bought not only by stock traders but also by a handful of Europeans who saw themselves as settlers.[48] Large mobs of Nandi and Kipsigis cattle were to travel the same route in subsequent years. By the time of the Gusii expedition of 1908 the sale of captured African cattle was seen not only as an inexpensive means of stocking up settler ranchlands, but also as a lever to force the entry of their erstwhile owners onto the labour market.[49] The beneficiaries of punitive expeditions were now very far from being other Africans in Nyanza. If these still participated in conquest they did so as constables under a sergeant of police rather than as spearmen behind a leader of their own. The conquest of western Kenya was over, and capital accumulation had begun.

It is now possible to suggest a periodization of the process.

British relationships with the African polities of Nyanza passed from coexistence to control, with British authority growing from just another power in Nyanza to the power over Nyanza[50] – as over the Uganda and East Africa Protectorates, between which in so many ways Nyanza occupied a middle position. In making the transition between Coexistence and Control British power passed through two intermediary stages that I call – after D.A. Low – Ascendancy and Domination.[51] Each stage or period differed from the others in the relative weight of the component characteristics of conquest that have already been outlined. Each phase also enlarged on the geographical confines of the preceding one and in so doing hardened the distinction between those who were within and those who were beyond the pale of British authority.

Coexistence accurately describes the relations that existed between British and Africans from 1890, when the first Imperial British East Africa Company treaties were signed with a few local leaders, until early in 1895. British assumptions were grand enough. Ever since Captain Lugard had passed through in 1890 they had refused to pay *hongo* or road-tolls; and from the same date they had refused to sell guns to Africans, if tolerating Swahili arms supplies to their Wanga allies.[52] Early in 1895 Frederick Jackson, Uganda's acting Commissioner, wished himself into believing that Africans shared the same assumptions as the British; the Bukusu, he told Hobley on his appointment to Mumias, knew that they had no right to purchase guns. The Bukusu knew nothing of the sort; they had just proved their right to guns by wiping out the British patrol sent to retrieve them. British authority extended barely beyond the Mumias station perimeter. They could protect friends neither near – Mumia; nor far – Kitoto. Conflicts of interest with Africans were entirely military in character, and at this stage the British were quite unable to exert any monopoly over firearms (column 24). Political accumulation was at a rudimentary stage, when authority could be exercised only by giving large segments of it away. Nearly three-quarters of the cattle captured on the first successful Bukusu expedition (incident 6) were taken by local allies; these were in any case fighting in their own cause against the Bukusu rather than defending any British interest. The food market remained under the control of Mumia as broker rather than the British as buyer. Hobley could not prevent Mumia from raiding the nearby Ugenya Luo (incident 7); but his retaliation – the expulsion from Mumias of Swahili traders who might hope to profit from Wanga predation – showed his appreciation of the importance of the external relations network of Nyanza in generating local political resources.[53]

The next period, of *Ascendancy*, was quite different in character. In the years 1895 to 1897 the British came to gain a hold over, but not to monopolize, external relations within Nyanza, to use this superiority to choose and support their African allies at the parochial levels, but to make very few demands in return. The period started with a decisive military victory, over the Bukusu.[54] This would have been impossible without the transfer from elsewhere of coercive resources, a power base – the Sudanese troops, and auxiliaries from Buganda under their great leader Kakungulu. The Nandi Field Force, also drafted from Uganda 'proper' and without the aid of any local auxiliaries, administered a crushing and bloody blow against the Luo Ugenya a few months later (incident 15). Auxiliaries were still able to extort much of the loot, but the British increasingly attempted to control their use. They were never the main force, and when they were present on an expedition the main force almost invariably included Sudanese companies posted from elsewhere to reinforce the Mumias garrison. By mid-1896 Hobley was trying to refuse the aid of auxiliaries altogether, if to little avail (incidents 19 to 21, 28 and 29). The British were determined to dominate their allies so as to diversify their alliance system. They were anxious to remove from their contacts with a widening circle of tribes the stigma of reliance upon one of them, the Wanga; for the relations of conquest, one might say, too easily became fetters on control. In this process, Anglo–African conflicts tended to change in character. Threats to British communications faded in importance as Hobley deliberately used dispute-suppression or arbitration to extend his influence (columns 3, 4, 27). British participation in peace ceremonies of blood brotherhood, with their ritualized expression of equality between the contracting parties, became less frequent as time went on.[55]

Political resources were thus being accumulated by diversification, by dispute suppression and, finally, by consultation, as a weekly assembly of Hobley's selected 'chiefs' met in Mumias from April 1896.[56] That African decisions were increasingly moulded by an appreciation of British ascendancy is perhaps indicated by the fact that there appears to have been only one case of local notables pushing forward a 'village idiot' figure to deal with the British; access to their support was more important than keeping them at a distance.[57] The British connection was meanwhile reinforced by the extension of the food market beyond Mumias, both through the despatch of food-buying parties under Swahili employees and the establishment of permanent food depots in Samia and Kabras, at Kakamega's and Kitoto's.

This growing British influence gave way to a second period of *Coexistence*, as the military props of ascendancy were knocked away, first by the diversion of Sudanese troops to quell the Buganda king Mwanga's rebellion in mid-1897, and then the mutiny of the Sudanese themselves. As the mutineers marched westwards across Nyanza towards Buganda they left a trail of destruction behind them, including a hundred dead in a burnt-out hut near Kakamega's. In an action that the British gratefully attributed to his loyalty, Mumia had to turn out his spearmen to defend his village and, incidentally, the government station against these erstwhile government servants. It was not surprising that in this period Mumia once again exercised the right of force against the neighbouring Luo; the 'British' in Nyanza now amounted to one Eurasian clerk at Mumias and a 'Bombay African' at Port Victoria.[58] He was hardly challenging a British ascendancy; it did not any longer exist.

The recovery of British authority was swift, and it entailed much more than picking up the threads of ascendancy. The period that followed was characterized by unmistakably economic clashes of interest, as the British for the first time pressed demands upon the parochial-level authorities, for labour especially (columns 8, 29). This was extracted by the exercise of an unequivocal *Domination*, military and political. Troops were once more available to the British as an Indian battalion was rushed to Uganda and as Swahili and Somali companies replaced the suspect Sudanese. And they were used. In an 18-month period from mid-1898 (incidents 32 to 41) seven out of the eight British interventions entailed the use of force, as compared with only six out of 17 in the period of

Ascendancy. The burden of the British demand for porters, needed to supply the greatly increased military establishment in Uganda proper, was so heavy that Nyanza's parochial-level supports buckled. Hobley faced his first crisis of collaboration. With the sole exceptions of Mumia and Odera Ulalo, he now found the tribal 'chiefs' whom he had recognized quite incapable of recruiting labour from any clan other than their own. He therefore displaced them and dealt direct with the other clan heads within each tribal settlement. This he found 'rather minute and somewhat tedious, but a recognition of these natural conditions vastly increases our hold upon these people'.[59] Previously he had diversified his African contacts beyond the Wanga base to reduce his dependence; now he multiplied his collaborators to enforce his demands.

In the final period, *Control* was firmly established over the centre of the new Nyanza system, with overt Anglo–African conflict moving out to its peripheries and regaining an old-fashioned flavour, being once again concerned with possession of firearms, now a symbolic rather than physical danger,[60] and attacks on British allies, as well as non-payment of tax. The essence of control was the multiplication of African roles under direct British command. In the crucial sphere of coercion, the British no longer relied on African military contractors: they now recruited Africans as individuals into a uniformed police force. In the field of civil administration, the channels of communication were widened by the appointment of interpreters, hut-counters and clerks. Perhaps most important of all for the maintenance of peace, the people of Nyanza generally were encouraged by the spreading network of Indian retailers and produce buyers no less than by tax demands to devote more of their domestic labour to production for the market. But even Control was marked by violence. The visible violence was on the periphery, as the growing British expectation of obedience was increasingly exasperated by its refusal. The latent violence was at the centre and was altogether more pervasive. In the 1890s African leaders had raided others as allies of the British; now they coerced their own people, as British subordinates. They collected tax on commission, compelled the cultivation of new crops, especially cotton, ordered out labour on local roads and recruited it for outside employers – all with the help of irregular bands of young toughs who might once have been warriors but who now were the first labour migrants returned from the areas of white settlement or the first fruits of mission education. Colonial rule would never lose this ambiguity in the politics of conquest, this lamination of a larger order with parochial disorders that were themselves so often caused by African attempts to deflect the costs of colonialism onto their fellows and to appropriate its benefits as their own.

Notes

1. Earlier versions of this chapter were presented at the Institute of Commonwealth Studies, London, in October 1973 and at the Eastern Africa Studies Program of the University of Syracuse in July 1975. I am indebted to the members of both seminars for their helpful comments. The analysis also owes much to discussion with Professor D.A. Low, the late Mr A.T. Matson, Mr Laurence Schiller and, at Cambridge, my colleagues John Dunn, John Iliffe, Gwyn Prins and Richard Waller.

2. Until 1902, the area under study was administered as part of the Eastern Province of Uganda being transferred in that year, along with much other territory, to the East Africa Protectorate, which was to become the Colony of Kenya in 1920.

3. For such generalization see my 'European scramble and conquest in African history', Ch. 12 in R. Oliver and G.N. Sanderson (eds), *Cambridge History of Africa*, Vol. 6: *1870–1905* (Cambridge, 1985).

4. As implied in John S. Saul, 'The state in post-colonial societies: Tanzania', in R. Miliband and J. Savile (eds), *Socialist Register, 1974* (London, 1974), p. 353.

5. As observed by Wallerstein, in P.C.W. Gutkind and I. Wallerstein (eds), *The Political Economy of Contemporary* Africa (Beverly Hills and London, 1976), pp. 43–4.

6. Ronald Hyam, *The Failure of South African Expansion, 1908–1948* (London, 1972), pp. 6–9.

7. G.H. Mungeam, *British Rule in Kenya, 1895–1912* (Oxford, 1966), pp. 171–80: G. Northcote to his father, 12 Feb. 1908: Kenya National Archives (KNA), DC/KSI. 4/1.

8. Commissioner of Public Works to W. McGregor Ross, 29 Jan. 1908: Ross papers, privately held.

9. For an important study of such a development in West Africa, see Ivor Wilks, *Asante in the Nineteenth Century* (London, 1976).

10. D.A. Low, 'Warbands and ground-level imperialism in Uganda, 1870–1900', *Historical Studies*, no. 65 (Melbourne, Oct. 1975), pp. 584–97.

11. General outline histories of the main Nyanza peoples are to be found in B.A. Ogot, *History of the Southern Luo*, 1 (Nairobi, 1967); G.S. Were, *A History of the Abaluyia, c. 1500–1930* (Nairobi, 1967); W.R. Ochieng', *A Pre-colonial History of the Gusii of Western Kenya* (Nairobi, 1974). The problem of cultural flexibility is discussed further in, for example, J.E.G. Sutton, 'Some reflections on the early history of Western Kenya', *Hadith* 2 (Nairobi, 1970), pp. 17–29; G.S. Were, 'Ethnic interaction in Western Kenya: the emergence of the Abaluyia up to 1850', *Kenya Historical Review* 2(1) (1974), pp. 39–44, M.J. Hay, 'Local trade and ethnicity in Western Kenya', *African Economic History Review*, 2(1) (Madison, 1975), pp. 7–12; J.M. Lonsdale, 'When did the Gusii (or any other group) become a tribe?', *Kenya Historical Review* 5 (1977) pp. 123–33.

12. For these various peoples, see James Dealing, 'Politics in Wanga, Kenya, c. 1650–1914' (unpublished Ph.D. thesis, Northwestern University, 1974); J.J. de Wolf, 'Religious innovation and social change among the Bukusu' (unpublished Ph.D. thesis, University of London, 1971); Richard Waller, 'The Maasai and the British 1895–1905: the origins of an alliance', *Journal of African History* 17(4) (1976), pp. 529–53.

13. A.T. Matson, *Nandi Resistance to British Rule*, 1 (Nairobi, 1972).

14. F.J. Jackson to C.W. Hobley, 2 Feb. 1895: Entebbe Secretariat Archives (ESA), A. 5/1.

15. For changes within 'traditional religion' in order to explain social changes see R. Horton, 'African conversion', *Africa* 41(2) (1971), pp. 85–107. For the prophets of western Kenya: G. Wagner, *The Bantu of North Kavirondo*, 1 (Oxford, 1949), p. 212; B.A. Ogot, 'British administration in the Central Nyanza District of Kenya, 1900–60', *Journal of African History* 4(2) (1963), p. 249; W.R. Ochieng', 'The Biography of Yona Omolo', in K. King and A. Salim (eds), *Kenya Historical Biographies* (Nairobi, 1971), p. 80; idem, 'Black Jeremiah', *Journal of the Historical Association of Kenya*, 1(1) (1972), pp. 6–21.

The Politics of Conquest in Western Kenya 1894-1908

16. Compare D.A. Low, in V. Harlow and E.M. Chilver (eds), *History of East Africa*, Vol. 2 (Oxford, 1965), pp. 11-12.
17. P.H. Partridge, 'Some notes on the concept of power', *Political Studies* 11(2) (1963), pp. 107-25; D.A. Baldwin, 'Money and power', *Journal of Politics* 33 (1971), pp. 578-614.
18. See the oral records in typescript evidence to Committee on Land Tenure in North Kavirondo (1930), p. 80: copy in Archdeacon W.E. Owen's papers, Church Missionary Society Archives, London; 'History of the Bukusu', Elgon Nyanza District Ethnological Records: KNA, DC/EN. 3/2/4; G.S. Were, *Western Kenya Historical Texts* (Nairobi, 1967), pp. 37-8, 43, 65, 119, 131-2; Dealing, 'Politics in Wanga', pp. 313-4, 319-22; M.J. Hay, 'Economic change in Luoland: Kowe, 1890-1945' (unpublished Ph.D. thesis, University of Wisconsin, 1972), p. 81.
19. On the importance of unintended results and misleading appearances in power relations, see Partridge, 'Concept of power'; G.T. Prins, 'Lewanika's achievement reconsidered: Europeans and Bulozi, 1878-1916', Cambridge University Commonwealth and Overseas History Seminar Paper, 1976. The classic exposition of collaboration theory has little to say on this aspect. See Ronald Robinson, 'Non-European foundations of European imperialisms: sketch for a theory of collaboration', in R. Owen and R.B. Sutcliffe (eds), *Studies in the Theory of Imperialism* (London, 1972), pp. 117-40.
20. See Table 3.1, columns 3 and 4. Further examples of peaceful arbitration or support for African judicial decisions are recorded in Hobley's personal diary, 8 Jan. 1896, 8 and 15 May 1896, 8 Nov. 1896, 8 Jan 1897. Deposited in Rhodes House Library, Oxford.
21. E.g. A.W. Southall, *Alur Society* (Cambridge, n.d., ?1955), especially Ch. VIII; Robin Horton, 'Stateless societies in the history of West Africa', in J.F.A. Ajayi and M. Crowder (eds), *History of West Africa*, 1 (London, 1971), pp. 106-19.
22. E.g. North Kavirondo [sc. Nyanza] Central Association, petition to House of Commons 13 June 1936: KNA, PC/NZA. 2/655; see also D.A. Low, in *History of East Africa*, Vol. 2 pp. 31-4.
23. C.W. Hobley to H.M. Commissioner, 15 Feb. 1896: ESA, A.4/4; same to same, 3 Aug. 1898 (A.4/12); and 26 Apr. 1900 (A.4/28).
24. B.A. Ogot, 'Revolt of the elders', in B.A. Ogot (ed.), *Hadith 4: Politics and Nationalism in Colonial Kenya* (Nairobi, 1972), pp. 134-49.
25. E.g., F. Spire to Col. H. Colvile, 15 Sept. 1894: ESA, A.2/2.
26. M. Perham and M. Bull (eds), *The Diaries of Lord Lugard* (London, 1969), 1, p. 402.
27. Hobley, diary, 24 Aug. 1896, 21, 22 and 26 Dec. 1896; Hobley to Sir Harry Johnston, 26 Apr. 1900: ESA, A. 4/28; Dealing, 'Politics in Wanga', pp. 330-1, 336.
28. Hobley to Berkeley, 12 Nov. 1895: ESA, A.4/3; Spire to Colvile, 11 Nov. 1894: A.2/3; Evidence to committee on land tenure in North Kavirondo, p. 80 (evidence of Revd. Alfayo Odongo).
29. Dealing, 'Politics in Wanga', p. 346.
30. Matson, *Nandi Resistance, passim*; S.K. arap Ng'eny, 'Nandi resistance to the establishment of British administration 1883-1906', in B.A. Ogot (ed.), *Hadith 2*, (Nairobi, 1970), pp. 104-26.
31. D. Apter, *The Politics of Modernization* (Chicago, 1965), p. 40.
32. The bulk of the relevant material is in the two Entebbe Secretariat series A.2: 'Staff and Miscellaneous, Inward', and A.4: 'Staff Correspondence, Inward'.
33. My thanks to John Iliffe for alerting me to these problems.
34. W. Grant to Jackson, 16 Jan. 1895: ESA, A.4/1; Hobley's report, n.d., enclosure in Johnston to Lord Salisbury, 5 Feb. 1900: Public Record Office (PRO), FO 2/297.
35. For a classic example, see Richard Brown, 'The external relations of the Ndebele kingdom in the prepartition era', in L. Thompson (ed.), *African Societies in Southern Africa* (London, 1969), pp. 259-81.

36. Compare Eric Stokes, 'Traditional resistance movements and Afro-Asian nationalism', *Past and Present* 48 (1970), pp. 100–18.
37. Compare A.G. Hopkins, *An Economic History of West Africa* (London, 1973), Ch. 2.
38. For which see Matson, *Nandi resistance*, I, *passim*.
39. Hay, 'Economic change in Luoland', Ch. 4.
40. Hobley to Berkeley, 17 Oct. 1895: ESA, A.4/3; Matson, *Nandi resistance*, 1, pp. 117, 328, 360; R.D. McAllister to Berkeley, 12 Sept. 1898: A.4/13; Hobley to Berkeley, 14 Jul. 1898 A.4/11; H.H. Austin, *With Macdonald in Uganda* (London, 1903), p. 253.
41. Hobley to Berkeley, 21 Dec. 1898: ESA, A.4/14.
42. Johnston to Capt. Gorges, 10 Feb. 1900: ESA, A.5/9; R.A. Manners, 'The Kipsigis of Kenya', in J.H. Steward (ed.), *Contemporary Change in Traditional Societies* (Chicago, 1967), 1, pp. 219–20, 248–51; S.C. Lang'at, 'Some Aspects of Kipsigis History before 1914', in B.G. McIntosh (ed.), *Ngano* (Nairobi, 1969), pp. 88–92.
43. Correspondence between J. Ainsworth, Spire and Jackson, 1911 to 1913: ESA, Secretariat Minute Paper 3022.
44. Hobley to Berkeley, 4 Feb. 1896: ESA, A.4/4.
45. Grant to Jackson, 16 Jan. 1895: ESA, A.4/1; Hobley to Berkeley, 13 Sept. 1895, A.4/2; Hobley, diary, 1–24 Aug. 1895; Dealing, 'Politics in Wanga', p. 233.
46. Hobley, diary, 1 and 12 Sept. 1896; *idem*, Report, enclosure in Johnston to Salisbury, 5 Feb. 1900: PRO, FO 2/297; Johnston to Hobley, 4 Jan. 1900: ESA, A.5/9.
47. The overall position, as demonstrated during the 1897 mutiny of Sudanese troops and the Ogaden (Somali) expedition of 1900–1, rested on the men of the sub-continental Indian barracks. See R. Robinson and J. Gallagher, with A. Denny, *Africa and the Victorians* (London, 1961).
48. Hobley to Johnston, 7 Mar. 1900: ESA, A.4/26; Matson, *Nandi Resistance*, II, Chapter 2. I am indebted to Mr Matson for a sight of the MS.
49. A.H. Le Q. Clayton, 'Labour in the East Africa Protectorate, 1895–1918' (University of St Andrews Ph.D. thesis, 1971), p. 350.
50. To borrow and adapt a phrase from R.E. Frykenberg, *Guntur District 1788–1848: A History of Local Influence and Central Authority in South India* (Oxford, 1965), p. 11.
51. D.A. Low, *Lion Rampant* (London, 1973), pp. 30–3.
52. *Lugard Diaries*, I, p. 402.
53. Spire to Colvile, 11 Nov. 1894; ESA, A.2/3; Hobley, diary, 8 Mar. 1895: it is uncertain for how long Hobley maintained their exclusion.
54. Ascendancy needed very much the same sort of reinforcement over the Luo in 1899, with the Uyoma-Sakwa-Seme expedition.
55. Compare H.A.C. Cairns, *Prelude to Imperialism: British Reactions to Central African Society, 1840–1890* (London, 1965), p. 70.
56. Hobley, diary, 8 and 15 Apr. 1896; and somewhat irregularly thereafter.
57. Compare Peter Worsley, *The Third World* (London, 2nd end, 1967), p. 320. The man in question was Kivini (Chibini) of the Isukha Mironge clan. Oral tradition remembers him as a weak man of no significance; Peter Itebete, 'Primary resistance among the Idakho of western Kenya' (University of Dar es Salaam, undergraduate research paper, 1965).
58. Matson, *Nandi Resistance*, I, p. 294. 'Bombay African' was the term applied to Africans freed by the Royal Navy's anti-slave squadron in the Indian Ocean and subsequently educated by the Church Missionary Society in India.
59. Hobley to Berkeley, 21 Dec. 1898: ESA, A.4/14.
60. G.F. Archer, Report on the work carried out by the Kitosh [Bukusu] Patrol between July 28th and September 1st 1908, enclosure in Jackson to Crewe, 20 Oct. 1908: PRO, CO 533/47/513.

Part II

Contradictions
& the Development
of the Colonial State

Four

❧❧❧❧❧❧❧❧❧❧❧❧❧❧❧❧❧❧❧❧❧❧❧

Coping with the Contradictions
The Development of the Colonial State 1895–1914

BRUCE BERMAN & JOHN LONSDALE

This is a preliminary sketch, a contribution towards the new study of the colonial state in Africa.[1] Our analysis is informed by the material experience of a particular colony, but among the 30-odd dependencies of tropical Africa Kenya has a better claim than most to be considered a representative type. In the period between the wars, up until 1953 indeed, British imperial designs towards Kenya appear to have been paralysed between the opposing demands of a 'West Coast' and a 'South African' policy – or, as we would prefer, between the conflicting requirements of peasant and settler political economy. Meanwhile, peasant and settler society were themselves continually in formation, each building up its own constraints upon the actions of the colonial state, and from within the state's institutions. We make two initial points therefore. Our focus is on the state as a complex historical process, not on governments – which are variously misconceived as sovereign actors, pliant instruments of economic interests, or mere reflections of civil society. Secondly, we believe that an analysis of early colonial Kenya, a political economy midway between the colonies of peasant export production and the colonies of white settlement, has much to contribute to the more general discussion of the colonial and post-colonial state that is now in train.[2]

Coping with the Contradictions

The colonial state and the articulation of modes of production in the world system

We start by outlining, rather baldly, our three underlying premises. If we begin with some of the consequences of capital, we go on to argue that the character of the capitalist state, and more particularly that of the colonial state, cannot be reduced simply to that of a loyal minister to capital's needs.

Late 19th-century imperialism in Africa was the final sortie by which the world capitalist system captured the last continent to remain partially beyond its pale. The system was comprised, then as now, of a hierarchy of many differing modes of production linked at the level of exchange and all under the domination of the most advanced forms of capital, whether that was based in the formally responsible imperial power or in one of its industrial rivals. The violence involved in the imperial seizure was occasioned by such varied contingencies that it can legitimately be seen as 'necessary'; certainly the men on the spot thought it to be so. Africa's precapitalist forms of production were subjected to a historic break in their autonomous development; in the terminology of the time they were literally 'opened up'. They became part-economies, externally oriented to suit the dynamic of a capitalism that had been imposed upon them from outside.[3] East Africa's productive forms were subjected to a particularly sharp ordeal of restructuring. By contrast with West Africa there was little continuity in the relations of exchange to bridge the transition from informal to formal empire; East Africa's precolonial relations with the global economy had been based too exclusively on the production of two rapidly wasting assets, slaves and ivory.[4] In the inland area that became the hub of Kenya there had barely been an exportable surplus at all when, suddenly, in the first decade of the 20th century, production was intensified beyond all previous experience by the demands of colonial rule and, concurrently, by the opportunities of the commodity boom, itself in part created by the political and capital investments with which the imperial powers competed for preferential access to markets and resources.[5]

The 'articulation' of differing modes of production, pre-capitalist and capitalist, that was thus achieved entailed for participants in the former a bewildering compound of change and continuity.[6] Elders who had organized the local circuits of reciprocity could convert them into funds of accumulation; services once rewarded with the means of production – women, livestock or land – might now be paid off with the means of subsistence only, food or cash, and thus become a source of surplus value.[7] The potential for distortions of property rights, marital rights, parental or filial obligations, were endless, as indigenous modes of production yielded up produce or labour to merchant or landed

78

capital. Yet, at an early stage in the process and for many perhaps even now, it was easy for those involved to interpret this restructuring in the idiom of continuity, as lineage or domestic growth, as the reconstitution of livestock herds after the visitation of epizootic disease in the late 19th century.[8] This combination of dissolution and preservation of forms of production in the service of the dominant dynamic of external capital was not the only complexity of 'articulation'. We have also to see 'articulation' as a political relationship in which the dominant groups in the mode of production thus joined to capital had the possibility of allying with capitalist classes to suppress those whom both exploited, whether peasants in the sphere of household production or labourers extruded from it.[9] Our initial premise, then, is that the 'articulation of modes of production' must form the basis for any theoretical analysis of the colonial state.

The colonial state is a variant of the capitalist state; we must first, therefore, consider more generally the role of the state in class societies. This is an enormously contentious issue within the Marxist tradition of scholarship, which is currently making the most interesting contributions to the subject.[10] The state, as we understand it ourselves, is the historically conditioned set of institutions in any class society that secures, more or less adequately, the social conditions for the reproduction of the dominant mode of production, in this case capitalism. That is easy to say but difficult to perform, since the state's role is necessarily contradictory. Capitalism depends on the accumulation of surplus value from labour power or, in other words, on its continuing domination of an ever-changing process of class struggle. Capitalism cannot secure this dominant position for itself; individual capitalists are too competitive with each other and, moreover, if coercion were to be seated overtly within the relations of production the intensity of class conflict would rise to intolerable levels. The history of capitalist states has therefore been a process of abstraction. By this we mean that the twin functions of guaranteeing the technical and legal conditions of capital that competition cannot provide – monetary and tariff rules, property laws and so on – and of maintaining the hierarchy of class domination have both been abstracted from the economic to the political level within each national social order.[11] The state has become the ultimate unit both of economic reproduction, or accumulation, and of political reproduction, or social control. But these essential roles are mutually contradictory, at two levels. The state's regulation of competition between individual capitalists invites dispute within the dominant classes, whose cohesion is a condition of their domination. And the legitimation of the class order has entailed the protection of labouring conditions, the provision of welfare services, the enfranchisement of the working classes: all of which may have tempered the self-destructiveness of capital, but all of which nonetheless constitute brakes fitted by the state onto the process of accumulation. The contradictions of its role have thus become embedded within the state's institutions in the metaphor of political conflict, but in reality as class struggle.

The state must therefore be construed as 'relatively autonomous' with regard to the dominant class forces, at least at the level of political practice.[12] In order to maintain its own legitimacy through the morality of class domination, the state must be seen to act on behalf of the social order as a whole; indeed it may have to act, as we have just suggested, against the perceived interests of particular segments of the dominant class in order to renovate the structures and ideology of domination and accumulation. Given the contradictory nature of the state, the content of 'relative autonomy' is therefore subject to continual dissension and redefinition in response to crises within the dominant mode of production. The need for the state to sanction an intensification of the work process or to reallocate public resources, in order to rescue the rate of profit from the claims of labour power, may well result in a crisis of state authority. Its relative autonomy may become eroded to the point where it acts, and is seen to act, as the direct instrument of the dominant class or of some of its fractions. The resolution of such a crisis, if it is not to be by violence, must, then, entail the restoration of relative autonomy within the changed context. Our second premise, therefore, is that the state cannot be the obedient servant of capital, only the protector of capitalist social relations – and these are relations of conflict.

The colonial state, finally, must be expected to face a still more complex task as the 'factor of cohesion' in a peripheral economy based on articulated modes of production.[13] It had to organize the reproductive conditions not of one dominant mode of production, but of a capitalist mode not yet dominant whose social integument included the other modes to which capital was articulated and whose own social relations and ideological charters it therefore threatened. As the guarantor of social order, the colonial state was obliged to cope with these 'dislocative consequences of the expansion of the capitalist mode'.[14] The colonial state indeed straddled not one but two levels of articulation: between the metropole and the colony as a whole as well as within the colony itself. It therefore bore a dual character: it was at once a subordinate agent in its restructuring of local production to meet metropolitan demand, yet also the local factor of cohesion over the heterogeneous, fragmented and contradictory social forces jostling within. This very material Dual Mandate defined the dilemmas of the colonial state.

In grappling with these dilemmas – and this is our third premise – the colonial state was obliged to intervene more directly in economic life than was characteristic of contemporary capitalist states. Conversely, lacking any very elaborate representative institutions, the early colonial state had to absorb the contradictions of the economic level more directly into the bureaucratic sphere. Disagreements were not between parties but between officials. The imperial insistence on financial self-sufficiency gave to each colony a sovereign self-interest in the orderly expansion of its forces of production. Kenya's colonial state, therefore, as in all other colonies, had to perform two major functions, in both of which it faced the ambiguous project of promoting change while supervising continuity.[15] First, the state had to convert its superior coercive force over Africans into a legitimate authority accepted by Africans and therefore mediated through their own pre-existing or emergent relations of power.[16] Secondly, in a process strikingly similar to but in essential contradiction with the first, imported capital had to be converted from a lifeless factor of production into an active social relation.[17] Capitalist social relations might be created through intervention either at the level of exchange or at the level of production. In Kenya the state actively assisted merchant capital (generally Indian) to stimulate a surplus production by household labour, often through the brokerage of tribal notables who may have been allies in the process of conquest and who were now official chiefs. This appeared to be the most obvious way of coping with the contradictions between accumulation and control, but it was challenged by a second branch of imported capital. For white settlers on the land a wage labour force had to be created. The degree of coercion that this entailed was contingent on the number of workers required, the price the capitalist was prepared to pay and the division of labour within the indigenous modes of production. Kenya's colonial state certainly practised primitive accumulation on the settlers' behalf in appropriating African land, confiscating livestock, taxing households and forcing out labour, but the early colonial workforce was nevertheless composed largely of young men not yet in command of the means of production at home.

The early Kenyan state thus laboured under a palimpsest of contradictions of accumulation and control. At the local level the conflict between peasant and settler accumulation was expressed as a competition, made vicious by racial antagonism, between landed and merchant capital over the surplus product of African labour power. This local competition was itself subsumed, at a higher level of articulation, into a contradiction between the claims of metropolitan accumulation, represented by the banks and large trading houses, and those of local producers, of whom the settlers were the most conscious of being exploited.[18] Metropolitan accumulation could thus very directly threaten the legitimacy of colonial domination. Nor did metropolitan interests resolve the question of priorities between the settler and peasant sectors. The product of settler farms and plantations was minuscule in the imperial scale,[19] and by the interwar period Kenya's neighbours, Uganda and Tanganyika, not to mention British West Africa, showed the viability of the peasant alternative.

In any case the expansion of either sector posed problems of social control. Primitive accumulation on behalf of the settlers might provoke violent African resistance in defence of their land; the extraction of African labour might foster the cohesive consciousness of class over the fragmented consciousness of tribe. The combination of accumulation and political control in one agency, as in the concessionary company era in the Congo, had also shown that coercive exploitation might destroy the base of labour's reproduction; 'the productivity of terror', it has been remarked, 'was evidently low'.[20] The partial separation of the political and economic spheres in the colonial state may be seen as a response to precisely this dilemma. Yet peasant expansion might also, from initially strengthening the patronage relations by which chiefs and others made their contribution to the politics of collaboration,[21] go on to transform these props of colonial authority into exploitative employers or landlords through the discontinuities of class formation. Ever since the Indian Mutiny, British colonial officials had nervously suspected that social change, however inevitable in the cause of accumulation, was nevertheless subversive of social order and colonial control.[22]

Our foundations in Kenya's historiography

Kenya's sulphurous history, rich in political conflict and colourful personality, has evoked a fertile historiography. One must therefore ask what is to be gained in reworking old themes, especially in a summary essay such as this, necessarily indebted to the labours of other scholars. All the themes we have just sketched in have been tackled: the foundations of government; the origins of white settlement and its effect on government's land and labour policies; the response of particular African peoples to colonial domination, the development of their peasant commodity production and the rise of their collaborating elites. Yet all these various dimensions have been treated largely in isolation from each other; too little attention has been paid to their interconnections and their contradictions, and the way in which these latter were incorporated into the structures of the state.

Three broad approaches have emerged to meet the problem of how to organize the totality of Kenya's historical experience. It is not possible to do more than touch on them here. One has been to regard the level of the state as a political arena for competing interests, with the settlers and the 'administration' as the chief protagonists; a second has portrayed the state as an independent actor; the third has taken the state to be the instrument of others, whether of Great Britain or of local white settlement. All three approaches (sometimes found within the covers of one book) have taken their point of departure from the first liberal-humanitarian critics of colonial Kenya, Norman Leys and McGregor Ross, both of them colonial officials,[23] perhaps especially from Leys' observation in 1924 that, to Africans, 'the Government is not *their* government. In their view, everything it does, the tax, labour regulations and all else, is done for the benefit of Europeans.'[24]

For Mungeam and Sorrenson, the contradictions of accumulation and control were posed largely in personal terms, as the administrator's dilemma, caught between the policy objectives of economy and morality;[25] it took an ex-official to argue that the morality of the Imperial trust towards Africans was firmly rooted in the material necessities of the politics of collaboration.[26] This last perspective is strikingly absent from the other treatments of the early history of the colony as a whole. In many ways the best synoptic treatments are to be found in the second volume of the Oxford *History of East Africa,* but it is characteristic of the historiography of the time that economic and political history are presented in separate chapters. The former, by Wrigley, shows how the economy was moulded by government but not how government policy was formulated. Low's chapter on politics before 1912 is a subtle analysis of the way in which district administrations took up the threads of indigenous legitimacy and fostered peasant expansion, but he reaches the abrupt conclusion, not adequately explained, that by 1914 the African population had been relegated to the status of 'the labouring proletariat'.[27] Clayton and Savage's great work on labour history has much the same perspective as Mungeam and Sorrenson, with white official and white employer united in their world view but bitterly divided over its ambiguous implications, the official back being strengthened not so much by the local realities of maintaining social order as by occasional stern reminders from the Colonial Office as to where the path of duty lay.[28]

Ghai and McAuslan paint the most straightforward portrait of the government as actor, changing its character with the growth of representative institutions, which in our view is to burke the issue of why earlier forms of representation were found to be inadequate for organizing social control. It is moreover symptomatic of all this past historiography that these authors have almost nothing to say on the evolving content of African customary law – though much on its administration.[29] Until this vast area has been researched into (and we have not done so ourselves) we are really in the dark as to the full meaning for Africans of the incorporation of their societies into the colonial state.[30] Studies of the regional impact of colonialism have so far been just that. Munro's and Tignor's admirable studies of the emergence of collaborative and dissident factions against the background of economic change have failed to articulate their several African societies into the institutions of the state, stopping short at their interface, no doubt faithful to the views of the men whose experience they enter into.[31]

The opposite criticism must be made of two works that understand the state as the instrument of capital, and that articulate Kenya to the global structures of imperialism or the capitalist world system, a dimension missing from the works mentioned so far. Wolff's uncomplicated perspective has a pliant Kenya being shaped to fit metropolitan needs. Brett's study, founded upon a real awareness of the complexities of articulation between metropole and colony, as well as the contradictions of accumulation and control, nonetheless focuses on the salient half-truth of Kenya's history, the way in which state institutions and policies were shaped to serve the settlers.[32]

None of these studies therefore provides us with a systematic understanding of the development of the colonial state in Kenya confronted with the complexities of its two levels of articulation. In particular, they cannot explain the two crucial paradoxes of colonial Kenya. The first is this, that peasant commodity production, far from being 'destroyed',[33] continually expanded despite the imposed dominance of settler production. The peasant economy did not merely nourish the expanded reproduction of a wage-labour force outside capitalist relations of production. In sharp contrast to the South African experience it also dominated the domestic cereals market as a whole between the wars and earned export incomes that normally increased from year to year, apart from a severe slump in 1929–31.[34] Unlike, or so it appears, other colonies in settler Africa, there were no real labour reserves in Kenya; the main sources of labour supply were also the centres of marketed African production. The second paradox consists in the obvious but hitherto not sufficiently investigated fact that the increasing scope and intensity of state intervention against the African population, in order to establish the viability of the settler sector, coincided with a rising level of conflict between the settlers and officials who were determined to defend African interests. Using the theoretical approach outlined earlier we turn now to attempt to reach a more synoptic understanding of the emergence of the colonial state in Kenya, within all the contradictions of the social forces that governed its subsequent development.

Peasant production and the foundations of political control

In the 1880s the inland areas of 'Kenya' comprised a web of subsistence economies that exploited complementary ecological niches suited either to predominantly pastoral or predominantly agricultural forms of production. Between cattlemen and cultivators there was a symbiotic exchange of commodities and intermittent adjustment of populations. Drought and pestilence brought famine; survival was achieved through intensified exchange, raiding, and the acceptance in more fortunate economies of neighbours made destitute through dearth. Ethnic boundaries were porous, with strangers securing entry by means of adoption, debt bondage, or by clientship, notably within the large *mbari* groups that advanced the frontier of Kikuyu colonization. Social boundaries themselves often enclosed complementary economies in a circuit of accumulation, both farmers in the hills and herders on the plains. During much of the 19th century the pastoral Maasai controlled the centre of this arena; to agricultural accumulators on their hilly peripheries their herds represented a vast savings bank to be drawn on either by trade or, at times of pastoral disaster, by the offer of succour. This arena was penetrated from the coast by the caravans of Arabs and Swahili and, from 1888, the Imperial British East Africa Company. These caravans, interested mainly in ivory exports, reinforced the position of accumulating notables in the agrarian economies, extending their markets and range of allies.[35]

Three decades later the economic and political structures of the region had been subjected to profound transformation, under the sway of a state apparatus linking them to the capitalist world economy. Maasailand was now the core of the White Highlands, which also overlapped the northern and southern marches of Kikuyu expansion. But the transformation was incomplete and contradictory, not least because of the haphazard manner in which the East African Protectorate (not to become Kenya until 1920) had been cobbled together.

Metropolitan interests in the formation of the East African Protectorate were extraordinarily confused; the process provides a classic illustration of the contortions forced upon the capitalist state in general, vitally concerned with allocating the fruits of accumulation but remaining outside the directly productive process. The Foreign Office, obliged to assume responsibility by the collapse of the Company in 1895, was without experience of African administration, particularly land administration, and was, moreover, preoccupied with Imperial strategy and thus with Uganda. The men on the spot within the Protectorate were generally old Company hands, of whom the Foreign Office thought little. The Treasury, by contrast, was concerned with recovery of the £5.5 million sunk in the railway, the essential prop of 'effective occupation',[36] and together with the Colonial Office pressed that the infant colonial state be assured a position as rentier of the landed assets that the railway alone had created. These two departments feared, rightly, that private land grants would alienate from the colonial state the returns on this speculative investment of metropolitan resources. But their reservations were a positive hindrance to solving the immediate problem of how to develop a local export production that would generate freight revenues for the railway and dutiable imports to sustain the

new state. The Foreign Office, goaded by Parliamentary criticism of
the growing Treasury grant-in-aid, could only compromise with an
Order-in-Council in 1901 that left the conditions of land disposal to a
wide local discretion. The uncertainties that continued to befog the terms
on which private capital was granted land would force the resignation
of two governors in less than a decade.[37] Stabilization of the relations
between metropolitan and colonial authorities and between them and
private capital was thus bedevilled by administrative anomaly. As a
factor of cohesion, then, the state could be descried only at the parochial
level, within African society. It was engine, first, of imperial conquest
and only secondly of white colonization.

The necessary precondition for establishing any form of export
production and of self-financing administration was effective authority
over the African population. While London and Nairobi bickered over
the larger dimensions of the colonial state and the conditions of capital
investment, the extension of British control proceeded on local initiatives. But conquest was expensive. In its first nine years military costs
swallowed nearly one-third of the Protectorate's budget; they exceeded
local revenue, and were chiefly to blame for the tripling of the annual
Imperial subsidy in the five years from 1896. It was essential that spasmodic displays of force be converted into the steady exercise of civil
power; that coercion be replaced by consent.[38] Meanwhile, the transfer
of metropolitan responsibility from the Foreign Office to the Colonial
Office in 1905 brought the Protectorate under the control of a department actively concerned with tropical development for metropolitan
needs.[39] The key prefectural structure of district administration was
consolidated, to be staffed increasingly, in replication of the Home Civil
Service, with the products of the public schools and Oxbridge, the
cultivated guardians of social order in a competitive capitalist world.[40]

The process of converting military force into civil power had already
begun in the populated areas strung out along the line of rail. It involved
a dual process, the appropriation and then redistribution of African
resources, as punitive expeditions transferred livestock, the circulat-
ing capital of household production, from recalcitrants to 'friendlies'.[41]
Collaborative access to British resources was the more attractive for coinciding with the ecological crisis of the 1890s, when cattle plagues,
small-pox and drought wiped out up to a quarter of the human population of some areas in central Kenya and set the survivors squabbling
over the means of subsistence.[42] Disaster and dearth enhanced the
value of patrons who could organize the means of survival and reproduction or, more concretely, defence, raids and exchange. In the devastated
areas of Kenya the British happened to be the best patrons available;
it was more apparent to them than it was to Africans that they had also
come as conquerors.

Coping with the Contradictions

The British accumulated power as they multiplied their allies and forced down the supply price of African assistance, retaining for government purposes an ever larger percentage of looted stock. They then bureaucratized the means of coercion, coming to rely on uniformed police rather than on African military contractors. This changing balance of power, which shifted from coexistence to British control, meant that collaboration had now to be rewarded not by loot but with markets, to satisfy both the British and their African allies in the changed context. For Africans had to be given the means to pay a hut tax, at once the sacrament of submission, 'an outward and visible sign that the [African population] had definitely accepted Government control', and very soon the single largest component of the Protectorate's domestic revenues, rising from 4.5 per cent in 1901–2 to nearly 29 per cent in 1904–5.[43]

While some of the earliest 'chiefs and headmen' were appointed from among the African military auxiliaries and camp followers of conquest, perhaps marginal men in their own communities, they were soon replaced – just as the old Africa hands were supplanted by Oxbridge men – by appointments from among individuals or lineages that had already come to the fore as accumulators of wealth and power. In the creation of a taxable base of marketed production, chiefs had to construct roads with gangs of unpaid labour (often they did so on their own account); the administration opened markets for Indian traders whose wares were extolled by officials on tour; improved seed was issued for marketable crops, paid for generally out of chiefs' tax commissions, sometimes out of officials' pockets. The expansion of commodity production (for which the best index is perhaps the huge increase in the internal stock trade) thus provided not only a material base for colonial domination but also, specifically, the funds of patronage for chiefs who with derisory official salaries nonetheless maintained a growing clientele, including the tribal retainers, the bully boys of colonial control. In Nyanza and Kikuyu, the years before 1914 were the first heyday of the progressive chief, both agent for the diffusion of the readily divisible benefits of peace and markets and the appropriator of his people's labour on his own fields, his self-interest backed by British power.[44] With conquest recent and consent fragile, the joint interest of commissioner and chief in funding their personal authority was the fulcrum of expanded household production. The legitimacy of the colonial state was hitched to the oxcart of African accumulation.

In a very concrete fashion, therefore, the legitimation of conquest and the poverty of the state articulated African household production to the capitalist world system, in the sense both of joining it to overseas markets through Indian merchant capital and of giving it political expression through the interests of the chiefs and district administrations. In 1910

Coping with the Contradictions

Governor Girouard reckoned that Africans paid up to 40 per cent of total revenues in tax and import duties, the settlers only 20 per cent. By 1913 products of African origin furnished perhaps three-quarters of export earnings. Primitive accumulation on behalf of settler farming was thus subject to clear limits; the state simply could not afford to let white mate black 'in a very few moves'.[45]

Private capital, settlers and the state

The importance of the African peasant economy was less clear to higher officials and to the settlers who entered the colony in increasing numbers after 1903, however obvious it may have been to district officials. While settlers had manifest ideological reasons for their myopia, there were concrete reasons too. The produce of Nyanza Province, by far the railway's best customer, may well have been almost entirely African in origin, but as late as 1910–11 nearly 70 per cent of its exports was derived from ivory hunting or cattle hides, not agriculture. British experience in tropical agriculture had been with plantation tree crops; it was not yet clear that peasant long-fallow cultivation could lead to export growth. The one determined experiment in this, the cotton-growing scheme in Nyanza introduced in 1907, was a crashing failure against the competing labour demands of household food production.[46] This missed chance of articulating a direct link between the peasant sector and a politically influential metropolitan industry was an incalculable loss to the cause of peasant expansion. Moreover, the more senior of the Protectorate's officials doubted whether African peasants could always be relied upon to feed themselves; they had died by their thousands in the 1890s.

Protectorate officials had already searched with some urgency for an alternative means to develop production from 1902, only a year after the first hut tax had been collected and before anybody could guess at its later fiscal importance. The state's early essays in immigration had an air of desperation about them: Punjabi peasants, Finnish homesteaders, persecuted Jews from Eastern and Central Europe, all had their passing attractions.[47] Even when settlers of British stock – if initially from South Africa – were attracted, the question remained whether the Protectorate was to be regarded as primarily a colonist's or a planter's country, an equatorial New Zealand or a mainland Ceylon. Each had its disadvantages. The Colonial Office feared the unproductive, land-locking evils of speculation by big capital; but its Australasian experience taught that pioneer colonists in an unproven environment required – if they were to play their Imperial role in export production and not simply live off the land – much more official assistance than the infant Protectorate could provide. So a strict line of policy was adopted towards both 'big' and 'small' men. Their land titles 'bristled with servi-

tudes'[48] designed to secure active development by owner-occupiers,
and to inhibit speculation on the unearned increments from state
expenditure.

These public constraints on capital were all undone in the eight years
of acrimonious negotiation that preceded the amendment of the Crown
Lands Ordinance of 1915. This created a virtually free market in land
in the White Highlands, subject only to the governor's veto on trans-
fers to non-whites. The conditional clauses in land titles, which were
designed to secure minimum levels of production, were more or less
abandoned, and had in any case never been effectively enforced. Big
capital was allowed to amass land unhindered; by 1912 some 20 per cent
of the alienated area was held by just five individuals and consortia.

This reluctant official acceptance that the Protectorate was, at least
in its formative years, a 'big man's country', was governed by four considerations, and had enormous consequences for the articulation of estate
and household production. First, the state needed some form of accommodation with the private capital on which it relied for export growth,
and land conditions were one of the causes of periodic settler uproar.
Next, conditional land titles frightened off the banks' finance capital,
without which expansion was stunted. Thirdly, by 1912 it was clear
that such growth of estate production as was beginning to occur was
largely the work of the 'big men', often aristocrats, while smaller settlers
more commonly lived off their African tenants by 'Kaffir farming'; it
appeared that speculation and production were not so contradictory as
the Colonial Office had feared. For rising land values – they shot up by
some 4000 per cent between 1908 and 1914, from 6d to £1 per acre
– were due as much to the expensive proving of new crops and appropriate forms of animal husbandry by big men as to the services provided by the state.[49] Subdivision of holdings and sale on a rising market
certainly gave the big concessionaires a handsome return on their exper-
imental investments, but the small men shared their speculative interest.
Generally located close to the line of rail, they too could hope to finance
improvements from subdivision, and rising land values gave them the
collateral needed to secure mortgage capital, as much from the private
capital market as from the banks. There was thus, finally, never any
sustained opposition from the small men to make the Colonial Office
hesitate in its increasing accommodation with large capital.

In the decade before the First World War the state's fumbling after
the goal of concessionaire development paralleled its construction of the
politics of collaboration with African chiefs. Relied on to provide the
returns on the initial imperial investment, the concessionaires had
become part of that investment themselves.[50] There was, however, a
vital difference between the two categories of collaborator in their
relationship to the state. The basis of the district-level politics of

collaboration with Africans was the antecedent accumulation of British power over them. The state's collaboration with land concessionaires, by contrast, required the loosening of control, both at the Protectorate level, since too stern a control over land tenure closed up the capital market, and at the district level in the Highlands where white landowners would not tolerate the form of autocratic paternalism wielded by district officials over the African population.[51] This was the first of the consequences of concessionaire development. The state was obliged to stand increasingly outside the immediate relations of capitalist production, while co-opting the leading concessionaires on to its one representative institution, the Legislative Council, set up in 1907. The Protectorate was too late and unproven a segment of the capitalist world's farming frontier for the state to dictate terms to capital. Not until after the war, when the state's revenues provided security for development loans raised in London, and when the pressing claims of social order demanded fresh administrative controls over labour relations and the farm work process, could the state be said to have begun to establish any real authority over the settlers. And it was not until the crisis of the Depression and the exigencies of wartime production in the 1940s that, in return for protected markets and public crop-financing, white farming accepted a position of state clientage.[52]

Meanwhile, the long-term position of white farming was fatally undermined by three further consequences of concessionaire development. The rise in land values before 1914 was based as much on anticipated potential as on demonstrated performance. In 1913 the two major settler crops, coffee and maize, accounted for only 16 per cent of domestic export values.[53] The concessionaires' interest in high land prices was constantly to foil government-sponsored schemes of closer white settlement between the wars.[54] Further, these unrealistically high land values forced up capital costs and concentrated the settler mind on the reduction of labour costs, by the use of extra-economic means to coerce a labour supply,[55] the single largest cause of friction between their needs for accumulation and the state's concern for social order. And, finally, the thousands of unexploited acres under speculative ownership provided, as elsewhere in settler Africa,[56] the means to attract a permanent labour force on to the settler manor by letting land to Africans under various forms of tenancy. In at least one White Highland district, it was officially reported in 1917 that agricultural progress was due almost entirely to the work of these African squatters.[57] Maasailand was being turned inside out, as African cultivators, the majority of them Kikuyu, now invaded the choicest areas of the pastoral plain, under the protection of its new overlords.[58] To these contradictions at the base of settler agriculture we now turn.

Coping with the Contradictions

African labour and the contradiction between estate and peasant production

The burden of our argument so far is that the authority of the young colonial state came to rest upon a compatibility of interest between the big men of both peasant and capitalist production. We conclude now by examining the nature of that compatibility, which has received scant attention in the literature.[59] This tacit alliance between chief and settler, which was the political form of the articulation of modes of production, was to come under increasing strain as settlers demanded more from the state. The tensions were engraved upon the institutions of the state, which was the alliance's broker.

The establishment of capitalist estate production depended upon the appropriation of African land. But this partial separation of Africans from their means of production did not have an immediately adverse effect upon their wellbeing save in the case of the pastoralists, who suffered immeasurably larger losses than the cultivators. On the contrary, African farmers enjoyed an enormous access of exploitable land, as the British *pax* enabled them to use areas previously left empty for reasons of defence, and white landownership made available to their tenants' hoes the acres that settlers could not yet afford to plough.[60]

The most concrete expression of the contradiction between estate and household production was over the African labour supply.[61] But it was not, as we hope to show, quite the contradiction it has seemed. The state, anxious to complete public works as cheaply as possible under the home Treasury's scrutiny, shared with the settlers their interest in keeping labour costs down. While the technical rate of labour exploitation remained low, with inexperienced labour gangs working under inefficient managements whose language they did not understand, the conditions of exploitation were arbitrary and harsh. The expedients to which the state was driven in its desire to extract an African labour force below the value of its labour power were also testimony to the buoyancy of the peasant agriculture that the state had earlier been obliged to assist. The evidence before the Labour Commission of 1912–13 bore ample witness to the ease with which Africans could earn a cash income from household production, free from all the terrors of unknown disease and irascible employers that disfigured the labour market. Moreover, the state's own desire for cheap wage goods forced its Public Works Department to buy from African rather than white maize producers 'if works [were] to be completed without excesses on the votes'.[62] By 1912 African domination of the domestic cereals market had obliged the settlers to organize themselves for marketing overseas.[63]

This competitiveness of peasant agriculture calls for an analysis of the early effects of labour policy more subtle than one that assumes peasant production to have been strangled to export its labour for settler estates.[64] The reverse was the case. The articulation of capitalist agriculture to the lineage mode of production through the extraction of labour was in fact facilitated by the very differentiations in African society that were inevitably increased by expanded commodity production. In obedience to settler demands the rate of hut tax was raised and a poll tax imposed 'to increase the native's cost of living';[65] but taxation encouraged domestic production as much as wage employment. Where it was not neutral was in its differentiation between individual African men. Some had land on which to expand production, close enough to Asian markets to head-load the produce,[66] fertile and well-watered enough for a secure subsistence; some had a wife or wives to perform most of the routine drudgery, or the cattle whose hides could now be marketed. Chiefs in particular could displace the costs of experimentation on to the labour of others. Others, the unmarried, propertyless young men in particular, enjoyed none of these conditions for domestic production. On the evidence of the Labour Commission it was these who went out to work, many of them voluntarily, to acquire the stock needed to start the domestic cycle of family formation, in much the same way as they had previously embarked on cattle raids.[67] Where chiefs' retainers, not only the bully boys of control but also the press gangs of accumulation, forced men out to work, they selected their victims from among the 'weaker and poorer class such as could not make trouble'.[68] In summary, the needs of estate production differentiated Africans between those who could produce, those whom the labour market pulled, and those who could be pushed.

The hidden pillar of the early labour supply was therefore the contradiction within the peasant sector between those who were able to maintain by domestic production their status in the inflationary spiral of communal obligation, especially in bridewealth payments, which resulted from monetization and the intensification of the market, and those who could only attempt to do so by wage labour.[69] It rested on the ambivalent position of the appointed chiefs.[70] It could stand only so long as the collaborative relationship between peasant economy and district administration retained enough autonomy to allow household production to continue its expansion, so giving the chiefs the resources with which to reward their own followings while picking on their opponents. The oppression of primitive accumulation on behalf of estate production was thus factionalized within the peasant periphery. Both settler and peasant production were able to expand before 1914, with their major contradiction raging half-hidden within the African labyrinths of lineage and clientage.

The contradiction was only half-hidden however. It began to obtrude into the relations between settlers and state from around 1908, as the influx of settlers coincided with the final fling of the Edwardian boom. The increasing outflow of African labour in both its forms, short-term migrancy and labour tenancy or 'squatting' on settler farms, began to undermine the authority of chiefs and district officials and so to threaten the shaky young framework of control. Two successive methods of recruiting migrant contract labour were tried; both had a subversive effect. Initially district officers were themselves recruiters – and government was the largest and often the worst employer. This administrative 'encouragement' of labour led to openly coercive round-ups by the chiefs, anxious to ingratiate themselves by filling their quotas. From 1908, acting on the concern of administrative officials, the state withdrew from its exposed position in the creation of capitalist relations of production and farmed out labour recruitment to professional recruiters and those settlers whose land bordered on the African areas. But this was to make bad matters worse. For recruiters and employers established direct personal ties with the chiefs that bypassed the ties between chiefs and officials; they therefore challenged the monopoly over external resources that was the basis of the district commissioners' local control. Direct relations between settlers and chiefs were being created, outside the mediation of the state, and yet potentially destructive of the very mechanisms of state authority that made those relations possible.

The squatter solution to the labour supply was no better. It did not initially involve coercion; command over cheap land resources was a sufficient attraction in the hands of the employer, particularly for the Kikuyu who experienced in its sharpest form the growing social differentiation of peasant production. Kikuyu peasant families were literally seeking 'Land and Freedom' on the Highlands, glad to exchange the initially light demands of settler overlords for the increasing oppressions of land concentration and labour recruitment at home.[71] But herein lay the threat to political order; the extraction of peasant resources could not tolerate political emigration from the jurisdictions of the chiefs.[72]

These manifold contradictions in the labour supply were played out at the political level in the growing ambivalence of officials towards the settler sector in their midst, support for which looked increasingly likely to undercut their politics of collaboration with Africans. Officials became more and more concerned about the corrosive effects of the individualism of wage labour on what was variously called 'tribal discipline' or, more quaintly, 'African nationalism'.[73] They were periodically alarmed by the tendency of exasperated settler employers to take the law into their own hands – a more immediate threat to political order than African resistance and perhaps a deliberate one, in that settlers were suspected of half-hoping for African rebellion, as a charter for fresh land grabs.[74]

The officials' solution to this self-destructive tendency of capital, its habit of promoting outright conflict with Africans while dissolving the communities of African society, was sought in an increasing administrative segregation between white and black, so unlike the confident hopes that their 'interpenetration' had held for Commissioner Eliot at the turn of the century.[75] With Colonial Office approval, Governor Belfield began to plan the division of the colony into settled districts under magistrates responsible to the Chief Secretary, and African areas under commissioners responsible to the new office of Chief Native Commissioner. The articulation of the economy was dividing the state. In May 1914 the Secretary of State forbade further thought of labour compulsion, on the grounds that it had contributed to the Ndebele rising.[76] Three months later, as if to confirm official fears, the Giriama rebelled against administrative measures to limit their peasant expansion and to move them within easier reach of tax collection and labour recruitment.[77] But the irony of the First World War, which trod on the rising's heels, was that it forced the colonial state, for all its sovereign concern for social order, to destroy the roots of Africans' collaboration by demanding their untold sacrifice in blood and livestock in the service of a metropolitan power under which, after all, the Kenyan state was merely a subordinate agent.

Conclusions: the centrality of the state in the political economy of colonialism

The complex experience of early colonial Kenya does, we believe, illuminate four points of more general importance in understanding the role of the colonial state in Africa. First, the state acted as the factor of cohesion, the focus of the contradictions in capitalism's articulation with indigenous modes of production, for both of which the state itself had provided the conditions for expansion. The contradictions that had emerged by 1914 were to provide the internal dynamic of economic growth and political conflict over the next half-century.[78] They subsequently found expression at the level of the state both in constant rows between secretaries of state and Kenya's governors and, locally, in the growing tension between the Provincial Administration based on the African areas, and the central Secretariat with its technical departments preoccupied with servicing settler accumulation.[79] But, secondly, these internal contradictions did not mean that the state was a disinterested if bewildered arbiter between the conflicting interests of civil society. The state never ceased to try to provide the conditions for the reproduction of settler capitalism, and to justify it through the myth of the indispensability of the large farm sector to the colony's exports.[80] What was at issue was the lengths to which the state could go before it was seen to be the settlers' instrument, at the risk of its legitimacy with Africans. The role of even-handed arbiter, of defender of the weaker, African, interest was an ideological position adopted by colonial officials, to make their own position tolerable while also maintaining the relative autonomy of the state. In practice they abstracted into the state, or bureaucratized, the coerced appropriation of African resources, and so pre-empted the sort of destructive settler resort to self-help that would have threatened the apparatus of control in the African areas. That the state also actively assisted the expansion of peasant production in the early 1920s and again in the 1930s was as much a reflection of the weaknesses of the settler export sector as of the disinterestedness of the state.

Thirdly, the growth of segregationist ideas among officials before the First World War illustrates the degree to which the state's ability to cope politically with the contradictions of the economy depended on the fragmented local containment of African political and economic forces, and their representation in state institutions according to ethnic categories.[81] The suppression of class formation outside these categories, which would have made the expansion of capital a still more explosive issue, was a constant theme of policy until the 1950s.[82] This colonial preoccupation with 'tribal cohesion' also tended to reinforce the early bias towards peasant commodity production, since this represented a 'dispersal of economic power and hence minimized the growth of economic entities within the colony that could put forward political demands upon the administration.'[83]

Finally, the steady expansion of the powers of the colonial state simply reflected its growing difficulties in managing the crises of its articulated economy. The concept of the colonial state as the 'overdeveloped' instrument of the metropolitan bourgeoisie – which might be abbreviated to the 'metrobogey', to catch the tone of some of the recent literature – ignores these local stimuli to the bureaucratization of the process of articulation. Nor was the paternalist interventionism of the colonial state, so much weightier than its metropolitan contemporaries, merely an archaic and irrational reaction, inhibiting more rapid development;[84] it was a response to very real dilemmas in fulfilling a colony's dual mandate, coping with the socially disruptive articulation of capitalist and indigenous modes of production that lay at the heart of the colonial situation.

Notes

1. Transatlantic collaboration has not proved to be easy. This final draft represents merely an arbitrary caesura in a continuing dialogue of exchanged ideas that we hope to pursue at more illuminating length elsewhere.

2. One of the earliest essays in this enterprise is the Introduction to G.B. Kay, *The Political Economy of Colonialism in Ghana* (Cambridge, 1972). The project has been carried furthest with regard to South Africa. For an instructive guide to the current state of the argument see Simon Clarke, 'Capital, fractions of capital and the state: "Neo-Marxist" analysis of the South African state', *Capital and Class* 5 (1978), pp. 32–77. Kenneth Good, 'Settler colonialism: economic development and class formation', *Journal of Modern African Studies* 14(4) (1976). pp. 597–620, emphasizes, as we do, the interventionist nature of the colonial state but without noting the constraints on its action with which we deal below.

3. Aidan Foster-Carter, 'The modes of production controversy', *New Left Review* 107 (1978), pp. 47–77.

4. Andrew Roberts, 'Nyamwezi Trade', in R. Gray and D. Birmingham (eds), *Pre-Colonial African Trade* (London, 1970), pp. 39–74.

5. A.G.Hopkins, *An Economic History of West Africa* (London, 1973). Chs 4 and 5; I. Wallerstein, 'The three stages of African involvement in the world economy', in P. Gutkind and I.Wallerstein (eds), *The Political Economy of Contemporary Africa* (Beverly Hills & London, 1976); J. Forbes Munro, *Africa and the International Economy, 1800–1960* (London, 1976), Ch. 4; C.C. Wrigley, 'Neo-mercantile policies and the new imperialism', in C. Dewey and A.G. Hopkins (eds), *The Imperial Impact* (London, 1978), pp. 20–34.

6. J. Iliffe, *Agricultural Change in Modern Tanganyika* (Nairobi, 1971); L. Cliffe, 'Rural class formation in East Africa', *Journal of Peasant Studies*, 4(2) (1977), pp. 195–224; D. Parkin, *Palms, Wine and Witnesses* (London, 1972).

7. M.P. Cowen, 'Capital and peasant households' (mimeo., University of Nairobi, 1976), 21.

8. Richard Waller, 'The Maasai and the British 1895–1905: the origins of an alliance', *Journal of African History* 17(4) (1976), pp. 529–53; D.M. Feldman, 'Christians and politics: the origins of the Kikuyu Central Association in northern Murang'a 1890–1930' (Ph.D. thesis, University of Cambridge, (1979), Ch. 2; P. Spencer, 'Drought and the commitment to growth', *African Affairs* 293 (1974), pp. 419–27; J.M. Lonsdale, 'How the people of Kenya spoke for themselves, 1895–1923' (mimeo., Proceedings of the African Studies Association (USA), 1976), extensively available in Terence Ranger, 'Growing from the roots: reflections on peasant research in Central and Southern Africa', *Journal of Southern African Studies* 5(1) (1978), pp. 128–31.

9. This insight is the particular contribution of P.P. Rey, *Les Alliances de classes* (Paris, 1973), as presented in Foster-Carter, 'Modes of production controversy'.

10. For helpful guides to the main arguments see Bob Jessop, 'Recent theories of the capitalist state', *Cambridge Journal of Economics* 1 (1977), p. 353–73, and the editors' Introduction, 'Towards a materialist theory of the State', in John Holloway and Sol Picciotto (eds), *State and Capital, a Marxist Debate* (London, 1978), pp. 1–31.

11. See in particular J. Hirsch, 'The State apparatus and social reproduction: elements of a theory of the bourgeois State', in Holloway and Picciotto (eds), *State and Capital*, pp. 57–107.

12. For discussions of this relative autonomy of the state, implicit and explicit, see R. Miliband, *The State in Capitalist Society* (London, 1973); and N. Poulantzas, *Political Power and Social Classes* (London, 1973). For an instance in the early development of relative autonomy see D. Hay, 'Property, authority and the criminal law', in D. Hay et al., *Albion's Fatal Tree* (London, 1975).

13. But the complexity is a matter of degree; as Perry Anderson reminds us in *Passages from Antiquity to Feudalism* (London, 1974), p. 22, this combination of different modes of production is to be found within all social formations.

14. Geoff Lamb, 'Marxism, access and the state', *Development and Change* 6(2) (1975), especially pp. 131–2.

Coping with the Contradictions

15. This schematic presentation is elaborated in later sections of this chapter.
16. For the distinction between force and power see E.M. Luttwak, *The Grand Strategy of the Roman Empire* (Baltimore, 1976), pp. 195–200.
17. Cf. Shula Marks with Stanley Trapido, 'Lord Milner and the South African State' (mimeo., Cambridge Commonwealth and Overseas History Seminar, 1979), p. 15.
18. R. van Zwanenberg, 'Primitive colonial accumulation in Kenya, 1919–1939: a study in the processes and determinants in the development of a wage labour force' (Ph.D. thesis, University of Sussex, 1971), Chs 1 and 2; for a fictional portrayal of antagonism between settler and banker, see Robert Ruark, *Something of Value* (London, 1955), p. 25.
19. Max Salvadori, *La Colonisation européenne au Kenya* (Paris, 1938); F.V. Meyer, *Britain's Colonies in World Trade* (London, 1948); Colonial Office minute by E. Melville, 10 June 1940, on Report of Delegation from the East African Territories: Public Record Office, CO 533/518/38103/2B.
20. By Douglas Rimmer, in his review article on L.H. Gann and P. Duignan (eds), *The Economics of Colonialism*, in *Journal of African History* 19(2) (1978), p. 269.
21. Ronald Robinson, 'Non-European foundations of European imperialism: sketch for a theory of collaboration', in R. Owen and B. Sutcliffe (eds), *Studies in the Theory of Imperialism* (London, 1972), pp. 117–40; M. Semakula Kiwanuka, 'Colonial policies and administrations in Africa: the myths of the contrasts', *African Historical Studies* 3(2) (1970).
22. D.A. Low, 'Empire and social engineering', in his *Lion Rampant: Essays in the Study of British Imperialism* (London, 1973), pp. 53–70.
23. Norman Leys, *Kenya* (London, 1924); W. McGregor Ross, *Kenya from Within* (London, 1927). For discussion of their role see Diana Wylie, 'Confrontation over Kenya: the Colonial Office and its critics, 1918–1940', *Journal of African History* 18(3) (1977), pp. 427–48.
24. Leys, *Kenya*, p. 318 (emphasis in original).
25. G.H. Mungeam, *British Rule in Kenya, 1895–1912* (Oxford, 1966), pp. 281; M.P.K. Sorrenson, *Origins of European Settlement in Kenya* (Nairobi, 1968), p. 241.
26. T.H.R. Cashmore, 'Studies in District Administration in the East Africa Protectorate, 1895–1918' (Ph.D. thesis, University of Cambridge, 1965), pp. 83–7, 118–19.
27. C.C. Wrigley, 'Kenya: the patterns of economic life, 1902–1945', and D.A. Low, 'British East Africa: the establishment of British rule', in V. Harlow and E.M. Chilver, with A.Smith (eds), *History of East Africa*, II (Oxford, 1965), pp. 209–64 and 1–56 respectively.
28. A. Clayton and D.C. Savage, *Government and Labour in Kenya, 1895–1963* (London, 1974).
29. Y.P. Ghai and J.P.W.B. McAuslan, *Public Law and Political Change in Kenya* (Nairobi, 1970).
30. A start has been made in H.F. Morris and J.S. Read, *Indirect Rule and the Search for Justice* (Oxford, 1972).
31. J. Forbes Munro, *Colonial Rule and the Kamba* (Oxford, 1975); R.L. Tignor, *The Colonial Transformation of Kenya* (Princeton, 1976).
32. R.D. Wolff, *The Economics of Colonialism* (New Haven and London, 1974); E.A. Brett, *Colonialism and Underdevelopment in East Africa* (London, 1973).
33. R. Palmer's conclusion with regard to Shona, Ndebele and Kikuyu agriculture in the 1930s, in R. Palmer and N. Parsons (eds), *The Roots of Rural Poverty in Central and Southern Africa* (London, 1977), p. 243.
34. At current prices African export earnings tripled from 1922 to 1929, from £180,000 to £543,000; and, after a slump to £214,000 in 1931, again more than doubled, to £488,000, by 1940. See tables in Salvadori, *Colonisation européenne*, p. 129; I.R.G. Spencer, 'The development of production and trade in the reserve areas of Kenya,

1895-1929' (Ph.D. thesis, Simon Fraser University, 1975), p. 367; P. Mosley, 'Agricultural development and government policy in settler economies: the case of Kenya and Southern Rhodesia 1900-1960', *Economic History Review* 35(3) (1982), pp. 390-408. That peasant export values could have increased still more rapidly without settler dominance is clear, especially if the prohibition on African coffee had been lifted before 1933; but the existing literature concentrates too gloomily on the *relative* decline in African exports compared with settler export production.

35. From a large literature see R.D. Waller, 'The Lords of East Africa: the Maasai in the mid-nineteenth century, *c.* 1840-1885' (Ph.D. thesis, University of Cambridge, 1979); G. Muriuki, *A History of the Kikuyu, 1500-1900* (Nairobi, 1974); M. Hay, 'Local trade and ethnicity in western Kenya', *African Economic History Review*, 2(1) (1975), pp. 7-12; J. Lonsdale, 'When did the Gusii (or any other group) become a tribe?', *Kenya Historical Review* 5(1) (1977), pp. 123-33; Cowen, 'Capital and peasant households', pp. 17-20; Munro, *Kamba*, pp. 7-30; P. Marris and A. Somerset, *African Businessmen* (London, 1971), pp. 25-47.

36. For the lack of Foreign Office policy see Mungeam, *British Rule*, pp. 33, 43, 68-72; and for the poor quality of many early officials, R. Meinertzhagen, *Kenya Diary, 1902-1906* (London, 1957), p. 132; Clayton and Savage, *Government and Labour*, p. 27. For the railway, see. G.N. Uzoigwe, 'The Mombasa-Victoria railway, 1890-1902: imperial necessity, humanitarian venture, or economic imperialism?', *Kenya Historical Review* 4 (1976), pp. 11-34.

37. Eliot (in fact Commissioner) in 1904, Girouard in 1912.

38. Sorrenson, *Origins*, pp. 29-30; Mungeam, *British Rule*, p. 132; Wolff, *Economics of Colonialism*, p. 50.

39. R. Hyam, *Elgin and Churchill at the Colonial Office, 1905-1908* (London, 1968), Ch. 12.

40. For the changing patterns of recruitment to the administration, see B.J. Berman, 'Administration and Politics in Colonial Kenya' (Ph.D. thesis, Yale University, 1974), Ch. 2.

41. For the connections between the politics of conquest and early district administration, see Waller, 'Maasai and British'; J.M. Lonsdale, 'The politics of conquest: the British in Western Kenya, 1894-1908', *Historical Journal* 20(4) (1977), pp. 841-70; Low, 'British East Africa'; Munro, *Kamba*, parts 1 and 2; Tignor, *Colonial Transformation*, Chs 1-6; Cashmore, 'District administration'; P. Rogers, 'The British and the Kikuyu, 1890-1905: a re-assessment', *Journal of African History* 20 (1979), pp. 255-69; M.A. Thomason, 'Little Tin Gods: the District Officer in British East Africa', *Albion* 7(2) (1975), pp. 145-60; Spencer, 'Production and trade'; Lonsdale, 'People of Kenya'; Feldman, 'Christians and politics', Ch. 1.

42. It was in the 1890s, according to missionary recollection, that the term Mau Mau was first coined to described a gang of bandits in southern Kikuyu; see Church of Scotland Foreign Missions Committee, *Mau Mau and the Church* (mimeo., Edinburgh, Feb. 1953), p. 5.

43. C.W. Hobley, *Kenya from Chartered Company to Crown Colony* (London, 1929), p. 124; hut tax proportions of revenue calculated from figures given in Mungeam, *British Rule*.

44. For these early chiefs see B.A. Ogot, 'British administration in the Central Nyanza District of Kenya, 1900-60', *Journal of African History* 4(2) (1963), pp. 249-73; E. Atieno-Odhiambo, 'Some reflections on African initiative in early colonial Kenya', *East Africa Journal* 8(6) (1971), pp. 30-6; W.R. Ochieng', 'Colonial African chiefs: were they primarily self-seeking scoundrels?', in B.A. Ogot, (ed.), *Politics and Nationalism in Colonial Kenya* (Nairobi, 1972), pp. 46-70.

45. Mungeam, *British Rule*, pp. 220-1; for Commissioner Eliot's unguarded comment, see Sorrenson, *Origins*, p. 76.

46. Nyanza's export figures from the Provincial Annual Report, 1910-11; H. Reed,

'Cotton growing in Central Nyanza, Kenya, 1901-1939' (Ph.D. thesis, Michigan State University, 1975), pp. 23-6; John Tosh, 'Lango agriculture during the early colonial period', *Journal of African History* 19(3) (1978), pp. 426-8, analyses an early failure with cotton almost exactly parallel to Nyanza's, not least in the African preference for surplus productions of sesame, an oilseed for which there was a world market (if not with British industry) as well as a domestic use in food preparation.

47. For land policies see Sorrenson, *Origins*; Ghai and McAuslan, *Public Law*, pp. 25-30, 79-83; M.G. Redley, 'The politics of a predicament: the white community in Kenya, 1918-1932' (Ph.D. thesis, University of Cambridge, 1976), Ch. 2; R.G. Weisbord, *African Zion* (Philadelphia, 1968), Chs 4-6.

48. To quote a local bank manager in 1914: see Redley, 'Predicament', p. 83.

49. For Lord Delamere's expensive pioneering, see Elspeth Huxley, *White Man's Country*, 1 (second edition, London, 1953), Chs 7 and 8; and for the state's assistance to agriculture, Wolff, *Economics of Colonialism*, Ch. 4.

50. *Ibid.* p. 55.

51. Berman, 'Administration and politics', Ch. 4.

52. Redley, 'Predicament', *passim*; Clayton and Savage, *Government and Labour*, Chs 4-7.

53. Wolff, *Economics of Colonialism*, p. 74.

54. Redley, 'Predicament', *passim*.

55. R. van Zwanenberg, *Colonialism and Labour in Kenya, 1919-1939* (Nairobi, 1975).

56. S. Trapido, 'Landlord and tenant in a colonial economy: the Transvaal 1880-1910', *Journal of Southern African Studies* 5(1) (1978), pp. 26-58; J.K. Rennie, 'White farmers, black tenants and landlord legislation: Southern Rhodesia 1890-1930', *ibid.* pp. 86-98; M.L. Morris, 'The development of capitalism in South African agriculture', *Economy & Society* 5 (1976), pp. 292-343.

57. F. Furedi, 'The social composition of the Mau Mau movement in the White Highlands', *Journal of Peasant Studies*, 1(4) (1974), p. 490.

58. Wrigley, 'Patterns of economic life', p. 229.

59. But see Mungeam, *British Rule*, pp. 283-5, for the first inklings.

60. Low, 'British East Africa', pp. 33-4; Wrigley, 'Patterns of economic life', p. 229; Feldman, 'Christians and politics', pp. 53-5; V. Uchendu and K. Anthony, *Field Study of Agricultural Change: Kisii District, Kenya* (Stanford, 1969), p. 47.

61. The fullest account of the Protectorate's labour policies is in A.H. le Q. Clayton, 'Labour in the East Africa Protectorate, 1895-1918' (Ph.D. thesis, University of St Andrews, 1971), now summarized in Clayton and Savage, *Government and Labour*, Chs 1-3; see also Leys, *Kenya*, Ch. 8; Ross, *Kenya from Within*, Ch. 6; Huxley, *White Man's Country*, pp. 1, 214-36, 274-6, for a settler view; M.R. Dilley, *British Policy in Kenya Colony* (second edn, London, 1966), Part IV, Ch. 1; R. van Zwanenberg, *Colonialism and Labour*, Ch. VII. The indispensable primary source for the views of officials, Africans and settlers is *Native Labour Commission, 1912-13: Evidence and Report*, (Govt. printer, Nairobi, n.d.), usefully summarized in Clayton & Savage, *Government and Labour*, pp. 55-62.

62. W. McGregor Ross to Commissioner for Public Works, 15 Oct. 1908: Ross papers, privately held.

63. E. Huxley, *No Easy Way: A History of the Kenya Farmer's Association and Unga Ltd.* (Nairobi, 1957), p. 4.

64. As in Wolff, *Economics of Colonialism*, Ch. 5.

65. In the words of Governor Belfield, 1913, quoted in Clayton and Savage, *Government and Labour*, p. 41.

66. In 1912 John Ainsworth calculated that Nyanza's agricultural exports represented 1.25 million headload-days per annum, Nyanza Province Annual Report (1911-12), p. 55.

67. The Kipsigis indeed used the same term to describe both cattle raids and wage labour:

I.Q. Orchardson, 'Some traits of the Kipsigis in relation to their contracts with Europeans', *Africa* 4(4) (1931), p. 468.

68. *Native Labour Commission 1912–13*, p. 135, evidence of Provincial Commissioner Ainsworth.

69. For the inflationary tendencies of monetization see P. Bohannan, 'The impact of money on an African subsistence economy', *Journal of Economic History*, 19(4) (1959), pp. 491–503; Wrigley, 'Patterns of economic life', p. 226.

70. Cf. Foster-Carter, 'Modes of production controversy'. For case studies, see R.L. Tignor, 'Colonial chiefs in chiefless societies', *Journal of Modern African Studies*, 9(3) (1971), pp. 339–59; J. Tosh, 'Colonial chiefs in a stateless society: a case-study from northern Uganda', *Journal of African History* 14(3) (1973), pp. 473–90.

71. For squatter motives see *Land Settlement Commission, British East Africa* (Nairobi, 1919), pp. 15, 17, 25; G. Kershaw, 'The land is the people: a study of social organization in historical perspective' (Ph.D. thesis, University of Chicago, 1972), pp. 100–1; F. Furedi, 'The Kikuyu squatters in the rift valley, 1918–1929', in B.A. Ogot, (ed.), *Hadith 5: Economic and Social History of East Africa* (Nairobi, 1975), pp. 177–94; R.M. Wambaa and K. King, 'The political enonomy of the Rift Valley: a squatter perspective', *ibid.* pp. 195–217. By the 1940s the squatters would seek 'Land and freedom' by other means, in the Mau Mau movement, when the increased capitalization of settler farming required that they be transformed from tenants to labourers.

72. For officials' cries of alarm see Cashmore, 'District Administration', p. 97; G.W.T. Hodges, 'African responses to European rule in Kenya to 1914', in B.A. Ogot, (ed.), *Hadith 3* (Nairobi, 1971), p. 95; Tignor, *Colonial Transformation*, p. 106; Munro, *Kamba*, pp. 92–3.

73. Governor E.P.C. Girouard, *Memoranda for Provincial and District Commissioners* (Nairobi, 1910), p. 6.

74. Hyam, *Elgin and Churchill*, p. 411.

75. Sorrenson, *Origins*, Chs 13 and 15.

76. Clayton and Savage, *Goverment and Labour*, p. 63.

77. Cynthia Brantley, *The Giriama and British Colonialism in Kenya: a Study in Resiliency and Rebellion, 1800–1920* (Berkeley and Los Angeles, 1981).

78. See Chapter 5, below.

79. These internal conflicts in the state are discussed in B.J. Berman, *Control and Crisis in Colonial* Kenya (London, 1990).

80. Colin Leys, *Underdevelopment in Kenya* (London, 1975), pp. 28–40.

81. Cf. M. von Freyhold, 'The post-colonial state and its Tanzanian version', *Review of African Political Economy* 8 (1977), p. 79. See also J. Iliffe, *A Modern History of Tanganyika* (London, 1979), Ch. 10; for the Kenya government's fear of pan-tribal consciousness in 1917, see J.M. Lonsdale, 'Some origins of nationalism in East Africa', *Journal of African History* 9(1) (1968), p. 132 n.

82. The exercise of social control in early Nairobi is a subject on which we await the findings of Frederick Cooper, Carla Glassman, B.A. Ogot and Luise White.

83. Wallerstein, 'Stages of African involvement', p. 41.

84. Cf. C. Ehrlich, 'Some social and economic implications of paternalism in Uganda', *Journal of African History* 4(2) (1963), pp. 275–85, and as implied in P.T. Bauer and B.S. Yamey, 'The economics of marketing reform', *Journal of Political Economy*, 62(3) (1954), pp. 210–35.

Five

𝔡𝔡𝔡𝔡𝔡𝔡𝔡𝔡𝔡𝔡𝔡𝔡𝔡𝔡𝔡𝔡𝔡𝔡𝔡𝔡𝔡𝔡𝔡𝔡

Crises of Accumulation, Coercion & the Colonial State

The Development of the Labour Control System 1919-29

BRUCE BERMAN & JOHN LONSDALE

Introduction: explaining the form of the colonial state (1990)

The most striking characteristic of the colonial state to most scholars has been the unusual scope and intensity of its intervention in the economic and social life of a colony. This increased steadily during the colonial period in Africa and was accompanied by the development of the colonial state from an initially simple administrative control apparatus into the complex and sophisticated institutions of social control and economic management of the 1945–60 period. Recognition that this development was a function of the socio-economic forces operating at the periphery of the world capitalist system brings us only as far as the real analytic issue: the specification of the linkage of these forces with the development of the colonial state in such a way as to account adequately for both its general form and the specific variations that emerged in different colonies; and, simultaneously, account for the particular role of such structural forms and practices of the state in shaping the development of the forces and relations of production and processes of class formation in those colonies.

The most prominent explanations of the colonial state at the time this chapter and Chapter 4 were written saw it either as 'overdeveloped' in response to the needs of metropolitan capital or as the conscious agent of the metropolitan bourgeoisie.[1] These corresponded to the then dominant theories of the state, respectively structuralist and instrumentalist, in both of which the forces determining the state as well as the forms of colonial production are identified as external to the colony itself. We wanted to demonstrate that both of these approaches were inadequate.

The structuralist analysis, in which the 'overdeveloped' colonial state was shaped by the systemic structural needs of metropolitan capitalism, operates at a level of abstraction capable of explaining only the most general form of colonial economies as primary commodity producers and of the colonial state as the agency directing that development and maintaining the continuity of primary commodity production. It cannot account for why particular crops were introduced in particular colonies or, more importantly, explain the variant forms of colonial production that developed in different areas, e.g., peasant commodity production, corporate plantation production, settler estate agriculture or, as in Kenya, the contradictory and conflicting development of a combination of estate and peasant production. Nor is it sufficiently powerful to explain the variant forms and differing trajectories of development of colonial state apparatuses in particular colonies. What is missing is a conceptualization of the structural forces *within* each colony and the consequences of their interaction with the imposed external forces emanating from the metropole. To note, as Mamdani does, that the specific nature of domination in a colony is determined by concrete historical circumstances simply begs the most compelling analytic question.[2]

An instrumental analysis of the colonial state as the conscious subordinate 'agent' of the metropolitan bourgeoisie, acting to meet the interests of that class, similarly neglects the issue of the influence of indigenous political and social forces, especially the accumulative interests of local colonial classes of producers. The available evidence is complex and ambiguous. For each instance of colonial authorities acting directly to further the interests of dominant sectors of the metropolitan industrial bourgeoisie, we can find other instances where these interests were not involved at all and metropolitan control of the actions of colonial states was weak and sporadic, even when those local authorities challenged metropolitan policy and interests. The view of the colonial state as the tool of metropolitan capital runs into particular difficulty when applied to settler colonies such as Kenya since there was a widely recognized antagonism between settler and metropolitan capitalist interests and a substantial degree of settler power and influence over local authorities.[3] What is missing is consideration of the contradictions and struggles that define the concrete tasks of political domination by the colonial state regardless of the willingness of local officials to act as the agents of metropolitan interests or the directions and pressures from the metropole for them to do so.

In Chapter 4 we attempted to define an alternative approach to analysing the development of the colonial state based on a theory of the state that 'derived' the specific forms of the state from the intersection of the contradictions of capitalist development in particular historical circumstances. The state plays a crucial but contradictory role in ensuring capitalist reproduction and accumulation while simultaneously sustaining effective control and legitimacy.[4] Thus, in so far as the coercive powers of the state are employed to create and sustain capitalist relations of production, particularly in the early stages of primitive accumulation when the direct producers are forcibly separated from the ownership and control of the means of production and the product of their labour, the legitimacy of state authority may thereby be threatened and the maintenance of the wider social order challenged by the resistance of dominated classes. The fundamental condition for the successful management of this contradiction is the relative autonomy of the state at two levels. First, at the level of structure, in the existence of the state as a separate and discrete institutional sphere in capitalist societies. Second, at the level of political practice, in the need for the state to be seen to act on behalf of the social order as a whole, or as a disinterested and impersonal arbiter of social relations and conflicts.

There are thus definite limits on the degree to which the state can act as the direct agent of capitalist accumulation before its authority and the wider social order are threatened by the struggle of dominated classes. At the same time, the state becomes the central object of class struggle. The crucial point is that there can be no functional stability of class domination, but only a relative and inevitably temporary equilibrium.[5] Domination and cohesive order is not a condition but a process, constantly undermined and reforged. The state, just like the sphere of production to which it is linked, is driven by crisis and struggle to the constant reformulation of its structures and practices. This is the basis for the constantly expanding scale and scope of intervention of the state in capitalist societies and for Marx's profound aphorism that the state is 'the résumé of society'.

As we noted in Chapter 4, the character and functioning of the colonial state was defined by the specific contradictory social forces over which it presided, and these were derived in turn from the complex articulation of capitalism with the indigenous modes of production in African societies. The form of articulation varied according to the particular character of capitalist penetration, the nature of the indigenous modes of production, and local ecology and resource endowment. The resulting variations in the subjugation and transformation of local societies and the degree to which capitalist forms of production were introduced also determined the differing patterns of class formation within and between colonies.[6] (See Chapters 8 and 9.)

In the colonial state the vital tasks of ensuring accumulation and legitimation made it into 'the primary mechanism of articulation', with a central role in managing its contradictions and struggles.[7] The colonial state actually straddled two levels of articulation, between the metropole and the colony, and, within the latter, between introduced forms of capitalist production and the various indigenous modes. It was involved in a complex process of social engineering in which the use of force was often necessary 'to achieve the two initial objectives: the extraction of a labour force for capitalist production in plantations, settler farms, commerce, administration and a modicum of industry, and to generate peasant production of export crops.'[8] However, state preoccupation with ensuring the conditions of primary accumulation also threatened political order. Having subdued and subordinated local societies, the colonial state had to convert superior force into legitimate authority based on a substantial degree of at least tacit consent from the subject population. The process of articulation raised the dilemma of how far metropolitan interests could be pressed against the interests of local producers in a colony, whether African peasants or European settlers, or, internally, of settlers over Africans, before provoking resistance and undermining effective state control.

In Chapter 4 we had tried to show how this process had been involved in the establishment of the contradictory foundations of the colonial political economy and the state in Kenya. In this chapter we attempt to carry the story further by examining how the crucial contradiction and recurrent struggles over the provision of African labour for settler estates shaped the developing structures and practices of the state and economic institutions in the colony.

Settler production, state coercion and African labour

The contradictions of articulation developed with particular sharpness in Kenya as a result of the establishment of both peasant commodity and settler estate production in the colony in the critical decade before the First World War.[9] Peasant production, building in a number of instances upon the activities of precolonial classes of accumulators in the major African social formations, had grown through both African initiatives and the encouragement of colonial officials seeking sources of tax revenue and a material basis for African acquiescence in British domination.[10] Settler estate production had been introduced in Kenya as the result of a specific conjunction of historical and geographical factors, and was from the start dependent upon land and labour drawn from the surrounding African societies. The resulting articulation of estate production with indigenous modes increasingly overshadowed the articulation of the latter with the metropole, while estate production itself was articulated with the metropole through mercantile and finance capital. While the settlers constantly pressured the state to provide the necessary infrastructure and inputs for estate production, labour recruitment and control were initially left in the hands of European labour recruiters and individual estate owners. The result was marked by fumbling experimentation and exceptional violence by the settlers unrestrained by systematic organization or institutional controls.[11] The ferocity and unpredictability of the settler assault on the African population threatened to undermine the whole apparatus of colonial control. In response, the state was poised by 1914 to extend its intervention and control of the African labour supply for estate production. While further direct action was postponed for four years during the war when state authorities were preoccupied with meeting military labour requirements, that wartime experience provided a crucial watershed demonstrating the efficacy of 'total' pressure and systematic organization. The introduction of massive forced conscription to the military Carrier Corps, which supplied porters for the British forces in East Africa, provided both the example of organization and a threat that drove Africans to work on settler farms to avoid being taken.

> The scattered and nonintegrated efforts to create such conditions before 1914 had henceforth to be streamlined in the light of the lessons of wartime experience . . . The difference after the war lay in the far more complete, systematic, and fully coordinated way in which partial pressures strengthened and complemented one another to produce a labor supply in peace time that matched the supply drawn out during the war.[12]

During 1918–19 settler producers in Kenya faced the task of restoring and expanding production for peacetime export markets with the African labour force of the colony severely depleted by appalling casualties from disease and malnutrition in the Carrier Corps and from the global influenza epidemic, which decimated the population of the reserves. At the same time, African peasants were attempting to reconstruct and expand commodity production, creating a conflicting application and demand for their labour. These particular historical circumstances reinforced the structural determinants of the extraction of African labour for estate production. First, the general condition of settler shortage of capital and a growing burden of debt for essential constant capital to bring the estates into production determined a desperate need to reduce the cost of variable capital (labour) as a condition of profitable operation. Second, the particular circumstances of Kenya, in which the major regions of labour supply for estate agriculture were simultaneously the major areas of developing peasant commodity production, meant that the settlers had to compete against alternative uses of African labour in commodity production as well as customary subsistence agriculture. The Kenya settlers could not operate within, or indeed survive, a fully deployed capitalist market of 'free' labour. This determined relations of production based less upon wages and more upon the resort to extra-economic coercion to extract semiservile labour from the peasant sphere at a price below its cost of reproduction. The necessary cheap labour was thus

> achieved not simply in a quantitative sense by keeping wages 'low' in absolute terms; for extra-economic coercion was also used to push wages below their 'value' (measured in terms of the socially accepted minimum to ensure the reproduction of labour power) . . . some of the means of subsistence [were] provided by the family's own 'subsistence' production.[13]

While the necessity of coercion remained, it was ideologically rationalized and, particularly during the crucial 1918–23 period, structurally contained, controlled, and legitimized by the state.

Ideologically the need for cheap labour led to a local version of the myth of African 'target labour' or, in its more intellectualized form, 'the backward-bending labour supply curve'.[14] This was based on the belief that African labour would not increase in supply with increased wages. Rather, quite the reverse was expected, since it was assumed that the African had limited cash needs attached to particular targets, primarily the payment of taxes and the purchase of particular nonsubsistence consumer goods. Thus, declared Ewart Grogan, 'three shillings give him as much satisfaction as three pounds', while at the 1913 Labour Commission 'almost all employers agreed that increased wages would not attract more labour.'[15] Governor Belfield concurred, adding that 'a rise in the rate of wages would enable the hut or poll tax . . . to be earned by fewer external workers . . . it follows that if we increase the rate of remuneration of the individual we decrease the number of individuals necessary to earn a given sum.'[16] It followed also that Africans must and should be forced to work if necessary, not solely for the benefit of the settlers, of course, but for their own good as well, since it would teach them the virtues of honest toil and the superiority of European methods. The ideological underpinnings of the labour system were completed by the rationalization of coercion through what Barnett calls the 'theory of the organization of native labour' which 'was influential within the entire imperial tradition':

> There are three assumptions in this strand of thought: first, native labour is by its nature recalcitrant, and therefore requires authoritarian treatment; second, native labour lacks initiative, and therefore requires very detailed directives and instructions; and third, native labour can, within certain limits, be improved, and the 'civilizing' function of authoritarian methods in some way legitimizes those methods.[17]

Thus, despite increasing settler paternalism towards African labour during the interwar decades, the underlying belief in the necessity of coercion remained. As a Member of the Kenya Legislative Council noted in 1941:

> I always treat my natives the same as I treat children, I try to be kind to them, and to advise and direct them, but when kindness has no effect you have to do the same as they do in the public schools at home and throughout the empire – use the cane.[18]

Structurally, a series of ordinances and policies enacted right at the beginning of and immediately after the First World War and brought into effect from early 1919 crystallized the relations of production in estate agriculture and brought the state definitively into their regulation and maintenance. Before examining the development of the role of the state more closely, however, it is important to examine briefly the character of the labour force that emerged during this period in terms of its total size; relative size in proportion to the adult African male population of the colony as a whole, and of the principal 'labour-producing' districts; and its internal structure in terms of sectoral, geographical and ethnic distribution.[19]

On the eve of the war in 1914, according to Clayton and Savage's estimates, a total of 110,000 Africans were employed for wages in Kenya in the peak seasons, some 10,000–12,000 of them by the railway and the Public Works Department.[20] By 1920, after the ravages of the Carrier Corps and the influenza epidemic, the average number at work was 90,000 at the moment acute labour shortage hit the efforts at postwar recovery and development. Thereafter, the number of African men in wage labour increased sharply, almost doubling to 169,000 by 1926, then declining slightly to 160,000 by 1929.[21] Even more important and revealing, however, are the statistics of the proportion of adult African men in wage employment. The total proportion for the colony as a whole in 1914 is estimated by Clayton and Savage to have been 24 per cent or less, but up to 32 per cent in South Nyanza and the districts closest to Nairobi.[22] From 1921, with the report of the Labour Bureau Commission, the Kenya government began more systematic estimates of the potential labour force, at first of all adult African men aged 15 to 30 and then, within a few years, of all those aged 15 to 40, judging that approximately half should be available for employment outside of their reserves.[23] Buell estimates that by 1926, 33.8 per cent of adult African men were employed for wages on average during the year. However, when compared with the total labour force and rate of participation in other colonies, Kenya is revealed to have had a larger total number of Africans in employment than any colony except the Belgian Congo, and a higher proportion of the African adult male population at work than any except the labour-producing territories of Southern Africa, the

Transkei and Basutoland.[24] Furthermore, given the short-term involvement of most African labourers, who worked for three to six months a year, and the consequent high turnover concealed in aggregate figures, the actual proportion employed *for some time in a given year* was probably much higher. As early as 1923 the administration estimated that, excluding the pastoral peoples and those medically unfit, almost 75 per cent of African men aged 15 to 40 had actually engaged in wage labour for some period during that year.[25] Again, disaggregating the colony-wide averages into the proportions employed from the principal labour-producing districts gives even more striking figures. The chief registrar of natives reported that in the first three months of 1927 the proportion of the adult male population in paid employment for Europeans was 72.28 per cent in Kiambu District (Kikuyu), 72 per cent in Lumbwa District (Kipsigis), 64.45 per cent in Nandi District, 50.3 per cent in Fort Hall District (Kikuyu), 48.2 per cent in North Kavirondo District (Luo and Luhya), and 44.91 per cent in North and South Nyeri Districts (Kikuyu).[26] To these figures we can also add a steadily growing number of women and children seasonally employed, especially for the harvesting of coffee, and numbering perhaps 30,000 by 1927.[27] Whether measured in absolute or comparative terms, the Kenya labour system was thus one that embraced a particularly high proportion of the African population, especially from the agricultural areas bordering the settled districts of the Highlands.

Significantly, only approximately half of the monthly employed labourers worked in estate agriculture, with the rest in various branches of government and commerce, with the state, including the railway, being by far the largest single employer in the colony. While a small number of semi-skilled artisans and clerical workers were beginning to appear, particularly in the urban areas and on the railway, the vast majority of African labourers in all sectors were temporary, unskilled migrants – a semi-proletarianized mass of single and temporarily single men moving back and forth between the African reserves, where their families remained on the land, and the settled districts and towns. A combination between private employers and the state in 1921 reduced the average wage by a third. However, under the pressure of settler economic expansion and continued growth of African commodity production, despite its increasing exclusion from export markets during the 1923–9 period, wages for unskilled labour rose from nine to eleven shillings a month, with a ration of maize meal, to twelve to fourteen shillings by 1923 and sixteen to eighteen at the end of the decade.[28]

These statistics on Africans working for wages on monthly contracts do not include a major form of African labour in the estate sector, indeed for many settlers the most important: the resident native labourers or squatters. More than any other aspect of the labour system, the growth of squatting expressed the inability of the smaller settler estates in particular to operate with fully capitalist relations of production, and the need to rely on a semi-servile relation between peasant and landlord. While squatting continued to provide a reasonably stable and secure labour force, as well as access to squatter stock for breeding and dung for fertilizer and to the casual labour of women and children during peak harvest and planting periods, it also involved key internal contradictions that threatened the settlers' position. First, the poorest and most undeveloped estates often engaged in 'Kaffir farming' or share-cropping, which created potential African tenants' rights in the Highlands. Second, and even more important during the 1919–39 period, since the squatters relied largely on their own produce rather than their meagre wages, they tended to emerge as independent commodity producers in competition with the settlers who provided them with plots on their estates. In so far as the settlers had difficulty making productive use of their assets, this was a real threat. In 1917, for example, the District Commissioner of Naivasha reported that 'Agriculture has made little progress except at the hands of native squatters.'[29] As a result, after 1918 squatters also were subjected to increasing state regulation and control that eliminated tenant rights and regularized and extended the elements of compulsion and involuntary servitude. In addition, as the settlers began to accumulate capital during the 1920s, they acted to bring the squatters further under their domination and to restrict their role as competitive commodity producers, largely by reducing the land available to them and the quantity of livestock they could own.[30] However, despite these restrictions, the number of squatters continued to grow, particularly as population pressures and land shortages began to be felt in the Kikuyu reserves. By 1931 the number of squatters in the Highlands reached 113,176 (the great majority of them Kikuyu), and they occupied no less than a million acres (about 400,000 ha) of settler land.[31]

Finally, the type and composition of the African labour force varied in different parts of the colony and in different types of enterprises. By the late 1920s the administration had divided Kenya into three labour zones. The first, in the Western Highlands, comprising the Trans Nzoia, Uasin Gishu and Nandi areas, involved settler estates employing primarily squatter labour, many of them Nandi and Kipsigis, although there was one sisal estate employing 600 workers and developing tea estates near Kericho already employing some 1600 workers. The second zone, Ravine, Nakuru, Navaisha and Laikipia, was the heartland of white settlement in the Rift Valley and involved primarily maize and stock production employing Kikuyu squatters. The third consisted of Nairobi and the nearby settled portions of Kiambu, Nyeri and Machakos in the Eastern Highlands, and the most distant, low-lying areas of Kitui,

Voi, Mombasa and the coast. The Eastern Highlands area, especially Kiambu and Nyeri, was the centre of coffee production and primarily used wage labour drawn from the neighbouring Kikuyu reserves. The lower-lying areas were dominated by the sisal plantations, which employed some 16,000 men by the late 1920s, and by the fuel and ballast camps for the railroad. At Mombasa a growing mass of casual labour worked at the harbour.'[32] In the two last areas, Nyanza labourers, Luhya and particularly Luo, predominated, having proved more resistant than the Kikuyu to the hotter malarial environments.

This labour force, termed by a contemporary South African observer 'probably the cheapest in the world,'[33] could not in the end have been created or controlled without the support and sanctions of the colonial state. The administration proved on the whole sympathetic to settler pressures, and the state applied direct coercion to deal both with the problem of recruitment and the problem of ensuring that African labourers stayed at work. The involvement of the Provincial Administration in the recruitment of labour for the settlers reached its greatest intensity in 1919–21, coinciding with the most serious labour shortage of the colony's history during the brief initial boom of postwar development and culminating in the crisis over the Northey labour circulars. Responding both to the acute shortage of labour and the vagaries of earlier instructions on 'encouragement' which left matters to the widely varying discretion of local district commissioners, Governor Sir Edward Northey, a South African general, ordered the chief native commissioner to produce a statement on labour recruitment policy. On 23 October 1919 the government issued a special labour circular stating, in part:

> All Government officials in charge of native areas must exercise every possible lawful influence to induce ablebodied male natives to go into the labour field. Where farms are situated in the vicinity of a native area, women and children should be encouraged to go out for such labour as they can perform.
>
> Native chiefs and elders must at all times render all possible lawful assistance on the foregoing lines. They should be repeatedly reminded that it is part of their duty to advise and encourage all unemployed young men in the areas under their jurisdiction to go out and work on plantations.[34]

At the same time, the government attempted to raise African taxes and in early 1920 introduced the Native Authority Amendment Ordinance. This empowered chiefs and headmen to order 'compulsory labour' of up to 60 days a year at wages below that of 'voluntary' workers for state purposes, especially for head porterage and railway, road, and public works projects. This was in addition to the already existing African obligation of 24 days a year (six days per quarter) of unpaid 'communal labour' on local projects. The fact that exemption from compulsory labour could only be obtained on proof of employment for wages during three of the previous 12 months indicates that a key intention of the law was that 'by threatening people with this type of work . . . the administration could increase the supply of labour to settler farms.'[35] The labour circular, tax increases and the compulsory labour ordinance combined in the new massive and co-ordinated application of state power to obtain labour for settler farmers. As a result, the Provincial Administration became directly and explicitly a recruiter of labour for private employers in the colony.

This effort ultimately foundered on both the emergence of African resistance to the escalation of official coercion involved and on the resistance to it both internally in the administration itself and from missionary circles in East Africa.[36] The heads of the Anglican Church and Church of Scotland in the area issued the 'Bishops' Memorandum' in November 1919 which raised the issue that 'to the native mind a hint and order on the part of the Government are indistinguishable', and warned of the abuse of power by chiefs and the deleterious consequences for African society in the reserves that would result from the policy.[37] The issue quickly spilled into the metropolitan arena, causing consternation in the Colonial Office in the face of an uproar over 'forced labour in Kenya' in humanitarian and Church circles and the Labour Party, as well as among prominent members of the Conservative and Liberal parties. This resulted in major criticism of the government in both the Commons and the House of Lords. In February 1920 a revised circular was hastily issued by the Kenya government reiterating the original policy in more circumspect language. This failed to mollify the critics, and the Colonial Office then intervened directly by drafting its own version of a third circular that reminded administrators that they had a duty to check abuses and favouritism by the chiefs, that Africans working on their own plots should not be pressured to go out and work, and that women and children could only work when they could return home each evening.[38] This too failed to have the desired effect on the political uproar created by the original circular. In 1921 Winston Churchill succeeded Milner as secretary of state. Sensitive to the labour issue in Kenya as a result of his 1908 visit, Churchill brought the immediate controversy to an end with a dispatch revising Kenya labour policy. While rejecting accusations that the administration was exploiting Africans, he ordered that 'encouragement' by administrators could not go beyond providing information on labour needs and resources for employers and potential labourers. In addition, while supporting the 24-day per annum communal labour requirement, he modified the compulsory labour policy for use, except for immediate government porterage needs, only on 'essential' government projects after permission had been explicitly requested from the Colonial Office for a specified purpose and period.[39] The pressure on the Provincial Administration to recruit labour directly thus abated, although a brief effort was made by Governor Grigg to respond to labour shortages in 1925–6 occasioned by the last major railway extensions by instructing field officers to 'do their utmost to promote the flow of labour'.[40] By the latter half of the 1920s, however, the indirect pressures of taxation and growing population pressure in some of the reserves and a growing African taste for cheap consumer imports combined to ensure an increasingly adequate flow of labour without further direct administrative coercion.

In the face of the gruelling labour demanded, the frequent cruelty of European and Asian employers, and the generally poor housing and diet provided for migrant labour, the principal expression of class struggle in Kenya, especially in the White Highlands, was the individualized protest of unannounced departure of African labourers from their work, or 'desertion', as it was termed. Retaining labour at work remained a continuing problem even as overall supply difficulties lessened, and it was in this area that the elements of involuntary servitude were most fully developed and consistently applied in the Kenya labour system. A body of legislation, enforced by the Provincial Administration and the Kenya police and periodically extended, constrained movement outside of the reserves by Africans and limited their freedom to enter and leave employment through punitive sanctions under which 'the infringement of labour laws is rated as a crime and the heaviest penalties can be imposed for minor acts of disobedience'.[41] This began with the Masters and Servants Ordinances of 1906 and 1910, and culminated in the Masters and Servants Ordinance of 1916, fully implemented after the war, which extended the maximum penalties for labour offences, including desertion, to a fine £5 of or imprisonment up to six months. In addition, offences were made cognizable by the police who could arrest and prosecute without a specific complaint from an employer.[42] Since labourers had no other legal redress against employers, the legislation provided for their 'protection', with penalties against the latter for withholding wages and other abuses. The 1910 ordinance, however, reduced employer penalties while introducing rules, extended in 1919, prescribing conditions of employment, food and housing to ensure 'fair treatment' of labour. After the war a small labour inspectorate was established as a branch of the administration to see that the rules were observed, but the resources of the inspectorate and the Provincial Administration were never sufficient to inspect regularly all employers, and evasion of the regulations was common.[43]

The keystone of the complex of labour controls, which made possible the efficient enforcement of punitive sanctions, was the Registration of Natives Ordinance, first passed in 1915, but only brought into force in 1919–20. This required every male African over the age of 15 to register before an administrative officer, where his fingerprints were taken and he was issued with a registration certificate, the *kipande*, which contained his personal particulars and a record of his employment outside of his reserve, including the type of work and the wages and rations received. Copies were sent to the chief registrar of natives in Nairobi. The *kipande* had to be carried at all times when moving or living outside of the reserves, usually in a metal cylinder hung around the neck, and each time an African entered or left employment the employer had to sign him on or off on the certificate. By the end of 1920, 194,750 certificates had been issued and this climbed to 519,056 by the end of 1924 and to 1,197,467 by 1931.[44] The registration system brought virtually the entire adult male African population under much more direct administrative control, and made it possible to trace back to the reserves and arrest deserters and other violators who failed to be properly signed off by an employer. The ordinance also created yet another category of labour 'crimes' as Africans became liable to fine or imprisonment for failing to carry, losing or destroying the *kipande*. Penalties were also applied to employers who failed to demand the *kipande* when hiring labour, failed to file with the registrar the particulars of the Africans they employed and failed to sign a worker off when the contract was finished. In addition, the *kipande* also assisted in the maintenance of the cheapness of labour by restricting 'both a man's freedom to leave his work and his freedom to bargain with an employer for a wage not necessarily related to that of his previous employment.'[45] Finally, the *kipande* also created opportunities for abuses by both employers and officials, especially with regard to the harassment of men identified as 'trouble-makers' or 'bad hats'. The efficiency of the registration system was revealed in its very first year of operation when 2364 of 2790 reported deserters were traced and prosecuted.[46] Little wonder that the *kipande* was the most hated of Kenya's labour laws and the one that came to symbolize for Africans their servile status.

Enforcement of these punitive sanctions fell heavily on the Provincial Administration. While the Kenya police pursued violators in the settled districts, the tribal police under the control of district commissioners did so in the reserves, and in both areas administrators dealt with the trial of cases in their capacity as local magistrates. Settler demands for immediate and severe punishment led to serious departures from accepted British judicial practice in the administration of labour laws, and 'several circulars reminded the magistrates that they should first investigate whether a contract of employment existed before punishing a person for an alleged breach of it.'[47] The level of coercion required to sustain the labour system in Kenya is suggested by the statistics on prosecutions for offences under the Masters and Servants (later Employment of Natives) Ordinances and the Registration of Natives Ordinance itself. In 1922 these totalled 2187 and 2949, respectively.[48] Even more revealing is the comparison of these figures with convictions for labour offences in other British colonies in Africa, which shows starkly the difference in the levels of coercion involved in sustaining the relations of production in Kenya and in colonies relying upon peasant commodity production.[49]

The squatters too were brought under the coercive powers of the state. Up to 1918 squatting was an attractive proposition for many Africans, especially from the densely populated Kikuyu reserves where many already lived as *ahoi* or tenants. It permitted escape from the oppressive hand of the chiefs, gave access to land and a chance to develop their own crops and large herds of livestock in return for three or four months of labour service for the settler at a wage of approximately four shillings a month plus rations.[50] The Resident Native Labourers Ordinance of 1918 sought both to encourage squatting as a source of labour and to bring it under systematic regulation. Kaffir farming was made illegal, squatters' rights as tenants were extinguished and they were reduced to the status of servants, while required labour service was extended to a regulated contract of 180 days per annum at around two-thirds the salary of contract labour and made applicable to all adult male members of the squatter's family aged over 16.[51] A key objective in ending conditions that produced a landlord–tenant relation was to 'destroy any rights the African might have in land by reason of the tenancy. A relationship of employer and employee involving elements of involuntary servitude was substituted, and one of the prime objects of later legislation in this field was to maintain the relation and prevent the development of a system of tenancy.'[52] Further legislation was soon required after a 1923 Supreme Court decision that held that a squatter was a tenant, not a servant, and thus not subject to the criminal penalties for desertion under the Masters and Servants Ordinance. An immediate effort was made to amend that ordinance to include squatters, but was disallowed by the Colonial Office, under a Labour secretary of state during the brief coalition government in Britain. The following year, 1925, a new Conservative minister permitted a new Resident Native Labourers Ordinance, which made the failure of a squatter to carry out his duties a punishable offence and prohibited residence on an estate other than under contract. In addition, the servile status of squatters was further reinforced by a provision that made their contracts transferable on the sale of a farm.[53]

African taxation, in addition to its function as a major source of state revenue and test of the efficiency of local administrative control, continued to play a major role in the labour system as a means of indirect coercion. Steady settler pressure resulted in an increase in the rate of hut or poll tax to five rupees in 1915 and efforts to raise the rate again in 1920 to eight rupees (16 shillings under the new currency then being introduced) as part of the co-ordinated pressures being applied to increase labour supply. Subsequent African protests and unrest, culminating in the 1922 disturbances, led to a reduction in the basic rate to 12 shillings, where it remained unchanged for most of the interwar period. Nevertheless, the tax weapon had its desired effect in forcing more Africans into wage employment, the Kikuyu in particular responding to its pressure.[54] The revenues from hut and poll tax rose in step with the increasing rate and the growing efficiency of collection, especially after chiefs operating on a commission were replaced by regular administrative officers as collecting agents, reaching £175,000 in 1914-15, £279,000 in 1919-20, and no less than £658,414 in 1920-21.[55] Thereafter it settled back to an annual average return of £500,000-600,000 per annum. In addition, Africans paid indirect taxes in the form of customs duties on imports at a rate from 1921 of 20 per cent *ad valorem* that added another £200,000-250,000 to their tax bill during the 1920s. The impact of this burden is suggested by Buell's estimate that the total value of cash crops marketed by Africans in 1924 fell short of the total African tax bill by some £320,000.[56] While the official theory was that the rate of annual hut or poll tax equalled an average wage for one month, for many Africans the actual tax bill was considerably higher than the base rate of 12 shillings since they paid on the hut of more than one wife as well as for kin unable to earn the tax on their own. The 1927 Labour Commission found an average cash income of families in the reserves of 90-110 shillings per year, of which no less than 28 shillings was paid in direct taxes by the head of the family.[57] This tax burden made it difficult for Africans to accumulate savings and ensured that their net income could supply a subsistence living only if they maintained access to land and production in the reserves or as squatters. Failure to pay tax was, of course, a punishable offence, and in the mid-1920s special detention camps for hut and poll tax offenders were established near district stations, where they provided administrators with a convenient source of unpaid communal labour for local projects.[58]

The establishment of official boundaries for the various African reserves in Kenya reflected contradictory impulses on the one hand to protect Africans from further alienation of land and allay widespread insecurity, and, on the other, employ the reserves as yet another method of forcing Africans out to work. In 1905 the settler-dominated Land Committee proposed setting up reserves containing the minimum land necessary for the current needs of various groups so that future population growth could only be accommodated by movement outside the reserves on to settler estates, while the 1913 Native Labour Commission repeated demands for reserves adequate for 'the current population only'.[59] In 1915 the Crown Lands Ordinance empowered the governor either to reserve land for the use of the African tribes or cancel the boundaries and exclude land deemed excess to their needs. Implementation of these provisions was delayed, however, by indecision over the extent of the reserve boundaries as the administration was caught between settler demands for restriction of the area of the reserves, and Colonial Office concern for reserves adequate for an expanding population. It was not until 1926 that the administration finally gazetted twenty-four "tribal" reserves covering 46,837 square miles, 14,600 of which were in the sparsely populated Maasai reserve. Even then Buell noted that the population density of the major labour-producing reserves adjacent to the White Highlands already exceeded that of many of the South African native reserves, and predicted a land shortage in 25 years.[60] Given the general underestimates of the African population that prevailed at the time, these pressures were actually felt much sooner. Demographic recovery after the disasters of the first quarter of the century saw population growth of 1–1.5 per cent a year by the late 1920s. From that time steadily increasing population pressure, primarily in the Kikuyu reserves and in the most densely settled areas of Nyanza, had some of the effect on labour supply the settlers had originally desired.

The scope and intensity of controls and pressures placed upon the African population in Kenya by the colonial state to provide labour for settler estates were far greater than those found in any other British colony in Africa under the overall authority of the Colonial Office, approaching and, in some instances, even exceeding those applied in the settler states of Southern Africa. The extremity of the coercive controls that emerged in Kenya can be more clearly understood not as the outcome of the particular cruelty or racism of the settlers and/or state officials, but as the surface expression of more profound underlying social forces, i.e., as a concrete example of the development of the forms of the state derived from the particular contradictions of capital accumulation and class struggle found in estate production in the colony. The dependence of settler agriculture upon, and its disruption by, the fluctuations and crises of metropolitan capital and international commodity markets; its constant shortage of capital and low level of constant capital; and its lack of technical skills determined a protracted and difficult process of primary accumulation within which estate production was unable to establish fully capitalist relations of production as the basis for the constantly expanded reproduction of capital. The essential condition for the expansion of production and the accumulation of capital within settler estate production was the increasing extraction of absolute surplus value through the development of more systematic control over the labour force, rather than through increased productivity as a result of the constant transformation of the means of production. This determined in turn the elements of servility and degree of coerciveness of the relations of production, as well as the extraction of labour below its cost of reproduction through a contradictory articulation of estate production with the indigenous African modes of production in which 'the tendency to the destruction of the indigenous mode had to be halted before the point where it ceased to provide for the reproduction of the labour power itself.'[61]

The sequence of crises over the labour supply to settler estates and the development of institutional forms and policies to deal with it during the early 1920s in Kenya is an instance of the 'process of constant reorganization by struggle and through crisis of capitalist social relations, economic *and* political'.[62] Pre-1914 experience in Kenya had increasingly shown that settlers and labour recruiters were through their individual actions incapable of recruiting a sufficient labour force or stabilizing the required relations of production, rather the brutality and unpredictability of settler privateering threatened to undermine the legitimacy of colonial domination in general. During the 1919–23 period, therefore, the state moved to provide the level of organization and coercion to sustain the relations of production for settler estate production as a whole. State structures and policies dealing with the recruitment and control of labour provided both for the extraction of labour from indigenous African modes of production and for the increase in absolute surplus value produced by African labourers, especially with regard to the increasing labour obligation of the squatters. At the same time, however, the state confronted the contradiction that it could only accomplish the stabilization and control of relations of production in the estate sphere if it retained its constitution as a separate and autonomous entity, thus 'taking the form of an impersonal mechanism of public authority isolated from society'.[63] The fundamental condition for the state acting in the interest of settler production was thus a limit on the degree to which it acted as the direct private agent of settler class interests, i.e., the state confronted the necessity of its relative autonomy as a condition of managing the contradiction between accumulation and legitimization. This was particularly sharply drawn in the colonial setting in Kenya, where the state was also a subordinate institutional and ideological emanation of the state and dominant class of the metropole, as well as the sole legitimate agency of public order resting on the maintenance of the tacit consent of the indigenous African population. If the state moved too far towards becoming an explicit instrument of settler class interests it faced the threat of direct intervention from above, unrest from below, or, indeed, both.

The condensation within the state of the contradictions of accumulation and control of the labour system is clearly visible, on the one hand, in the growth in Kenya of a field administration exercising far closer and more intensive control over the rural African population than was found in other British African colonies. Simply on the level of the proportion of field administrators to population, Kenya reached a ratio approaching twice that of Uganda and four times that of Nigeria, both of which relied upon the development of peasant commodity production.[64] In addition, the corpus of legislation discussed above conferred on the Provincial Administration not only an exceptionally high degree of control over Africans both in the reserves and in their movements outside to find work, but also an unusually wide scope for intervention into indigenous social structures in the reserves. At the same time, the institutional structures of the state were modified by the creation of specialized agencies such as the chief registrar of natives to maintain the relations of production in estate agriculture, while the development of agricultural and veterinary services to Africans, which could have stimulated more rapid growth of competitive peasant commodity production, were retarded to a level well below that of Uganda and Tanganyika.[65]

On the other hand, however, the legitimacy of state authority in the reserves was also tied to commodity production as the material basis for a developing class of peasant accumulators and for the directly collaborating stratum of chiefs and lower-level state functionaries. For the Provincial Administration the relative autonomy of the state was tied in practice to the maintenance of peasant commodity production, and local administrators continued to encourage its growth wherever it did not directly challenge the settler sphere. As a result, the principal labour-producing districts in Kenya were simultaneously the major areas of peasant commodity production, with the Provincial Administration having to maintain a tenuous balance in the contradictory articulation of the peasant and settler spheres. The marketed output of African agriculture actually continued to expand during the 1920s, directed not towards the export sector increasingly dominated by the settlers, but towards an internal goods market to feed the African labour force on the estates, particularly on the coffee and sisal plantations.[66] In addition, influential elements of metropolitan mercantile capital throughout the interwar period remained sceptical about the economic viability of settler estate production, and some firms remained involved in the marketing of African crops.[67] Counter-pressures for the expansion of peasant production thus existed within both the colonial state and metropolitan capital, gaining strength at moments when the estate sphere stumbled.[68]

Furthermore, the state apparatus of labour control, as well as settler attitudes towards Africans and the way they treated them, greatly intensified the authoritarian paternalism of the Provincial Administration. This response is clearly illustrated in a letter sent home in 1920 by a young assistant district commissioner, H.R. Storrs-Fox:

The European settlers as a class are out to exploit the nigger. They

[sic] try to drive him out of his reserve (where he certainly doesn't do very much work but cultivates his own bit of ground and lives quite happily) by the Hut tax. Thus he is quite gently persuaded to go out and work for a white settler who pays him the princely sum of 5–7 rupees per month and as often as not takes no pains to look after his housing and comfort and treats him pretty harshly . . . It is the old capital and labour stunt, but labour can't stick up for itself here.[69]

These remarks reveal not only the administration's sense of detachment from the confrontation of white settler and black labourer, its belief in its own autonomy, but also its sense that this very detachment required its essentially disinterested intervention to moderate the class struggle and correct an oppressive and unbalanced relationship. Administrators' belief that only they could provide the African with protection from unreasonable and overly harsh oppression led to internal struggles within the state over each of the various aspects of the labour control system and efforts to modify in practice those that most bluntly compromised its presumed autonomy. Administrative paternalism was further enhanced, moreover, as the new breed of public school and Oxbridge administrators, so distrusted by the settlers, increasingly dominated the administration and moved into its most senior positions during the 1920s.

Nothing more compromised the ostensible autonomy of the state, particularly the delicate balance maintained by the Provincial Administration, than its conversion into a labour-recruiting agency for settler farmers. Before the First World War, when administrators were given repeated ambiguous instructions about 'encouraging' African labour, a fragmented struggle emerged between many field officers trying to avoid involvement in recruiting labour from their districts, and settlers trying, often successfully, to force the transfer of uncooperative officials. Within the crisis over the Northey labour circulars and the outbursts of African unrest and resistance in the 1919–22 period, the Provincial Administration was caught between the Nairobi authorities' commitment of the state to recruit labour for the settlers and the most serious challenge to administrative control since its establishment in the early years of the century. At this point opposition to the policy became generalized throughout the administration, even among the secretariat officials who had originally been involved in its formulation and quickly came to understand that a critical limit of state power had been transcended. This internal opposition, which simmered largely out of public view, was organized by John Ainsworth, the chief native commissioner over whose signature the first circular had been issued; H.R. Tate, the provincial commissioner of Kenya (later Central) Province, which contained the Kikuyu districts that were the most important source of African labour; and no less than C.W. Bowring, the chief secretary. The

'Bishops' Memorandum' discussed earlier was actually written after consultation between leading missionaries and the three senior administrators, with the final draft typed in his office by Bowring or one of his staff. 'A Chief Secretary concerting a protest against his Governor's policy represents a remarkable event in colonial history,' while Churchill's 1921 dispatch relieving the Provincial Administration of direct involvement in labour-recruiting was hailed by Tate as the 'Emancipation act for which the administration had fought long and persistently'.[70]

The elimination of direct responsibility for labour recruitment permitted the Provincial Administration to attempt to reassert its disinterested role as paternal protector and equilibrator. However, the consequences of the indirect coercion of Africans and the removal of a large proportion of the male population from the reserves still posed serious problems of control.[71] Administrators confronted the contradictory destruction/preservation of indigenous society concretely in terms of African workers leaving the reserves, especially the squatters who took their families with them and escaped the authority of the administration and the chiefs for the settled districts where administrative controls were weakest. The contradictory pressures tearing at the state showed here in administrators' uneasy anticipation of the consequences of labour migration and the decay of indigenous institutions in advance of actual evidence of disruptive effects. Administrators insisted on the maintenance of jurisdictional boundaries,

> believing that the best means of maintaining order in the reserves . . . was to ensure that every African remained under the authority of his chief and that individuals were not able to leave locations without good reasons. Flight from locations tended to undermine the chiefs' authority. For this reason the British were concerned lest labour demands undermine tribal economic and political stability, especially the position of the chiefs, and lead to violence.[72]

After the First World War administrative concern found expression in aspects of labour legislation and in measures to expand the authority of chiefs

> to ensure that labor was recruited under carefully regulated circumstances and did not lead to the collapse of tribal authority . . . [and that] the African population would leave the reserves only as legitimate wage laborers and . . . there would be no possibility of individuals leaving to escape tribal obligations and the authority of chiefs.[73]

Thus, while the Native Registration Ordinance facilitated the application of punitive sanctions on behalf of settler employers, it also gave to the Provincial Administration a greater sense of control by enabling it

120

to keep far more accurate track of men from a district both inside and outside of the reserve.

The fear of social disintegration and the loss of control also led to conflict within the administration over taxation and reserve policy. While administrators saw the necessity of tax as a source of revenue and as a means to stimulate economic development, they were often uneasy about its use as a coercive mechanism to force Africans to work for the settlers. In 1913 the District Commissioner, Machakos, complained that 'to increase taxation in order to drive natives out to work is forced labour under a subterfuge and it is impossible to get away from the fact'.[74] Again, in 1920 field officers were sharply critical of efforts to increase African taxation and their pressures were instrumental in gaining a reduction. Tate wrote to the chief native commissioner that the tax increase was 'repugnant both to our feelings of justice and to the paternal relationship which we bear to the natives . . . I feel so strongly on the injustice of increasing at present the native hut and poll tax that if the proposal becomes law I shall . . . be compelled to give effect to a measure which neither I nor I believe the majority of my colleagues can defend in any way.'[75] Similarly, administrative indecision over the demarcation of the reserves arose from the clash of settler pressures to make them small in area to force out labour and administrative desires to use reserves of adequate size to isolate Africans from all but the most inescapable and carefully regulated economic and social contacts with the settler sphere and preserve the integrity of tribal society.[76] The ill-fated attempt between 1917 and 1927 to create separate field administrative structures for the African and settled districts owed as much to administrative efforts to isolate Africans from disruptive contacts as it did to settler efforts to grasp greater control over their own local administration. The isolationist attitude remained, however, as an influence on the exercise of administrative paternalism until the 1950s.

The extent to which these administrative reactions could soften the harshness of relations of production sustained by state institutions was limited by a key internal contradiction, i.e., the extent to which the state itself relied upon the forced and often unpaid labour of Africans to meet its own needs. The use of call-ups for communal or compulsory labour for porterage, road works, and the construction of markets and government buildings in the reserves, as well as for large-scale state infrastructure projects on the railway, continued throughout the 1920s and only declined into insignificance during the next decade. Furthermore, abuses often occurred when local administrators were able to employ compulsory labor at their own discretion, while the conditions for compulsory labor supplied to contractors on large government works projects, such as the Uasin Gishu branch line of the railroad, were as bad as on any settler estate and the death rate extremely high.[77]

Crises of Accumulation, Coercion & the Colonial State

The 'labour problem' in Kenya was thus rooted in the need of settler estate producers for a mass of semi-servile migrant and resident labourers and their inability to supply the requisite coercion without generating African resistance and threatening the basic framework of colonial domination. In consequence, a process of increasing state intervention that had begun before 1914 culminated in the early 1920s in a massive application of official coercion to ensure the recruitment of labour and sustain the necessary relations of production in estate agriculture under the paternal authority of the Provincial Administration. At no point in the process did the administration contest the basic premise that Africans had to supply the necessary labour for European estates, although for many officials it was a necessary evil if the colony was to be developed, nor did they deny that some forms of compulsion would be necessary. The contradictions of the process of accumulation and relations of production in estate production, and its contradictory articulation with indigenous modes of production, were condensed within the state in the sharp reaction to the use of officers of the Provincial Administration as recruiting agents, which compromised the visible autonomy of the state and its role as paternal protector of the African and disinterested agent of social order, and to when the extraction of labour from the reserves threatened to undermine effective control. The state had, in effect, abstracted the relations of force from the immediate process of production, eliminating their crudest elements and giving them an organized order and predictability in their application; but this was possible only in so far as the state remained, and was seen to remain, a separate, relatively autonomous and disinterested apparatus acting in the general interest. Within the limits of state maintenance of the labour system, what the administration demanded of the settlers was that they live up to the obligations of paternalism themselves and cease their capricious and brutal treatment of African labour. In short, by replacing private oppression with state sanctions, the colonial state in Kenya made possible the more intense exploitation of African labour through the increasing extraction of absolute surplus value.

Notes

1. M. Mamdani, *Politics and Class Formation in Uganda* (London, 1976); H. Alavi, 'The state in post-colonial societies: Pakistan and Bangladesh', *New Left Review* 74 (1972); and J. Saul, 'The state in postcolonial societies: Tanzania', in R. Miliband and J. Saville (eds), *Socialist Register 1974* (London, 1974).
2. Mamdani, *Politics and Class Formation*, p. 139.
3. A. Emmanuel, 'White settler colonialism and the myth of investment imperialism', *New Left Review*, 73 (1972); and on settler politics in Kenya, E.A. Brett, *Colonialism*

and *Underdevelopment in East Africa* (New York, 1973); M.R. Dilley, *British Policy in Kenya Colony* (London, 1966); M.G. Redley, 'The politics of a predicament: the white community in Kenya', Ph.D. dissertation, Cambridge University, 1976.

4. The 'derivationist' approach adopted here emerged in Germany out of debates over the theory of the capitalist state in the early 1970s. See the essays translated in J. Holloway and S. Picciotto, (eds), *State and Capital: A Marxist Debate* (London, 1978), especially Holloway and Picciotto's overview in 'Towards a materialist theory of the state' and Joachim Hirsch, 'The state apparatus and social reproduction: elements of a theory of the bourgeois state'.

5. Our approach thus rejects the functionalist assumptions of, for example, Poulantzas, because of the resulting difficulty in explaining the limits of state action and the material basis for the continual revisions and crises of state structures and policies.

6. L. Cliffe, 'Rural class formation in East Africa', *Journal of Peasant Studies* 4 (1977).

7. G. Lamb 'Marxism, access and the state', *Development and Change* 6(2) (1975), pp. 131-2.

8. Cliffe, 'Rural class formation', p. 203.

9. For an analysis of the origins of peasant and settler production and the state see Chapter 4, above.

10. On the development of peasant commodity production in Kenya, see R. van Zwanenberg, 'The economic response of Kenya Africans to European settlement 1903-39', *Hadith* 4 (1973); and *idem*, 'The development of peasant commodity production in Kenya', *Economic History Review* 27 (1974); J. Forbes Munro, *Colonial Rule and the Kamba: Social Change in the Kenya Highlands* (London, 1975), Ch. 9; J. Newman, 'First steps in rural capitalism: Machakos before the Second World War' (Paper presented to the Cambridge Conference on Political Economy of Kenya, 1975); M.P. Cowen, 'Differentiation in a Kenyan location' (Paper presented to the East African Universities Social Science Conference, Nairobi, 1972).

11. Buell concluded that for the first 15 years of white settlement, no effective standards for labour existed in the colony, and under the umbrella of colonial control, 'the employer was nearly free to do as he liked'. R.L. Buell. *The Native Problem in Africa* (New York, 1928), I, p. 351.

12. R.D. Wolff, *Britain and Kenya, 1870-1930: The Economics of Colonialism* (New Haven & London, 1974), pp. 110, 113.

13. L. Cliffe, 'Rural politics economy of Africa', in P.C. W. Gutkind and I. Wallerstein (eds) *The Political Economy of Contemporary Africa* (Beverly Hills, 1976), p. 115.

14. J. Weeks, 'Wage policy and the colonial legacy: a comparative study', *Journal of Modern African Studies* 9(3) (1971); p. 364.

15. E.S. Grogan, *From Cape to Cairo*, as quoted in A. Clayton and J. Savage, *Government and Labour in Kenya 1895-1963* (London, 1974), p. 22; and *ibid*, p. 58.

16. Clayton and Savage, *Government and Labour in Kenya*, p. 75.

17. T. Barnett, 'The Gezira Scheme: production of cotton and the reproduction of underdevelopment', in I. Oxaal, T. Barnett and D. Booth (eds), *Beyond the Sociology of Development* (London, 1974), pp. 200-1.

18. Lt. Col. J.G. Kirkwood, MLC for Trans Nzoia in Colony and Protectorate of Kenya, *Legislative Council Debates*, 28 Nov. 1941.

19. Statistics of African labour in Kenya vary from one official source to another and must be taken as rough estimates, particularly for the pre-1914 period, both because of the crude statistical procedures employed and, after the First World War, the failure of some employers to fill out the official forms for the registration of all Africans they employed. Nevertheless, the general magnitudes and trends of development do emerge and can be taken as basic indicators of the parameters of the system, being probably underestimates rather than overestimates of the number of Africans at work in the colony at any particular time.

20. Clayton and Savage, *Government and Labour in Kenya*, p. 65.
21. *Ibid.*, p. 151. Clayton and Savage use figures drawn from the annual reports of the Native Affairs Department. Buell, drawing on the report of the chief registrar of natives, gives a total of 185,409 Africans in employment during the first three months of 1927. Buell, *Native Problem in Africa*, 1, p. 345.
22. Clayton and Savage, *Government and Labour in Kenya*, p. 65.
23. Buell, *Native Problem in Africa*, 1, pp. 344–5; and Wolff, *Economics of Colonialism*, pp. 114–16.
24. The percentage of adult men employed from the Transkei in 1927 was 41 per cent, for Basutoland, 35 per cent. Conversely, for Nigeria the percentage in employment was only 2.1 per cent, in Tanganyika, 15.5 per cent, and even in the Belgian Congo, with the largest absolute number of Africans in employment, the proportion was only 14.3 per cent. See Buell, *Native Problem in Africa*, 1, p. 346.
25. Colony and Protectorate of Kenya, Native Affairs Department, *Annual Report* (Nairobi, 1923), p. 30.
26. Buell, *Native Problem in Africa*, 1, p. 345.
27. Clayton and Savage, *Government and Labour in Kenya*, p. 151.
28. The standard published source suggests that 'although a substantial minority of workers were earning rather higher rates overall, those of unskilled labour represented little or no increase in purchasing power when the increased price of African consumer goods and increased taxation were taken into account.' (Clayton and Savage, *Government and Labour in Kenya*, p. 148.) Van Zwanenberg estimates that real wages in 1939 were essentially the same as they had been in 1909, see R. van Zwanenberg, *The Agricultural History of Kenya to 1939* (Nairobi, 1972), p. 34. However, this estimate may conceal considerable fluctuation during that period, especially during the economic expansion of the 1923–9 period and the depression in 1930–6. Calculations by M.P. Cowen and J. Newman in an unpublished study show a substantial increase in real wages between 1924 and 1931 ('Real Wages in Kenya', mimeographed, Nairobi, 1975). If accurate, this is both congruent with the continued growth and competition for African labour of peasant commodity production, and suggests the limits of settler and state control of the labour market.
29. Quoted in F. Furedi, 'Kikuyu squatters and the changing political economy of the White Highlands' (Paper presented to the Conference on the Political Economy of Colonial Kenya, Cambridge, 1975), p. 3.
30. *Ibid.*, pp. 4, 8–9.
31. *Ibid.*, p. 5; also C. Leys, *Underdevelopment in Kenya: The Political Economy of Neo-colonialism* (London, 1975), p. 47.
32. R.L. Tignor, *The Colonial Transformation of Kenya: The Kamba, Kikuyu and Maasai from 1900–1939* (Princeton, 1976), pp. 179–80.
33. T. Sleith, *Report on Trade Conditions in British East Africa, Uganda and Zanzibar*, as quoted in Wolff, *Economics of Colonialism*, p. 130.
34. The circular is reproduced in *Despatch on Native Labour*, House of Commons Special Prints, 33, Cmd 873 (London, 1920). Administrators were also instructed to keep to record of whether chiefs and headmen were or were not helpful in recruiting labour.
35. Tignor, *Colonial Transformation of Kenya*, p. 172.
36. Administrative resistance to the circulars will be discussed below. In order to hold this paper to reasonable length, African resistance in 1921–2 will not be treated in detail. For a standard account see C. Rosberg and J. Nottingham, *The Myth of Mau Mau: Nationalism in Kenya* (New York, 1966), pp. 35–64.
37. The 'Bishops' Memorandum' first appeared in the *East African Standard*, 8 Nov. 1919, and was reprinted in Cmd 873.
38. Circular no. 3, 14 July 1920, reprinted in Cmd 873.
39. Clayton and Savage, *Government and Labour in Kenya*, pp. 117, 136–7.

40. *Ibid.*, p. 125.
41. S. and K. Aaronovitch, *Crisis in Kenya* (London, 1947), p. 113.
42. The last provision was eventually cancelled by the Colonial Office in 1925, but was in force during the 1919-23 period as part of the massive application of state coercion to recruit and control African labour. Clayton and Savage, *Government and Labour in Kenya*, p. 147; the Masters and Servants Ordinances are reprinted in Cmd 873.
43. Buell, *Native Problem in Africa*, 1, pp. 351-3. In 1939 the Mombasa Labour Commission noted, with regard to the employer's obligation to supply housing for his workers, that 'We were astonished to find that both government and private employers have been ignorant of this provision in the law or have disregarded it.' *Report of the Commission of Inquiry Appointed to Examine Labour Conditions in Mombasa* (Nairobi, 1939), paragraph 20.
44. W. McGregor Ross, *Kenya from Within: a Political History* (1927, repr. London, 1968), pp. 189-90; 1931 figure from Tignor, *Colonial Transformation of Kenya*, p. 160.
45. Clayton and Savage, *Government and Labour in Kenya*, p. 132.
46. McGregor Ross, *Kenya from Within*, p. 189.
47. Y. Ghai and J.W.P.B. McAuslan, *Public Law and Political Change in Kenya: A Study of the Legal Framework of Government from Colonial Times to the Present* (London, 1970), pp. 142-3. One former administrative officer reported that while serving in a settled district in the 1920s, Africans would arrive at the district station with notes from their employers demanding that they be immediately punished for various labour violations (interview by B. Berman with S.V. Cooke, May 1969).
48. Buell, *Native Problem in Africa*, 1, p. 358; and Clayton and Savage, *Government and Labour in Kenya*, p. 153. Convictions under the Registration of Natives Ordinance reached a peak of 4,244 in 1929.
49. Charges Under the Masters and Servants (or similar) Ordinances in East and West Africa Territories . . . during the year 1929:

	No. of charges	No. of convictions
Kenya	2,105	1,492
Nyasaland	771	755
Tanganyika	666	500
Uganda	238	190
Zanzibar	115	67
Gold Coast	7	4
Nigeria	180	154

(Colonial Labour Committee Papers, 1931-41, cited in Clayton and Salvage, *Government and Labour in Kenya*, pp. 159-60.)
50. Furedi, 'Kikuyu squatters and the changing political economy', p. 2.
51. Buell, *Native Problem in Africa*, 1, p. 326.
52. Ghai and McAuslan, *Public Law and Political Change*, pp. 83-4.
53. Ghai and McAuslan's assertion that this 'clearly indicated the feudal aspects of the relationship' (ibid.) errs by failing to consider the relations of production in their wider structural (capitalist) context and their origin in the inability of settlers to appropriate surplus value from 'free' labour.
54. Tignor, *Colonial Transformation of Kenya*, pp. 182-3. During the same period the settlers successfully resisted the administration's efforts to impose a light income tax on the immigrant European and Asian communities (McGregor Ross, *Kenya from Within*, pp. 154-8).
55. Wolff, *Economics of Colonialism*, p. 117.
56. Buell, *Native Problem in Africa*, 1, p. 332. Calculating on a different basis, Leys estimates that taxes equalled no less than three-quarters of the average African wage of 1 million per annum in 1920-3 (Leys, *Underdevelopment in Kenya*, p. 32). The African tax burden

and lack of return in state services became a source of internal controversy in the Colonial Office during the 1929–31 Labour government (see papers in Public Record Office (PRO), CO533/391/15904/1929) and was criticized by both of the official commissioners appointed to investigate the colony's fiscal situation during the depression. See *Report by the Financial Commissioner* [Lord Moyne] *on Certain Questions in Kenya*, Cmd 4093 (London, 1932); and *Report by Sir Alan Pim on the Financial Position and System of Taxation of Kenya*, col. 116 (London, 1936).

57. Wolff, *Economics of Colonialism*, p. 119. With wages for farm labour as low as eight shillings per month in some areas during the mid-1920s, Africans often had to work two to four months a year simply to meet their direct taxes. Since few worked for a full year at a time, there was little left over for consumption or saving.

58. In 1922, 2,216 Africans were convicted of nonpayment of tax (Buell, *Native Problem in Africa*, 1, p. 358); and this later soared to 8,709 in the depression year of 1933 (*Report by Sir Alan Pim*).

59. East African Protectorate, *Report of the Commission on Native Labour* (Nairobi, 1913).

60. Buell, *Native Problem in Africa*, 1, p. 323.

61. Cliffe, 'Rural political economy', p. 115.

62. Holloway and Picciotto, 'Towards a materialistic theory', p. 26.

63. E. Pashukanis, *General Theory of Law and Marxism*, quoted in *ibid.*, p. 19.

64. Buell, *Native Problem in Africa*, 1, p. 361. Buell comments that the ratio 'would indicate that a comparatively large European population demands administrative attention and also that a firmer control over the native is needed in a White Settlement Colony than in a native state'.

65. *Ibid.*, pp. 384–8.

66. On the relationship between peasant commodity production and the legitimacy of state authority, see B.J. Berman, *Control and Crisis in Colonial Kenya* (London, 1990), Ch. 6.

67. Brett, *Colonialism and Underdevelopment*, especially pp. 178–9. On the development of the interests of British mercantile capital in African commodity production, see K. Stahl, *The Metropolitan Organization of British Colonial Trade* (London, 1951), pp. 213–14, 283–9.

68. The combination of local and metropolitan pressures led, briefly, in the aftermath of the 1921–2 depression and the 1919–23 political struggles (the so-called Dual Policy), and again during the depression in the early 1930s, to an official policy of encouraging peasant production by the central authorities in Nairobi. In both instances the resources actually committed by the state were minimal compared to the assistance demanded by and offered to the settlers, and faded completely with subsequent recovery of the settler sphere, leaving the encouragement of peasant production largely up to the discretion of local administrators. (Brett, *Colonialism and Underdevelopment*, pp. 205–8; and Berman, *Control and Crisis*, Chs 5 and 6.)

69. Rhodes House Library, Oxford, Colonial Records Project, Storrs-Fox Papers.

70. Clayton and Savage, *Government and Labour in Kenya*, p. 153.

71. Buell, *Native Problem in Africa*, 1, pp. 379–80, 396–7.

72. Tignor, *Colonial Transformation of Kenya*, p. 153.

73. *Ibid.*, pp. 153–4.

74. Quoted in T.H.R. Cashmore, 'Studies in district administration in the East African Protectorate, 1895–1918' (Ph.D. dissertation, Cambridge University, 1965), p. 104.

75. H.R. Tate to Chief Native Commissioner Ainsworth, 16 Jan. 1920. Quoted in Clayton and Savage, *Government and Labour in Kenya*, pp. 162.

76. Ainsworth was the leading exponent of strong reserves and segregation of Africans from disruptive contact with Europeans. Expression of his views can be found in PRO, CO533/130, especially Ainsworth to CO, 8 Aug. 1913; and Kenya National Archives PC/NZAZ/3 'Memorandum on the Question of Natives who Leave their Reserve', 19 Oct. 1911.

77. Buell, *Native Problem in Africa*, 1, pp. 354–5.

Part III

Capitalism & the Colonial
State in Theoretical
& Comparative Perspective

Six

☙☙☙☙☙☙☙☙☙☙☙☙☙☙☙☙☙☙☙☙☙☙

The Concept of 'Articulation' & the Political Economy of Colonialism

BRUCE BERMAN

'Articulation' is the most distinctive and important concept to emerge from the Marxist critique of dependency theory in the so-called 'modes of production controversy'. It has become, however, increasingly controversial and must be approached with care to sort out the various meanings attributed to it and the serious conceptual problems that some of them present. Articulation was initially developed from the structuralist concept of a 'social formation' – consisting of the hierarchic linkage of several modes of production under the dominance of the capitalist mode – as a vehicle for explaining underdevelopment and the apparent persistence of precapitalist forms and relations of production at the periphery of the global system. The focus of the issue was the continuity of the peasantry as the most numerous segment of the population in Africa. The key problem was to answer the question: 'How does capitalism become dominant in regions such as Africa without replicating itself in each instance?' This question, in turn, is derived from Marx's notion of the 'formal subsumption of labor', since 'capital always takes labor as it finds it' so that 'the question is what it does with labor'.[1] After a century of colonial rule and independent national existence in Africa 'the relations of production in which the peasantry are involved are necessarily posed in relation to the development of capital'; in analysing the persistence of the peasantry 'the passive notion of "survival" is dropped and the question changes to that of the *reproduction* of the peasantry and its functions for imperialism'.[2]

The reproduction of the peasantry and apparently precapitalist forms of production are thus seen as necessary and functional for capital. For Claude Meillassoux, for example, the reproduction rather than expropriation of the peasantry in Africa represents a continuing process of primitive accumulation that is an intrinsic part of capitalist development.[3] In the 'strongest' model of articulation, in the work of Pierre-Phillipe Rey, the subordinated mode of production continues to exist for a considerable length of time, retaining a significant degree of autonomy in its transactions with the dominant capitalist mode, and capital may even encourage the emergence of new non-capitalist modes.[4] Typically, the existence of subordinate and dominated precapitalist modes is argued to be essential for the continued expanded reproduction of capital in metropolitan centres of development.[5]

As Jonathan Crush points out, however, 'extravagant claims have been made for its utility, but very little has actually been demonstrated in practice'.[6] Much of the problem stems from the structuralist origins of 'articulation' reflected in the abstract emptiness of the concepts, especially that of 'mode of production', the ahistorical and teleological character of its functionalist mode of explanation, and the economistic isolation of its focus that prevents any effective treatment of class struggle or the state.

The most immediate difficulty is with the notion that what are being articulated are 'modes of production'. On a theoretical level, the concept of a mode of production is an abstract and formal specification of relations that provides an essential tool for the analysis of historical experience, but does not necessarily have any concrete existence in its 'pure' form. Thus, a difference exists between the abstract model of the capitalist mode of production created by Marx and the historical crystallization of social forces and relations in the varied national capitalisms encountered in actual experience; and the more we are involved in the study of actually existing societies, the broader and more complex the system of relations that have to be analysed.[7] Reliance on an abstract formal concept of mode of production results in a tendency to identify the existence of a mode by the presence or absence of a particular form of labour process or exploitation of labour such as the patriarchal peasant farm or wage labour. However, these are, as Jairus Banaji points out, 'simple categories' or simple abstractions in Marxist terms that can exist within different historical societies dominated by the 'laws of motion' or developmental tendencies of different modes of production and that take their particular character from the manner of their involvement in those wider relations.[8] Thus, peasant production in itself cannot constitute a mode of production as such, but is rather a form of production that can exist and takes on its particular historical character within the dominant dynamic forces of different societies that determine the conditions of its reproduction or transformation.

The Concept of 'Articulation' & the Political Economy of Colonialism

Failure to recognize the conceptual limits of a 'mode of production' has led to 'a desire to link immediately observable features of society . . . directly to the defining features of various modes of production without setting them in the context of a historical process'.[9] This has meant, for example, that in some instances each different labour process has been identified as a separate mode of production in a multiplication ad infinitum in which a single Latin American *latifundia* is said to contain several 'modes of production'. In so doing, the utility of the concepts of 'mode of production' and 'articulation' disappear in a reductio ad absurdum of micro-forms.[10] There is also the reverse danger of making the capitalist mode of production contain such a diversity of forms and relations of production that any sense of where it begins or ends disappears, and it becomes 'a vacant and homogeneous totality' synonymous with the global system as such. This is particularly apparent when capitalism is defined at the level of exchange rather than at the level of production, as in Immanuel Wallerstein's world system analysis.[11]

This difficulty in dealing with modes of production so abstractly conceived is avoided (or at least side-stepped) by defining articulation as the linkage of two societies, neither exemplifying a mode of production in its 'pure' form, but each nonetheless dominated by a different developmental dynamic. In this version, according to Henry Bernstein, a dominant capitalism

> subjects the elements of other modes of production to the needs and logic of its own functioning and integrates them, more or less, in the mechanism of its reproduction . . . there is no question that the 'autonomy' of the pre-capitalist modes or relations of production are preserved, nor any doubt that the law of motion governing the articulation is determined by capital.[12]

The key issue is then the nature and forms of penetration of peasant production; and the essential moment of the process is the destruction of the cycle of simple reproduction of the indigenous domestic economy via the monetization of at least some elements of material reproduction. The initial break in the self-sufficiency of precapitalist production in Africa was accomplished either peacefully through the activities of merchant capital ('market incentives') or through the colonial state by extra-economic coercion in the form of taxes, forced labour, or the compulsory production of cash crops. The result was that the peasantry was forced to supply agricultural commodities and/or labour power. In areas deliberately developed as labour reserves, capital and the state forced peasants to periodically enter the labour market by ensuring that the material conditions of production in the reserves were insufficient to meet the needs of simple reproduction, commodity purchase, and tax payments.[13]

The indigenous productive systems were thus subject to powerful

forces of transformation. At the same time, however, the preservation
of domestic production was necessitated by the fact that neither the
wages of migrant labour nor the prices received for marketed commodities were sufficient for the reproduction of the worker/farmer or his
family. The resulting reproductive gap was displaced onto the continued
production of use values by domestic precapitalist forms and relations
of production. Conversely, the partial continuity of the domestic sphere
of production permitted capitalist plantations and mines to hold wages,
and merchant capital to hold commodity prices to exceptionally low
levels. Articulation thus resulted in the subjugation and exploitation of
peasant labour on the basis of the partial restructuring and partial preservation of precapitalist forms with a minimum of capital investment.[14]
While precapitalist forms appear to persist at the surface of social relations, their significance and continued existence is actually transformed
and determined by capital. Domestic production is no longer an autonomous mode of production but a form of the reproduction of labour
power within capitalism.

This formulation of articulation is useful insofar as it directs our
attention to the extraction of African labour power and commodities
and the simultaneous persistence of precapitalist domestic production as
the key features of the process. But such a formulation remains incomplete and misleading. Its structuralist origins are manifest in a rigid
and·teleological structural determinism. Articulation is seen as a static
and self-reproducing relationship that, once established, continuously
and unproblematically serves the 'needs' of metropolitan capital. 'The
ultimate prime-mover in the third world,' according to Nicos Mouzelis,
'is always the changing reproductive requirements of western capitalism';[15] whatever happened to indigenous African societies was a
response to those requirements. These indigenous societies are thus
treated as essentially passive receptors of external forces, acted upon but
having no active effect on the process; or as Banaji states: 'modes of production entirely deprived of their own laws of motion, vegetating on the
periphery of an industrializing Europe like a vast reserve of labour
power periodically called into action by the spasmodic expansions of
metropolitan capital'.[16]

The structuralist concept of articulation, then, shares the conceptual
failings of the structuralist theory of the state in its inability to deal with
the relationship between structural determination and human agency
and with the effects of contradiction and conflict on historical processes.
As Frederick Cooper aptly notes: 'so we have dominance and articulation, without dominators or articulators . . . Such an argument defines
away all possibility of incomplete domination, of resistance to capitalism,
or of African societies being ordered in any way except to maximize the
advantage of capital . . . This is Marxism without class struggle'.[17] It

is impossible to explain with the structuralist version of articulation either the diverse and possibly temporary and contingent forms within the process or the influence upon these variations of particular sectors of capital, the pre-existing structures of indigenous societies,[18] and the crises and struggles that regularly punctuated colonial rule.

How can we conceive of articulation in a way that can more adequately meet such explanatory objectives? First, articulation should be seen as a process of struggle and uncertainty, the particular historical field in which European capital and the colonial state attempted to control the labour power and production of African societies. Everything that happened, especially the kaleidoscopic variations of transformation and preservation in indigenous societies, did not happen merely 'to serve the needs of capital', either as an expression of structural necessity or the conscious agency of European interests. We confront instead a process of uneven capitalist development in which logical necessity confronted the historical reality of conflict and the limitations of instrumental capability. The diverse patterns of transformation and preservation equally represent unforeseen and unintended outcomes, reflecting both African resistance to capitalist penetration and the inability of European capital and political forces to overcome such resistance in specific contexts:

> [We must recognize] how difficult it was to get Africans off the land, how hard Africans fought to maintain their agricultural cycle and to manipulate new markets as much as to avoid total commitment to them and hence how little alternative capital had to some form of migratory labor.
> The limited extent of primitive accumulation, the lack of generalized wage labor, and the continuation of extensive non-market production may not have been mere aspects of a profit-maximizing mechanism for a somewhat vaguely defined capitalist system, but important constraints on the dynamism of capitalism.[19]

Second, beyond such immediate confrontations between Africans and Europeans, articulation also contained structural contradictions operating on two distinct levels that prevented the achievement of any long-term stability in the pattern of tranformation/preservation and generated the bases for new forms of conflict. On the one hand, the penetration of capital, however partial, progressively undermined the ability of domestic forms of production to reproduce themselves. Bernstein, following Meillassoux, notes:

> This exploitation undermined reproduction in two ways: a) by the withdrawal of productive labour; and b) by substituting in the sphere of necessary consumption, commodities for use values previously produced within the domestic community or acquired through simple

exchange. Once established this process is irreversible and effects the degradation of the conditions of existence of the domestic community not only through the transfer of value but through the erosion of an entire culture of production . . . [A]rticulation has a transitional character not only theoretically but historically . . . the reproduction capacities of the domestic community are run down through the regular course of its articulation with the capitalist mode.[20]

If capital 'needs', or at least uses to advantage, the precolonial forms of domestic production, it simultaneously incapacitates them. From this flows the physical decay, decline of productivity (especially of food) and widespead pauperization that began to appear in parts of colonial Africa as early as the 1930s and is characteristic of wide areas of rural Africa today.

This process of decay and impoverishment, on the other hand, is not found uniformly through the social landscape of rural Africa. All peasants were not equally subject to immiseration. Evidence is steadily accumulating of active processes of not simply differentiations of wealth and poverty, but of actual class formation in colonial rural Africa. This stratification suggests the second level of contradiction in the process of articulation. In the relationship between the external social forces of capital and the pre-existing social forces of an indigenous society, we have a confrontation of two sets of forces, each propelled by its own tendential 'laws of motion'. The crucial point is that the indigenous societies were not simply passive receptors or active resistors of the penetration of capital, but they often contained reactions to it that led to the emergence of a distinct and contradictory *internal* transition towards capitalism. This key paradox was recognized 70 years ago by Rosa Luxemburg when she noted that capital required links with non-capitalist areas for its expanded reproduction; yet as it penetrated these areas, it set off within them a contradictory transition to capitalism.[21] Within the process of articulation, then, capital tends to produce its own antithesis in internal capitalist forces struggling with it to accumulate and appropriate the surplus value produced.[22]

In concrete terms, this involved the emergence of pockets of wealthy peasants employing wage labour and attempting to accumulate capital, i.e., in transition to capitalist production as well as using the proceeds of investments in trade and savings from wage labour for reinvestment in agriculture or even petty manufacturing. This interior transition to capitalism directly confronted the merchant capital that served in the colonial period as the active agent of articulation, linking the petty commodity production of Africa with metropolitan industrial capital. The contradiction in the process of articulation can thus be seen from a slightly different perspective as what Geoffrey Kay defines as the 'contradictory tendencies of merchant capital to both stimulate and repress the development of the forces of production and to both open and block the way for the full development of capitalism'.[23] Moreover, the process of the emergence of a class of capitalist producers within indigenous societies implied the dispossession and proletarianization of other members of the community and generated new forms of conflict over the accumulation of land and control of labour that, to paraphrase Adam Przeworsky, were struggles about class before they were struggles among classes.[24]

Consistent with structuralist practice of accepting the separation of the economic and political instances and treating them largely in isolation, earlier concepts of articulation have tended to be narrowly economistic. While there has been some recognition that the colonial state was actively involved in the process of articulation and the penetration and domination of capital is an arena of political struggle, only Rey among the major theorists of articulation has stressed the contradictions and struggles involved as 'a combat between the two modes of production, with confrontations and alliances which such a combat implies: confrontations and alliances essentially between the classes which these modes of production define'.[25] Geoff Lamb has further developed the point by positing the role of the state as the 'primary mechanism of articulation between modes of production'. He notes further:

> The essential point is that the state takes on the central role of managing and representing the myriad encounters and struggles between classes and agents of different modes. The state provides economic, social, and political services for capitalist penetration, orchestrates the de- and re-structuring of elements of the pre-capitalist mode . . . and copes, so to speak, at the level of cohesion of the whole social formation with the dislocative consequences of the expansion of the capitalist mode.[26]

Lamb's formulation exaggerates the omniscience and omnipotence of the colonial state as the instrumental agent of metropolitan capital. What is missing from these accounts is an understanding of the uncertainty and instability of colonial domination and exploitation, of how the colonial state was itself caught and enmeshed in the contradictions of articulation, and of how this shaped the form both of the state and of the contradictions as well. We need, instead, an approach to the state that can satisfy Cooper's suggestion that 'by stressing the give and take of these processes' we can begin 'to draw a picture of change and the limits of change that transcends images of mechanical responses to markets or implacable domination'.[27]

Colonial states unquestionably deliberately acted to stimulate the supply of local labour and primary commodities, and thus to ensure the broader conditions for accumulation by metropolitan and settler capital.

This involved repeated direct involvement in the structural transformation of indigenous forms of production and in the extraction and control of labour and commodities from the peasantry. This meant, in effect, that property, production, and market relations were increasingly contained within the political and juridic forms of the state. However, nowhere in colonial Africa was the separation of the direct producers from the land achieved completely. Insofar as generalized commodity production and/or generalized wage labour were incompletely established, the coercive force of markets remained weak, and market and production relations required a continuing strong degree of extra-economic coercion and state control. The crucial separation of economic and political spheres could not therefore be effectively achieved and the process of legitimation of the colonial state as an apparently autonomous and disinterested arbiter remained a constant dilemma for the colonial authorities. Colonial domination could not incorporate Africans as ostensibly free 'citizens' incorporated as producers or workers in 'free markets' but only as servile and dependent 'subjects' of authoritarian state control. The coerciveness of the state was masked ideologically in the claims of imperial paternalism, and in practice by intervention to 'protect' Africans from 'unfair' exploitation by regulating the conditions of labour and the marketing of commodities to constrain the extremes of capitalist accumulation.

The contradictions between the processes of accumulation and legitimation in which the state was involved generated a dialectic in which each effort to extend capitalist production and exchange relations was slowed and often halted by the colonial authorities' fear of provoking African resistance and disrupting the degree of stable control already achieved. This enables us to understand the very real limits on the power of the colonial state and its capacity to act as the agent of metropolitan capital and the degree to which it had to attend at least to some degree to the interests of various segments of the African population. As Kay noted in one of the first Marxist analyses of the colonial state more than a decade ago:

> It was managed by extreme caution. The political administrators of the colonial state were instinctively aware, if not fully conscious, of the frailty of their position and knew they could never maintain their power in the face of organized opposition among the mass of the Ghanaian people . . . The attempt, wherever possible, to avoid such opposition by exercising deliberate restraint, runs like a thread through the official actions and statements: colonial administrators were practiced exponents of the maxim that those who wish to rule must first learn to govern themselves.[28]

However, the process of legitimation and the maintenance of stable control required more than state protection of Africans from 'abuses'. It also contained a real material base that required attention to the incomes and conditions of peasant farmers and labourers to demonstrate the real benefits of colonial 'progress'. This link to indigenous interests was reinforced by the constant metropolitan demands for colonial fiscal self-sufficiency, which made the state heavily dependent on the tax revenue drawn from Africans for its own reproduction. Furthermore, the shortage of European personnel, money, and coercive force available to colonial states created a pressing need for local collaborators and intermediaries to fill the lower rungs of the state apparatus and consequently to maintain order at the local levels. Since the salaries paid to these African collaborators were generally meagre, the state was forced to find a stable way of rewarding them and ensuring their loyalty through opportunities for accumulation on the basis of regular production and exchange relations. As a result their position had to be established on a class basis within the political economy of the colony. If not, whether they were 'traditional' rulers relieved of the previous internal constraints on their power or 'new men' elevated by the colonial authorities, they tended to prey upon the local population through extortionate pressure and appropriations that undermined the order they were supposed to maintain. Colonial officials tended to promote the opportunities for internal accumulation and the emergence of a nascent indigenous capitalist class of 'progressive' Africans that traditional rulers could be encouraged to join and/or from which the class of collaborators could be recruited. The state itself therefore reinforced one of the central contradictions of articulation.

Conversely, the colonial state also found control and legitimacy threatened by the destruction and transformation of indigenous precapitalist societies and by the class struggles, particularly over land, generated by the processes of class formation in the countryside. At the same time, colonial officials feared the emergence of a permanent, class-conscious, combative African working class, completely detached from the land. This led to deliberate efforts to preserve and even resuscitate precolonial social forms as a basis for social order. The state was thus involved, paradoxically, in both sides of the dialectic of destruction and preservation of indigenous societies. This was reflected in the characteristic ambiguity of its policies: it provided the conditions for external capitalist penetration, but placed limits on its operations; it partly destroyed and restructured indigenous social forms but also moved to prop up and sustain them; it encouraged internal accumulation and a transition to capitalism but also blocked its full development and consolidation.

Stripped of its structuralist baggage, articulation is a concept of considerable utility for understanding the dynamics of the political economy of colonialism. Insofar as it focuses our attention on the particular modalities of the processes of accumulation and class formation, the forces and relations of production, and class struggle in the confrontation of capitalist and precapitalist social structures in Africa, it represents an important step beyond dependency/underdevelopment theory. Articulation must be understood, however, not as a self-reproducing condition 'serving the interests of capital' but as a complex, conflict-ridden, and unstable process through which precapitalist indigenous societies were, with considerable difficulty, penetrated and dominated in varying degrees by the forces of capitalist imperialism. We must also recognize both the crucial and contradictory role of the colonial state in this process and the importance of the variable responses of indigenous societies to imperial penetration, sometimes actively resisting and sometimes pursuing the spread of capitalist social forces. Articulation was neither a consciously instrumental agency of exploitation nor a determined expression of a teleological systemic 'logic', but rather it was a partly deliberate and partly unforeseen and unintended process of uncertainty and struggle that, while establishing the dominance of capital, rarely corresponded precisely with the intentions or interests of the historical actors. The primary theoretical contribution of the concept of articulation is in helping us to explain more adequately the diverse patterns of the transformation, destruction, and preservation of indigenous societies in colonial Africa.

Notes

1. Frederick Cooper, 'Africa and the world economy', *African Studies Review* 24 (2/3) (1981), p. 14.
2. Henry Bernstein, 'Capital and peasantry in the epoch of imperialism', Economic Research Bureau, University of Dar es Salaam, Occasional Paper 7(2) (1977), p. 4.
3. Claude Meillassoux, *Femmes, greniers et capitaux* (Paris, 1975).
4. Pierre-Philippe Rey, *Les alliances des classes* (Paris, 1973); Aidan Foster-Carter, 'The modes of production controversy', *New Left Review* 107 (1978), p. 51; Bernstein, 'Capital and peasantry', p. 19.
5. John G. Taylor, *From Modernization to Modes of Production* (London, 1979), Ch. 13.
6. Jonathan Crush, 'The Southern African regional formation: a geographical perspective', *Tijdschrift voor economische en sociale geografie* 73(4) (1982), p. 200.
7. Foster-Carter, 'Modes of production controversy', p. 66; Ernesto Laclau, *Politics and Ideology in Marxist Theory.* (London, 1977), pp. 42, 47–9; Anthony Brewer, *Marxist Theories of Imperialism* (London, 1980), p. 265.
8. Jairus Banaji, 'Modes of production in a materialist conception of history', *Capital and Class* 3 (1977), pp. 9–10, 30–1.
9. Nicos Mouzelis, 'Modernization, underdevelopment, uneven development: prospects for a theory of Third World formations', *Journal of Peasant Studies* 7(3) (1980), p. 367.

10. Norman Long, 'Structural dependency, modes of production and economic brokerage in rural Peru', in I. Oxaal *et al.* (eds) *Beyond the Sociology of Development* (London, 1974), pp. 253–82.
11. Laclau, *Politics and Ideology*, pp. 43–6.
12. Bernstein, 'Capital and peasantry', p. 35.
13. *Ibid.*, pp. 14–15, 28–9; Banaji:, 'Modes of production', p. 33.
14. Bernstein, 'Capital and peasantry', pp. 10–14.
15. Mouzelis, 'Modernization, underdevelopment, uneven development', p. 367.
16. Banaji, 'Modes of production', p. 14.
17. Cooper, 'Africa and the world economy', p. 15.
18. Barbara Bradby, 'The destruction of natural economy', *Economy and Society* 4(2) (1975), pp. 127–61.
19. Cooper, 'Africa and the world economy', pp. 40, 16.
20. Bernstein, 'Capital and peasantry', p. 15
21. Rosa Luxemburg, *The Accumulation of Capital* (London, 1963), Chs xxvii–xxx.
22. Foster-Carter, 'Modes of production controversy', p. 64.
23. Geoffrey Kay, *Development and Underdevelopment: A Marxist Analysis* (London, 1975), pp. 95, 104–5.
24. Adam Przeworsky, 'Proletariat into class: the process of class formation from Karl Kautsky's *The Class Struggle* to recent controversies', *Politics and Society* 7 (1977), p. 372.
25. Rey, *Les alliances des classes*, p. 15.
26. Geoffrey Lamb, 'Marxism, access and the state', *Development and Change* 6(2) (1975), pp. 131–2.
27. Cooper, 'Africa and the world economy', p. 21.
28. Geoffrey Kay, *The Political Economy of Colonialism in Ghana* (Cambridge, 1972), p. 9.

Seven

🌀🌀🌀🌀🌀🌀🌀🌀🌀🌀🌀🌀🌀🌀🌀🌀🌀🌀🌀🌀🌀🌀

Structure & Process in the Bureaucratic States of Colonial Africa

BRUCE BERMAN

Introduction

Contemporary studies of European colonialism in Africa present us with
two very different and apparently contradictory images of the colonial
state.[1] On the one hand there is the 'strong' state, the potent bureaucratic agent of imperialism. By coercion, indirect pressures and material
inducements it smashed the self-sufficiency of indigenous precapitalist societies and managed their subordinate linkages to metropolitan
capital. Its continually expanding apparatus intervened in ever wider
areas of the colonial political economy, directing change to serve the
interests of the metropole while containing and suppressing indigenous
social forces. This colonial state was a powerful instrument of political
domination and structural transformation. As Mamdani argues:

> Colonialism is the implantation of a state apparatus in the conquered
> territory. The colonial state was a geographical extension of the
> metropolitan state; it was directly subordinate to the latter . . .
> Simply put, the colonial state represented an *absentee* ruling class, the
> metropolitan bourgeoisie, and it performed the functions of both
> state and ruling class in an 'independent' nation. The colonial state
> created the structures of the underdeveloped economy at both the
> levels of production and exchange . . . [it] destroyed and created
> entire classes.[2]

On the other hand, however, there is the 'weak' colonial state, the
paternalistic mediator struggling to maintain a precarious sovereignty

140

over the contending interests of colonial society. Constantly strapped for resources, plagued by poor communications and inadequate information, and possessing limited coercive force, it appears as a facade of power sustained by a delicate game of bluff and wit, combining exhortation and threat with the cooptation and accommodation of indigenous social forces. Rather than being the agent of change, the colonial state feared the consequences of change emanating from social forces over which it had little effective control. Colonial order, argues Kay, for example, was ultimately a 'close run thing', constantly threatened by crisis and struggle.[3]

That both of these accounts were written by Marxist scholars makes the contrast between them even more striking. The essential point, however, is that there is no choice to be made between these images of the colonial state. *Both* are valid as reflections of the two faces of a single reality. The most striking characteristic of the colonial state was the ambiguous, indeed, contradictory character of its structures and processes. This reflected the contradictory social forces of colonial society, social forces that both determined the development of the colonial state and were in turn shaped and modified by it. The colonial state cannot adequately be understood without consideration of its role in the political economy of colonialism, and vice-versa. To do so requires that the colonial state be situated theoretically as a specific form or variant of the modern capitalist state.

The development of the forms of the state is derived from the central social relations of capitalist production. This is the starting point of the 'historical derivationist' approach to the theory of the state, which focuses on the historical specificity of state forms and the central role of class struggle in their development.[4] This involves an explicitly political reading of Marxist theory in which, as Wood points out, 'relations of production are . . . presented in their *political* aspect, that aspect in which they are actually *contested* . . . the object of this theoretical stance is a practical one, to illuminate the terrain of struggle by viewing modes of production not as abstract structures, but as they actually confront people who must act in relation to them'. She goes on to note that these relations of production are encountered in historical experience within the very forms of the state itself as 'not mere secondary reflexes but constituents of the production relations themselves . . . the material base is itself articulated through juridical-political forms'.[5]

In the historical derivationist perspective the state is neither a neutral, disinterested 'arbitrator' nor an 'ideal collective capitalist', but rather a system of political domination that takes the form of a separate and *apparently autonomous* complex of institutions and practices that establish and maintain in juridical and political forms the social relations that ensure the reproduction and accumulation of capital. This means, on the one hand, that the central contradictions of capitalist social relations are reproduced within the structure of the state itself; while, on the other hand, if the state acts as a direct agent of class domination imposing these relations, it undermines their essential fetishized appearance as free and equal contractual exchange between capital and labour. The state is an agency of capitalist development, but it cannot be based solely on the continuous application of compulsion without generating diverse forms of resistance rather than compliance and becoming the focus of increasingly costly, disruptive and unpredictable struggles.

The state must establish and maintain, therefore, an effective degree of legitimacy if political domination is to be achieved by means other than naked force. In capitalist society effective control and legitimacy rest upon the sharp separation of the economic and political spheres and the ability of the state to act as an apparently neutral and disinterested arbiter among contending class forces and as an 'impersonal apparatus of public power' on behalf of an asserted higher general or 'national' interest.[6] The apparent autonomy of the state is thus a fundamental expression of its contradictory role in capitalist society. The ability of the state to act as an 'ideal collective capitalist' or as the explicit instrument of particular sectors of capital is limited by the need to maintain the apparent autonomy of the state itself. The interests of the state authorities diverge from the interests of capital over the need of the state to sustain the conditions of its own legitimacy. At the same time, the state remains tied to capital by its dependence on the process of accumulation for the fiscal conditions of its own reproduction.[7]

Accumulation and legitimation are then the two central and dialectically related 'tasks' of the capitalist state. They are imbricated in virtually all areas of state activity and their mutual contradictions underlie the dilemmas of governance. In particular, the autonomy and legitimacy of the state are the outcome of contradictory and conflict-ridden processes in which force and consent are interrelated in complex ways. ' "Legitimacy" and "active consent" ', as Corrigan, Ramsay and Sayer point out, 'are not static or abstract, but are extremely turbulent descriptions', and 'all state forms under capitalism are constituted through continuing conflicts, struggles and contradictions, despite their seeming natural and civilized appearance *above* society.'[8] The autonomy and legitimacy of the state, even the fundamental separation of the economic and political spheres, must constantly be maintained and repaired in the face of the state's actual involvement in accumulation and class struggle.

The state can be understood, then, as a set of consciously instrumental structures and practices for the reproduction and expansion of capitalist society and the patterns of production relations and class domination within it. The very notion of state 'policy' expresses the drive to extend control over social structural forces that has led to the development of a sequence of techniques to manage the recurrent crises and struggles of capitalism. If we examine the structural forms and practices of the capitalist state, however, we find not a finely tuned structure of domination, in which every action serves the interests of capital and each part has consciously been shaped to a particular role in the smooth functioning of the whole, but rather a more diverse and ambiguous collection of parts created at different historical junctures to deal with varying crises and struggles. Moreover, these are partly integrated and partly in conflict with each other. Despite increasing efforts to develop its instrumental capacities, the state remains ultimately beyond the will of its human personnel. The diverse forms of the state apparatus 'can be seen as the institutional fossil of past struggles to impose bourgeois forms',[9] and as an index of the scope and limits of its capacity to deal with the contradictions of capitalist society.

Bureaucracy has played an increasingly dominant role in the capitalist state as its purposive interventions have become more continuous and complex. With its graded hierarchy of permanent professional officials, functional specialization of units, and emphasis on 'disinterested' expertise and the rational calculation of means and ends, bureaucracy is the principal expression of the drive to increasing instrumental control over social structure and practice. At the same time, far from being a neutral instrument, bureaucracy increasingly comprises the immediate context of the real crises and struggles of social life. Classes confront each other within and through bureaucracies in both the state and capital. The specific forms of the bureaucratic state apparatus have been determined by the tasks of reproduction/accumulation and control/legitimacy in the context of particular historical forces that subject the abstract 'logic' of capital to the realities of conflict.

Structural logic thus does not always correspond to real historical outcomes. The state authorities do not automatically know the 'best' way of resolving a particular crisis and restoring the conditions for accumulation and domination, and their choices have to be made in the context of struggles whose outcomes remain to some degree unpredictable.[10] Bureaucracy is the immediate context in which such choices are made, and, as Wright suggests, we must place the analysis of bureaucracy within the broader social context of structural forces and class relations, and also deal with the internal dynamics of bureaucratic organizations as they shape state action and its impact on the development of capitalism.[11] The decision-making or policy processes of state bureaucracies are an important element of the way specific states actually 'work': a crucial determinant of the capacity or incapacity of the state to deal with the structural contradictions and crises of capitalism and, hence, also of the multiple and often idiosyncratic trajectories of national development within the capitalist world system. Bureaucratic processes are a key mediating link between the state as a *determined* outcome of the structural forces of capitalism, and the state as a *determining* factor shaping the further development of those forces.[12]

Turning to European colonialism in Africa, it is important to recognize that it represents one of the most consequential modern efforts to modify or create entire social structures. For a large portion of humanity it continues to be of enduring importance in defining their socio-economic and political circumstances. It should not surprise us, however, that colonial projects of social engineering did not succeed as planned. While the actual practice in most colonies was far less coherent and intellectually elaborated than the schemes of colonial theorists, colonialism was nevertheless the most conscious and deliberate aspect of capitalist imperialism. What is significant is the intentional reach of such projects as well as the ensemble of factors that shaped both their intended and unintended outcomes. From the start, the principal agency of colonial projects of social transformation was the colonial state and this consisted for most of its history primarily of a bureaucratic apparatus for the domination and exploitation of the subject population.[13] The colonial state is in fact one of the most striking historical examples of bureaucratic authoritarianism. Indeed, as we shall see below, the development of its administrative organizations and policies for socio-economic intervention and control often preceded their application and refinement in the metropole. The bureaucratic apparatus is thus the necessary focus of the study of the colonial state.

The distinctive structures and practices of the colonial state in Africa *circa* 1880–1960 derived from the particular character of the social forces over which it struggled to preside, a character rooted in the complex process of 'articulation' through which the precapitalist and precolonial forms of African societies were penetrated and dominated by exogenous capitalist forces. Under the aegis of the colonial state African societies were subjected to contradictory patterns of transformation, destruction and preservation of their internal structures that resulted in a wide variety of intermediate and hybrid forms. This process did not occur instantaneously or uniformly, but in a variety of forms and phases encountering different local conditions and responses. The resulting variations emerged from the particular forms of external capitalist penetration, the heterogeneous structures and responses of the indigeneous societies, and the diversity of local ecology and resource endowments. Articulation also involved widespread coercion by colonial states and frequent, if uneven, active and passive resistance from Africans. The differing impacts on and reactions within African societies also determined the emergence of distinctive processes of class formation and struggle.[14]

Throughout colonial Africa the state struggled to perform two contradictory tasks: first, to secure the conditions for the extraction of commodities and accumulation of capital by metropolitan interests by managing their articulation with indigenous forms of production and, second, to provide, as an essential precondition for accumulation, a framework of stable political order and effective control over the indigenous population. In the rest of this chapter we shall examine the role of the colonial state as an agency of accumulation and domination, employing by way of illustration empirical material drawn from the experience of the French and British colonies of West, Central and East Africa.[15] In the last section the structures and processes that have been treated analytically will be brought together in a consideration of the real historical sequence of the development, decline and eventual displacement of the colonial state.

The colonial state as an agency of economic change: articulation and accumulation

Recent studies have revealed with increasing clarity and detail the development of the political economy of colonialism in Africa. The 'scramble' for Africa gained momentum in the 1880s initially as an extension of traditional patterns of treaty links between African and European states to protect trade in the face of growing inter-imperial rivalry and increasing internal upheaval in African societies. By the 1890s, however, the rapid industrial expansion, growing class struggles and rising commodity prices of the 'second industrial revolution' emerging out of the 'Great Depression' shaped the European thrust into Africa towards violent conquest and a drive to control African labour and production.[16] The basic structures were erected in the quarter-century before the First World War, consolidated in the interwar decades, and have endured until today, with little significant modification until the post-1945 period.[17] The colonies provided low-cost raw materials for export to their respective metropoles, and a market for manufactures imported from them. Up to the Second World War the capital investment in this trading economy was extremely limited and comprised only a fraction of the total foreign investment of the metropoles.[18] The total public and private investment in all of West Africa between 1870 and 1936 amounted to £147 million. Half of this constituted public investment, largely spent on railways and harbour facilities to provide the infrastructure for the trading economy, and was disproportionately concentrated in the cities of the coastal colonies, which served both as the principal ports and seats of the colonial central governments. Only 20 per cent of the total was invested in the colonies of French West Africa, with the rest in the smaller but more populous British colonies.[19]

145

In West Africa in particular, and Central and East Africa to a lesser degree, the trading economy was dominated by metropolitan mercantile and finance capital, increasingly concentrated in the hands of a small number of trading companies and banks that controlled and financed the bulk of exports and imports.[20] In French Equatorial Africa in particular, and some areas of East and West Africa, concessionary companies operating in mining, timber and plantations were also important. However, with the exception of a few colonies such as Kenya, where settler farmers dominated export production, and Northern Rhodesia, where copper mining became predominant in the interwar period, the principal focus of African colonial economies was peasant-produced primary commodities.[21]

The trading economy was based on state-protected monopolies and monopsonies, which made possible large and sustained profits, especially for merchant capital.[22] Colonial states provided restrictive tariffs and differential duties, legally protected monopoly concessions and even direct subsidies to help secure an exclusive or predominant position for metropolitan firms in colonial production and marketing.

Colonialism also involved momentous changes for the African societies of the rural hinterlands. This was the focus of the process of articulation linking them with the intrusive forces of metropolitan capitalism. Although some regions of coastal West Africa had earlier became involved in commodity production and trade, especially during the brief era of 'legitimate trade' that succeeded the end of the slave trade, for the societies of the interior of West Africa and virtually all of East and Central Africa their incorporation into the world economy was coterminous with the extension of effective colonial political control in the 1890–1914 period.

The varying patterns of capitalist penetration and the diverse forms of the indigenous African societies produced a number of basic patterns of change and numerous local versions of each of them. The basic forms included peasant commodity production for international markets, which was probably the most common and important colonial 'development' throughout Africa, as well as directly installed capitalist production in European-owned mines and plantations. In addition there were areas such as the interior regions of French West Africa, northern Uganda and the Northern Territories of the Gold Coast that were deliberately maintained as undeveloped labour reserves to supply migrants for the cash-crop areas and mines; as well as peripheral and apparently backward regions largely inhabited by pastoral peoples.[23] Regional variations meant that more than one and sometimes all of these forms were present within each colony, although one was typically predominant. In the Gold Coast, for example, African commodity production in the coastal and Ashanti regions predominated, although European mining capital was also important and the north-ern part of the colony served as a labour reserve for the south. Kenya and Tanganyika both contained areas of peasant production, settler and plantation estate agriculture, and labour reserves; with estate production dominant in the former and peasant production in the latter.

The initial break in the self-sufficiency of indigenous economies had already occurred in the period of precolonial trade in important coastal regions of West Africa, and was in some instances during the colonial era accomplished peacefully through a combination of the activities of merchant capital and willing African response to market incentives.[24] More commonly, however, the colonial state employed substantial coer-cion to force Africans to enter commodity production or wage labour. The most common forms of state intervention were taxation, forced labour and compulsory crop production. The imposition of head – or hut – taxes on Africans was widely used not only to supply essential revenue for the colonial state, but also to generate an immediate need for money.[25] Where the general pressure of taxation proved inadequate to supply particular needs, the more direct coercion of forced labour for the state and private employers and compulsory production of specific commodities was frequently employed.[26]

Once the initial application of pressure had generated a migrant labour force and peasant production of commodities, metropolitan capi-tal and the colonial state were faced with continuing problems of maintaining and, indeed, increasing the labour supply and the level of commodity production. As Lonsdale points out, 'no official had any faith either in the productivity or reliability of free peasantries' and believed peasants required 'political supervision or the discipline of employ-ment.'[27] All of the colonial powers, therefore, developed elaborate sys-tems of labour control to ensure not only the supply of labour but also that workers would remain at work for stipulated periods, and based in varying degrees on 'legal' coercion by the state. The systematic appli-cation of coercion was particularly marked in French colonies. To supplement 'free' migrant labour, local administrations also provided 'provoked' migrant labour to recruit workers for both large-scale public works and private employers.[28] In addition, under the terms of the *indigénat* (native legal code), local administrators could conscript adult men for ten days of unpaid corvé labour on local roads and public works. British colonies relied on similar administrative pressures on a more sporadic basis, particularly in a colony such as Kenya that required large numbers of migrant labourers for plantations and settler farms, as well as for state infrastructure projects.[29] The control and discipline of African labour was similarly coercive. In French Africa escape from con-scripted labour was, of course, a punishable offence. In British colonies the state regulated relations between workers and employers through local 'Masters and Servants' Ordinances (modelled on 18th-century British laws) that made leaving or quitting work before the end of a contractually stipulated period the punishable crime of 'desertion'.[30] In sum, the recruitment of labour and the regulation of relations of production was increasingly assumed by colonial states, rather than being left to unpredictable 'market' forces or the direct confrontation of labour and capital.

Control over peasant agriculture was initially partial and sporadic. This led to coordinated efforts by merchant capital and the colonial state to control the inputs, quantity, quality and price of agricultural commodities. Direct coercion in the form of compulsory planting of cash crops continued to be used, especially for crops such as cotton where the minimal prices paid provided little economic incentive for African production. In Tanganyika, for example, the state's 'grow more crops' campaigns during the Great Depression of the 1930s 'involved considerable use of force (such as minimum acreages of cotton to be cultivated, or threats of conscription for those who could not pay tax)'.[31] In addition, however, more sophisticated and less directly coercive means of control were developed. Peasant cooperative societies, for example, provided control beneath a facade of African participation.[32]

In French Africa the equivalent institutions were the Sociétés indigènes de prévoyance (Native Provident Societies). By the 1930s they had spread throughout French West and Equatorial Africa. Membership and dues in the SIPs were compulsory for peasant farmers and the local commandants de cercle served as ex-officio presidents. The societies advanced seeds for cash crops to their members at 25 per cent interest; constructed wells and feeder roads, made loans and during the depression of the 1930s assumed responsibility for marketing their members' produce.[33] Peasant commodity production was thus not only placed under state control, but actually brought within the bureaucratic apparatus of the administration. As one contemporary observer put it, 'La société est la chose, au sens le plus absolu du mot, de l'administration'.[34]

Supplementing co-ops and provident societies, or operating in areas where they did not exist, administrations also created official markets or trading centres, particularly in or near local government headquarters. In Tanganyika 'these were designed to concentrate trade, to attract more people to central locations, to accelerate acceptance of East African shillings and cents as the dominant media of exchange, and to enable local officers to interweave tax collection with local market cycles'.[35] The central markets facilitated control over the collection and sale to the mercantile companies of commodities produced in scattered villages. In French West Africa the local commandant controlled the market and ensured that the produce was divided among the trading firms.[36]

The activity of the colonial state in promoting the spread of capitalist social forces and securing the conditions for the accumulation of capital reveals the extent to which articulation was not simply the outcome of impersonal structural forces, but also the result of conscious and deliberate state action. As Warren points out, colonialism 'involved the explicit use of non-democratic political and military force against the colonial population together with the much stronger element of deliberate motivation implied by the assumption of governing responsibility'.[37] While colonial officials were hardly aware of being actively involved in the process of 'articulation', they clearly worried a great deal about stimulating 'trade', both to supply the tax revenue to maintain the state itself and to meet the needs of metropolitan interests. In the process they spurred the penetration of capitalist forms of production, exchange and wage labour that began to transform indigenous societies and articulated them to metropolitan capital and the wider world economy.

This instrumental role of the state also left its mark on the structural apparatus of colonial states. The development of specialist technical departments in agriculture, forestry, veterinary services, public works, transport and communications were all largely shaped to supply the research and extension services, roads and railways, port facilities, post and telecommunications links required to facilitate commodity production and trade. Even in the realm of the social services in health and education supplied on a limited basis to Africans, the conscious motive of state policy was to improve the work capacity and level of skill of African labour.[38] Indeed, the level of state intervention in the political economy of the colonies significantly exceeded that of the state in the metropolitan political economy throughout the colonial period. In the words of the distinguished French colonial official Robert Delavignette,

> although in France the State still allows some degree of economic liberalism, in the colony it has already decreed compulsory labour service, fixed commodity prices and wages, and regulated production. In no colony of Tropical Africa does the state confine itself to police functions: everywhere it tries its hand at fulfilling those of providence.[39]

Indigenous domestic economies were thus subjected to powerful forces of transformation. The outcome of articulation, however, was only a partial restructuring of indigenous social forms, which continued to function throughout rural Africa. Instead of a transitive process, articulation turned out to be contradictory and syncretic, producing a partial transformation, destruction and preservation of African societies contained in a myriad of intermediate and hybrid forms scattered across the countryside.[40]

To a degree the partial nature of the transformation reflected the deliberate actions of the state authorities. Neither the wages of migrant labour nor the prices received for peasant-produced commodities were normally sufficient for the reproduction of the worker/farmer and his family. The resulting reproductive gap was displaced into the continued household production of use values. Articulation produced, in effect, a situation in which African labour and commodities were appropriated below their value through the partial preservation of the precolonial domestic sphere of production.[41] In the Gold Coast, for example, the authorities were aware of the exceptional cheapness of locally produced cocoa and the colonial state actively moved to preserve the traditional land tenure and use system and prevent the further commercialization, alienation and concentration of landholdings; decline of food production; and increasing dependence on cocoa production and unstable world market prices. In effect, the state attempted to block the further capitalist transformation of Gold Coast production.[42]

In much of colonial Africa the colonial authorities also deliberately acted to prevent permanent African residence in cities, especially in family units, and long-term commitment to wage labour. This reflected a pervasive fear in colonial states of the development of a genuine African urban proletariat and the class struggles it threatened to bring with it, and a commitment to the maintenance of the migrant labour system.[43] Such policies also acted against the emergence of capitalist industrial production.

The incompleteness of change also reflected, however, the inefficacy of the pressures of European capital and the colonial state in the face of African *resistance* to wage labour and cash crop production. Cooper stresses 'how difficult it was to get Africans off the land, . . . and hence how little alternative capital had to some form of migratory labour'; and the orneriness of the peasants 'who would produce a little but not a lot, who resisted what extension agents regarded as improved techniques, and who rejected cash crops that the state encouraged'.[44]

At the same time, the reproduction of the syncretic complex of capitalist and precapitalist social forms was inherently unstable not only as a result of the immediate threat of African resistance to the exploitation and coercion it involved, but also because of the long-term structural threat of the contradictions within the process of articulation itself. First, the monetization of material elements of social reproduction and the diversion of labour power to commodity production led in varying rates and degrees to a reproductive 'squeeze' or crisis of indigenous domestic production.[45] Before 1945, the development of peasant commodity production was not accompanied by any significant improvements in productivity. Peasant agriculture remained based on precolonial hoe techniques. The introduction and expansion of commodity production was accomplished through the extension of cultivated area and increase of labour time at the expense of food production and traditional grazing and fallowing practices. Combined with increasing rural population, this produced soil depletion and erosion, declines in relative and absolute productivity (especially of food crops) and the spread of malnutrition and pauperization in the countryside.[46]

Second, articulation also produced various indigenous processes of capitalist development whose conditions of reproduction and accumulation clashed with those of metropolitan capital in a confrontation of interior and exterior dynamics of change.[47] While colonialism reduced and even destroyed indigenous social classes – African merchants in coastal areas of West Africa or the ruling classes of African states that forcibly resisted colonial domination – it also produced particular processes of class formation that undercut or reinforced precolonial patterns of stratification, depending on the specific characteristics of the process of articulation. In many places a class of wealthy farmers began to orient their production to the market, hired wage labour, attempted, in howsoever small way at first, to accumulate land and capital, and even started to use more modern and productive methods and technology. In sum, they began to move towards more fully capitalist forms of production. African merchant capital continued to survive or appeared *de novo* in the interstices of the trading system, sometimes as local agents of and sometimes in competition with metropolitan mercantile capital, with profits in some places invested in agriculture or even petty production.[48]

Metropolitan capital tended to produce its own antithesis within the process of articulation – it both required the spread of African commodity production, wage labour and exchange, and was threatened by the internal dynamic of accumulation, class formation and rural decay they produced.[49] Furthermore, the activity of the colonial state in creating the conditions for accumulation by metropolitan interests created circumstances that posed constant potential threats to political control and social order. To understand how it was possible in these circumstances to maintain an effective system of domination, we must look more closely at the internal structures and processes of the colonial state and its methods of local administration.

The colonial state as an agency of political domination

By the interwar period Britain and France had achieved a relatively stable and orderly system of control over their African colonies. While there were often local incidents of unrest and, less frequently, violent uprisings even more violently repressed, once the apparatus of domination was put in place, it rarely collapsed except in relatively restricted areas and then for only brief periods of time. No serious threat to the continuity of colonial control in the form of a mass anticolonial movement emerged in colonial Africa. Moreover, control was maintained with the most slender administrative and military resources: a relative handful of European administrators and small, meagrely equipped garrisons of African recruits led by a very few European officers.[50] Colonial domination turns out, in fact, to have been an extraordinarily complex social process involving far more than the use of force. Indeed, 'examples of colonial states backing off in the face of African opposition are becoming increasingly apparent'.[51] Equally important, effective administrative control and social order in the countryside was based upon achieving a 'concordat of coexistence' involving the active collaboration of a minority and the tacit acquiescence of the majority of the African population within a process of bargaining in which colonial officials often 'were participants . . . not its arbiters'.[52] Coercion then faded into, although never disappeared from, the background of day-to-day governance.

Throughout the colonial period the immediate agents of domination were the field administrators posted in the territorial subdivisions of a colony. This prefectural organization of local administration was the most common and distinctive feature of colonial bureaucracy and remained the key factor linking colonial states to indigenous social forces. For France, in particular, where prefectural administration achieved its archetypical development, it represented a well-known and practised instrument of control. For Britain, however, it was a state form unknown in the metropole, but explicitly adopted and refined in the encounter with indigenous social forces in the non-white colonies of the Empire, particularly in India after the upheavals of 1857–8, whence it was transferred to the new colonies of Africa at the end of the century.[53]

The prefectural field officers, up to the end of the Second World War, were the principal and sometimes the sole state actors at ground level, exercising a diffuse and wide-ranging responsibility for virtually all state activities – for 'law, order and good government' as the typical British formula put it. Until postwar development programmes brought a growing number of technical officials into rural areas, for most Africans the white administrator *was* the colonial state. As Heussler put it, 'few general practitioners in human history were as powerful and active in the whole sweep of community life'.[54] They constructed and maintained in highly personal fashion the varied local structures of control and collaboration, and this was made possible by the characteristic internal processes and ideology of the state apparatus.

For the prefectural agent the central dilemma was to determine how far he could press central directives and promote commodity production and trade before the extraction of taxes, labour and commodities provoked local disobedience and resistance, thus threatening the order he was also expected to maintain. For the central authorities the issue was the degree to which the field agents' accommodation of local social forces could be tolerated before they became in fact agents of those interests against the centre.[55] In colonial states the contradictions between metropolitan and indigenous social forces shaped the dialectic of centralization and fragmentation along two axes of cleavage. The first was in the relationship between the metropolitan state and the state apparatus in each colony; the second was within the latter in the relationship between the central administration in the colonial capital and its prefectural agents in the field. During most of the modern colonial era in Africa a chronic shortage of financial resources, primitive communications and the diversity of local social forms and ecological conditions generally favoured the discretion of the field over control from the centre.

Comparative analysis of the internal dynamics and practices of colonial states has been hampered, however, by a conventional wisdom that defines British and French colonial administration as essentially different in structure and methods; the former tending towards decentralization and diversity, the latter towards centralization and uniformity. This view is based on certain differences in formal structure and, in particular, the articulated colonial 'doctrines' of each metropole. But, as Kiwanuka noted in 1970, 'few scholars have addressed themselves to the difference between what was said and what actually happened'.[56] When we do probe beneath the surface of formal structure and rhetoric, we find that the experiences and internal processes of French and British colonial administration were not only similar, but also in many instances practically identical.

At the metropole–colony level the British system allowed the governor and senior officials of each colony substantial discretion in formulating and implementing policies that guided the colony's articulation within the larger structures of imperialism. Rigid rules and centralized controls were consciously avoided. Each colony dealt directly with the metropolitan authorities as a discrete entity, and this meant that 'there was no machinery for enforcing a centrally agreed policy'.[57] The oft-repeated dictum 'Trust the man on the spot' expressed a set of pragmatic judgements on the difficulty of controlling the action of distant imperial agents. The Colonial Office generally articulated only vague 'principles' of policy that it expected would be adapted by the local colonial government to fit the varied circumstances of individual colonies. Furthermore, large areas of policy were often not covered by even general metropolitan statements. As Perham pointed out: 'The Colonial Office rarely promulgated general principles about the form for the structure of that part of government which chiefly affected the native population'.[58] The structure and practices of the prefectural apparatus were thus left almost wholly to the discretion of the local officials of each colonial state, with historical precedents modified to fit the particular indigenous social forces they confronted.

Despite a more clearly articulated formal hierarchic structure, including the distinctive additional level above the individual colonies of the colonial Federations of West and Equatorial Africa (AOF and AEF) each headed by a governor-general responsible directly to the minister for the colonies in Paris, French colonial administration was similarly decentralized in practice. Ministers and ministry officials in Paris had only limited influence on policy or direct control over what went on in the colonies. The colonial portfolio had little prestige and ministers changed so frequently, especially during the interwar period, that most ministers had little time or motivation to learn much about colonial affairs or leave their mark on policy. The corps of colonial inspectors was far too small and thinly spread to provide the metropolitan authorities with detailed information about all of the various colonies and did little to enhance their effective control.[59] Metropolitan policy after the structures of the state and political economy were put in place in the colonies, settled into a preoccupation with the promotion of trade and the exploitation of African resources at the lowest cost to France. Authority for supervising and implementing colonial development was delegated to the governors-general of the colonial federations, and this translated into a preoccupation with large-scale infrastructure projects and the expansion of export trade in close collaboration with the dominant mercantile houses.[60] After 1945 the growth of a federal bureaucratic apparatus that operated in the various colonies resulted in a significant degree of centralization, but the governor-general and the federal apparatus for many years exercised little direct control over the colonial state apparatus within each colony. According to Hubert Deschamps, a Governor and later a noted student of French colonialism, 'L'administration locale, sauf contrôle intermittent des ministres, est omnipotente'.[61] As far as such vaunted colonial doctrines as 'assimilation' and 'association' were concerned, he noted that while these were well developed logically, they had only a limited effect and often reflected rather than directed actual colonial practice. 'Les coloniaux,' he concludes, 'ont fait les colonies et la politique coloniale.'[62]

The metropolitan authorities were particularly active at the beginning of colonial rule when critical decisions had to be made to occupy a territory, commit military and financial resources to extend effective control, establish a civil administration, and determine the general lines of economic development. Even then, however, the process also involved

154

the officials on the spot, who often took initiatives the metropole was forced to accept.[63] Thereafter, major metropolitan policy initiatives clustered around the periodic crises of metropolitan capital, such as the major programmes of 'colonial development' set forth during the depressions of the early 1920s and the 1930s, and in the period of postwar reconstruction after 1945. In the first two instances, implementation remained in the hands of the local colonial administrations. The last, however, would bring, as we shall see below, a major shift of power to the metropole and precipitate the final crisis of the colonial state.

One potent metropolitan instrument of control was its superintendence of colonial finances. Both Britain and France operated on the hallowed principle that each colonial state had to be self-sufficient on local sources of revenue. In British Africa any colony unable to meet the costs of its administration passed under the supervision of the Treasury, which inspected its budget and mercilessly pruned expenses until it was satisfied all possible economies had been made. Only then would it authorize a grant-in-aid for any outstanding costs. French Africa was held on a similarly tight rein under a 1900 law that mandated the 'financial autonomy' of the colonies. In addition, colonies had to contribute from their revenue to the costs of the military, communications and educational services provided by the metropolitan state. This policy of fiscal autonomy ensured that without further supervision each colonial government had a continuing interest in developing a level of commodity production and trade at least sufficient to provide a tax base to meet the costs of its own reproduction. Also, metropolitan grants to the colonies for capital investments in infrastructure and development were meagre and colonial governments had to rely on interest-bearing loans raised from metropolitan finance capital on the London or Paris money markets, thus adding growing debt-servicing charges to their other financial burdens.[64]

Metropolitan meanness, however, had several further consequences that both constrained the level of economic activity in the colonies and limited metropolitan control. First, it led to revenue hunger on the part of colonial governments expressed in efforts to tax or impose fees on every possible commodity or transaction, and a tendency to accumulate budgetary surpluses wherever possible as a reserve against unforeseen financial exigencies. This acted both as a disincentive to economic activity and kept state activities constantly restricted and underfinanced.[65] Second, and even more important, it tied colonial states to indigenous production and trade as the source of their own fiscal reproduction, and gave them a vested interest in retaining internally as much of the local surplus product as possible, rather than having it transferred to the metropole as trading profits. This was reflected in the degree to which state revenues rested on direct taxes of the African population, especially various forms of hut and head (poll) taxes, or indirect duties on imports and exports, also paid largely by African producers and consumers.[66] As a result, colonial states were directly involved in the contradictions between metropolitan and indigenous accumulation, and in a way that encouraged an ambivalent relationship with the latter.

The one area in which the metropolitan authorities did gain an increasing, albeit indirect control over their colonial agents was in the recruitment, training and posting of individual officials. The essential corollary of the dictum 'Trust the man on the spot' was that he had to be the 'right man' who could be trusted to act in ways acceptable to the central authorities where they could not exercise effective direct control over him. Up to the end of the 19th century, however, the recruitment process was a haphazard affair, with governors commonly hiring officials as they were needed. These early officials were the human detritus of European imperialism with diverse and often unsavoury backgrounds, and they gained a reputation for incompetence, unreliability, insubordination and brutality. In 1879, for example, the Governor of Senegal noted that the colony 'drew persons who if not compromised at home were at least incapable of earning a livelihood in it', and that the men attracted to colonial administration were 'the lost children of the mother country'; while as late as 1910 the Governor of Kenya complained that 'the time is past when we should recruit our staff from so-called pioneers and cowpunchers'.[67]

Between 1890 and 1914 metropolitan authorities in both Britain and France ended the local recruitment of officials, organized them into a formal administrative service similar to the elite cadres of the metropolitan bureaucracy, and assumed firm control over the recruitment and training of administrators to ensure their competence and reliability. By the interwar years the colonial administrations of both countries were preponderantly drawn from the upper middle class of the metropole, especially from the administrative and professional families rather than from among the commercial and industrial bourgeoisie.[68] They thus shared a common background of experience and ideas with their counterparts in the metropole and this gave the latter a degree of 'remote control' over their actions, reinforced by metropolitan control over promotions to higher-level positions.

Within each colony a similar tendency towards decentralization prevailed in the relations between the centre of the colonial state and its prefectural agents in the field. While the governor and his senior officials in the capital of a colony could establish the basic policies, the interpretation and implementation of policy remained in the hands of the district commissioners and commandants de cercles. As one district commissioner in Kenya put it, the communications from the centre

'were guidelines and suggestions, more than definite instructions'.[69]
The isolation of bush administrators from immediate contact with their
superiors; primitive internal communications that improved only slowly
due to the financial penury of the state; their broad responsibility for
general administrative, police, judicial and tax functions; and the general shortage of specialist and technical officers, all combined to give
them an exceptionally high degree of discretion over the whole range of
government activities and the autonomy to take the initiative in other
areas as well. This situation was broadly accepted by the central authorities. The British district commissioner, known in the popular epithet
as 'the king in his castle', thus found his counterpart in the French commandant, 'le roi de la brousse'. The broad discretion they enjoyed permitted, indeed encouraged, the exercise of a high degree of personalism,
and this was raised to the level of a principle of administration by some
officials. Joost Van Vollenhoven, the celebrated Governor-General of
French West Africa, solemnly declared that '*only one's presence, personal
contact counts*. The circular is zero'; while Robert Delavignette told
the students at the Ecole Coloniale that 'there is an inner principle proper to territorial colonial administration: the personal authority of the
administrator and, in the final analysis, his personal character expressed
in the exercise of authority'.[70]

Bush administrators were able to administer their districts in ways
that reflected the idiosyncrasies of personal style. The fiercely defended
independence and frequent eccentricity of bush administrators is a common element of the history and folklore of colonialism in Africa. Field
officers had substantial opportunity to modify or ignore policies from the
centre they disliked. They often acted on their own and then either failed
to inform the centre or told the higher authorities what they wanted to
hear. In Northern Nigeria 'the Resident Bornu candidly advised a junior
to learn what things to keep to himself and what to pass on'.[71] Discretion was thus protected by a claim to a unique understanding of local
conditions and effective control over the information passed up official
channels. As a result, the field officers not only shaped the percep-
tion of local conditions by the higher authorities, but also indirectly
influenced central policy by defining the available range of policy
options.[72]

The discretion of field administrators, however, was neither unlimited
nor did it involve governance by mere whim or caprice. Bush administration was a serious, complex and sometimes dangerous business that
was the central pillar on which the whole colonial edifice rested. While
the prefectural agents of the state were left free to work out the particular
local adjustment to the dominant structures of production and political control, they had little power to question or modify those structures. They could adapt or develop methods to extract African labour,

encourage commodity production and collect taxes, but they could not question the basic commitment of the state to do these things. Moreover, while the central authorities could not control the day-to-day activity of field administrators, the flow of labour, commodities and taxes from a district provided an index of effectiveness and they could sanction officers who failed to supply them in the required amounts. At the same time, however, while the field administrators had broad coercive powers to punish African refusal to supply labour, commodities and taxes, or even for 'not showing proper respect', this coercion could not be exercise through the constant resort to overt force. The object of this force was to generate submission and obedience, not continuing resistance on the part of the African populace, and its constant application represented the very negation of state authority and the failure of prefectural control. Given the limited means of force immediately available to each field officer, continual reliance upon it showed diminishing returns, since it tended to require outside assistance and invited central intervention. The central authorities judged the performance of field officers not only on the basis of their success in providing labour, commodities and taxes, but also, as one British governor put it, by 'the ability they have displayed in procuring the contentment and satisfaction [of] their districts'.[73]

Field administrators thus reached the limits of their discretion when they either failed to supply what was required by capital and the central authorities; or when in doing so they relied too heavily on force and provoked African resistance. The contradiction between tasks of accumulation and control was reproduced in the role of each district commissioner or commandant de cercle. The internal tension of bush administration was to find the way to act as the agent of a coercive system of exploitation and at the same time gain African compliance. Coercive power had to be transformed into authority that commanded obedience to orders with the force of 'law', and applied force in the controlled and predictable form of the 'punishment' of individual offenders rather than in armed assaults against collective resistance. It was precisely the decentralized discretion of the field administrators that permitted them the flexibility to work out local arrangements balancing the mobilization and exploitation of production and labour with effective political control in a stable 'concordat of coexistence'. This very real degree of autonomy enabled them to construct the *apparent autonomy* of the colonial state not simply as a disinterested arbiter among conflicting interests, but even as a benevolent guide and protector, rather than just being the agent of metropolitan interests. Colonial domination was thus disciplined by an ultimate dependence on local consent and this required a degree of responsiveness to indigenous interests and grievances. It was 'the paradox of rule', Lonsdale notes, 'that power could not be exercised without giving some of it away.'[74] The contradictions on which it rested were reflected in the preoccupation of administrators with achieving, on the one hand, an apparently unchallenged and absolute control over the African population, and on the other, their tacit acceptance of a complex political substratum of bargaining and accommodation.

To accomplish their contradictory tasks administrators worked at a number of levels. First, they staked a claim to ideological terrain that asserted both the authority and the disinterested benevolence of the colonial state they personified. This effort to achieve a degree of ideological hegemony rested on the ideological forms of authoritarian paternalism. Heussler noted of British administrators that 'year in and year out they lived the lives of little kings in an epoch when their home-based brothers had exchanged kingship for bourgeois democracy'.[75] Even more vividly Hubert Deschamps, not only an administrator but an active socialist, wrote:

> We leave France to become kings. And soon because there will be revolutions, we shall be the only kings on earth. And not do-nothing kings either, but artists at our job, enlightened despots organizing our kingdoms according to maturely reflected plans.[76]

Both French and British administrators readily saw themselves as a ruling class uniquely fitted to rule, on behalf of Africans too naive and backward to rule themselves. The 'consent' they demanded from Africans was obedience to a ruling class of demonstrated superior will and capacity, but one that magnanimously governed on behalf of a disinterested understanding of the commonweal and a paternal regard for the wellbeing of its subjects. In return for the deferential loyalty and obedience of the ruled, the ruler had the high-minded duty of promoting their mental and spiritual wellbeing.[77] This, or something similar, was the bush version of the 'dual-mandate' or 'mission civilatrice' proclaimed by colonial pundits and apologists. Demands for commodity production, wage labour for metropolitan enterprise or labour on public-works projects could then be depicted as being carried out for the benefit of Africans themselves to help them achieve 'civilization', 'progress' or, as it later came to be styled, 'development'.

The extent to which Africans willingly accepted the ideological claims of the colonial ruling cadres or submitted out of fear, resignation or rational calculation of possible rewards, is difficult to determine. It is clear, nevertheless, that the demands of the rulers for obedience also contained a promise of African participation in the benefits of a controlled process of change towards a new and superior social order on European forms. The ideological exhortation of Africans was linked directly to a material element consisting of their participation in the rewards of education, jobs, public works and an increased surplus product.

The appeal to African self-interest, based on the promise that obedience would pay and the threat that disobedience would not, provided the material grounds for local accommodation and effective control.

Second, field administrators actively sought a class of collaborators in indigenous society. They wanted, in the words of Lord Lugard, 'a class who in a crisis can be relied on to stand by us and whose interests are wholly identified with ours'.[78] The primary beneficiaries of the promise of reward for cooperation were a minority who both collaborated in the power of the conquerors and accumulated new forms of wealth under their aegis. The small number of white prefects and the large areas and often widely dispersed population under their charge made the recruitment of a cadre of indigenous functionaries imperative for the maintenance of a continuous colonial presence in every corner of the countryside. The key elements of this cadre of collaborators were the chiefs or headmen in every village and, more important, the chiefs placed in charge of the administrative subdivisions of the districts or *cercles*. French West Africa, for example, contained more than 47,000 village chiefs and some 2,206 *chefs de canton* directly responsible to the commandants.[79]

Understanding of the development of these African cadres and of the process of collaboration more generally is obscured, however, by a 'myth of indirect rule' that has stressed the fundamental difference of British and French administrative methods in the bush. According to this view, the French employed direct administration (*administration directe*) through a cadre of administrative chiefs directly appointed and controlled by the commandants, while the British administrators acted largely as advisers ruling 'indirectly' through the largely preserved African 'native authorities'. A full discussion of the mythology of this formulation is beyond the scope of this chapter, but we can note briefly that it is very doubtful whether indirect rule actually worked this way even in Northern Nigeria, which is usually taken as the paradigmatic example. Lugard, who established the Northern Nigeria administration and created the concept of indirect rule, 'made the point as strongly as he could that all chiefs, even the Sultan of Sokoto, were henceforth agents of the government . . . and that the authority of the local residents was above theirs. Legally this was vassalage and not a treaty relationship'.[80] Chiefs in British Africa were free to act only in ways the British approved, were ordered to carry out policies whether they liked them or not, and were deposed and replaced with more pliant men when they were found incompetent, corrupt or insubordinate.[81] Conversely, while the French created their chiefs as direct subordinates of the field administration, they took increasing pains to recruit them from the chiefly families of the precolonial society; as Delavignette noted, 'we are well aware that it is essential to preserve the native character of the canton chief and to make use of the traditional feudal spirit which still survives in him; on the other hand, the very fact of colonization forces us to shape him to our administrative outlook'.[82]

The central underlying issue is the process of collaboration essential to the extension or stabilization of colonial control. Where willing collaborators could not be found within indigenous precolonial structures they were created, and the actual practice in the field was formulated by the administrative officers on the spot in response to local exigencies. The presence or absence of centralized precolonial state forms, or whether these were adapted or destroyed by the colonial administration, do not seem to be the factors that determined the development of a group of strong and effective collaborators. The key variable, rather, appears to be the degree to which the process of class formation, notably the emergence of an indigenous class of accumulators of wealth within the narrow opportunities provided by the colonial political economy, overlapped with the indigenous levels of the political control apparatus. This class was far broader than the chiefs and headmen. It comprised not only wealthy peasants who gained an increasingly large proportion of the revenues from cash crops and invested savings in expanding their holdings and output, and African traders and merchants who found profitable if limited niches within the trading system; but also school teachers, artisans and clerks who found employment in private firms and the expanding bureaucratic apparatus of the state and at salaries often substantially higher than the miserable wages paid to the mass of unskilled labourers.[83] All these elements benefited in some degree from the colonial political and economic presence and comprised a potential base of support for it.

The different elements of this emerging class were generally encouraged by local administrators. It contained the 'progressive' Africans who willingly pursued the development of commodity production, trade and wage labour without administrative pressure. Administrators often deliberately sought to bring the 'progressive' elements into more direct collaboration by recruiting them to subordinate state positions, especially those requiring a degree of Western education, or into largely coopted local institutions such as the 'councils of notables' created in the *cercles* of AOF or the 'local native councils' in the districts of Kenya.[84] At the same time, they encouraged chiefs and headmen, in particular, to take the lead in opportunities for accumulation through production and trade, both as an example to others, and to provide legitimate material rewards to supplement their generally meagre official salaries and inhibit their abuse of their authority through direct exactions from the peasantry. This brought the prefects directly into the process of class formation. Their discretion and the resources at their disposal gave them sources of patronage to encourage and reward the members of the African proto-bourgeoisie. Access to Western education, especially the post-primary education that was the key to higher salaried jobs, was one of the most important, and in French and British Africa this was deliberately directed towards the sons of chiefs and other notables. Institutions such as the SIPs and co-ops could be employed to provide loans and advances to wealthy 'progressive' farmers who were often local chiefs and other notables as well; while the local native councils in Kenya provided lucrative contracts for small local public works.[85] All of this meant that the administrators mediated access to many of the sources of accumulation and the state increasingly became the necessary focus of the emerging proto-capitalist class.[86]

The patronage and other local resources controlled by local administrators could also to some extent be spread more widely among the peasantry. At one level, the wealth accumulated by the chiefs and other local notables enabled them to construct wide networks of patron-client relations. More directly, the discretion of local administrative officers enabled them selectively to administer or modify the policies and apparatus of the state in ways that both softened its most coercive features and distributed some small material rewards. This included disciplining the exploitation of Africans by external capital in such a way that the administrator's role as benevolent protector was affirmed.[87] Hearing and adjudicating local disputes was another crucial function of the administrators' public role. In so far as Africans came before them as supplicants and petitioners appealing for justice, their legitimate authority and paternal domination was tacitly affirmed.

Third, and finally, the discretion of field administrators focused African political and economic aspirations and grievances on the district commissioner or *commandant* as the source of authority, principal decision-maker and broker of access to benefits and new forms of wealth. Greater centralization would have forced local administrators to clear their actions with higher authority or subjected them to more detailed directives from the centre. African demands and opposition, in turn, would have quickly been communicated to the very centre of the state. Instead, from the local administrator's discretion and the general decentralization of the prefectural apparatus emerged the colonial version of 'divide and rule': *African political and social forces were fragmented, isolated and contained within the framework of local administrative units, which both protected institutions of the colonial state from constant involvement in diverse local issues and conflicts, and inhibited the coalescence of African opposition and resistance into a colony-wide challenge to the colonial order.* Administrators worked to prevent the growth of horizontal linkages that could generate African opposition across the main axes of structural cleavage in a colony. The reliance on chiefs was tied to the principle of 'tribe' as the basis for administrative subdivisions and to encouraging precolonial ethnic groupings as the basis of local identity. A principal objective of 'indirect rule', in fact, was to prevent the mobilization of the peasantry within the context of a trans-ethnic anticolonial struggle.[88] In Senegal, 'the patron–client politics fostered under the wings of the colonial state helped to manage the adaptation to the peanut market and keep political tensions divided and, in large part, contained within villages and compounds'; while in Tanganyika administrators operated on a 'principle of optimal fragmentation of various local levels' since 'cross-district or cross-ethnic communication might ignite combinations of people, groups and resources which could become alternatives to official indirect rule politics'.[89]

Managing this containment on a day-to-day basis taxed all of the administrators' political skills. They saw themselves involved in a game of wits with the African population in which their authority was constantly challenged and their strength and shrewdness tested. The conventional wisdom of bush administration provided a series of proverbs or maxims to guide the field officer in the various situations he was likely to encounter.[90] At the same time, the authority of the state had always to appear unchallenged, even as administrators played the 'game' of local politics. Neither the state nor any individual officer could openly admit to error or failure, even in reversing previous policy. No action could be taken that might appear to be a concession forced by African demands or resistance; all policy had to appear to be the result of the autonomous will and benevolent regard of the state and its local agent. Administrators thus constantly sought the combination of threat and force, exhortation and paternal tutelage, patronage and material benefits that would maintain a stable local order. In the process they learned the limits of their authority. From Nigeria in 1909 and Kenya in the 1950s two officers stated the same maxims:

> The first rule was never give an order unless you could enforce it . . .
> The second rule was never give an order that was likely to be disobeyed.[91]

Conclusion: centralization, development and the decline of the colonial state

The creation and maintenance of a stable mode of domination in the countryside that balanced the imperatives of accumulation and control, metropolitan and indigenous interests, exploitation and material rewards, coercion and collaboration was the principal achievement of the prefectural apparatus of the colonial state. A system based so heavily, however, on the personal authority and skill of individual officers was inevitably beset with considerable local and temporal variation in the quality of domination achieved. On the whole, although the evidence is far from conclusive, the British were probably more successful at it than the French, not because they were more able, but because they were given more time in which to understand local conditions and create the social relations and practices of an effective modus vivendi. British officers generally spent their career in a single colony and regular tours of two to three years in a single district, while their French counterparts were deliberately rotated frequently not only from *cercle* to *cercle*, but from colony to colony. The time French administrators spent in a single colony actually fell during the interwar years to 5.4 years from the average of seven years in the 1880–1919 period.[92] Even though they were increasingly carefully recruited and better trained, French commandants, according to some observers, became less knowledgeable about their cercles and may have been less effective as time passed.[93] In contrast, the cadres of field administrators in British colonies developed a strong sense of cohesiveness and group solidarity that helped protect their discretion against the central authorities, facilitated communication and probably enhanced their effectiveness.

What the prefects achieved, however, was a flexible method of 'static adjustment' reproducing the local political and economic structures of a very partial capitalist transformation, and marked by an increasing tendency towards *immobilisme* during the interwar years. Lord Hailey, for example, noted of Tanganyika that 'the progress of the territory as far as native affairs are concerned seems to have come to a standstill. Improvements continue to be made in the machinery, but as a whole, the machine does not move forward'; while Cohen has more recently observed that French administrators 'in the inter-war period . . . maintained a form of stability that easily led to stagnation'.[94] This growing stagnation reflected the inability of the system of domination to deal with African social forces when they could not be contained at the local level and directly confronted major structural issues; and the prefects' growing fear of further change as a threat to order and control. Colonial prefectural administrations found it exceptionally difficult to deal with change except through incremental modifications of their existing practices, and this gave considerations of short-run expediency precedence over vague long-term objectives. From an agency of capitalist transformation in the countryside, the prefectural apparatus became an increasing restraint on further change. As Cooper points out, 'the limited extent of primitive accumulation, the lack of generalized wage labour, and the continuation of extensive non-market production may not have been mere aspects of a profit maximizing mechanism for a somewhat vaguely defined capitalist system, but important constraints on the dynamism of capitalism.'[95]

The fabric of colonial domination required constant attention and repair, as successive equilibria were disrupted by deepening contradictions that undermined the autonomy and discretion that enabled the prefects to balance the conflicting demands of accumulation and political order. Colonial officials, especially the prefects in the field, found themselves subject to social forces over which they exercised only limited control and to which they could respond with only ad hoc improvization.

The growing threats to the stability of colonial domination emerged, first, within the colonies themselves from the process of collaboration and indigenous class formation. The chiefs, upon whom great hopes were placed, especially in West Africa, for their development as a viable dominant class controlling land, labour and production, often became sources of disruption rather than agents of control. They showed constant tendencies to extort money from the populace, especially where they were responsible for collecting tax and received a cut of the proceeds as part of their rewards; to accumulate land and other property by means fair or foul; and to become the focus of intense local political struggles. Increasingly seen by the populace as creatures of the state, the chiefs compromised its authority as they undermined their own position.[96] A more direct challenge came from other elements in the emergent African bourgeoisie. While they benefited from their association with the colonial authorities, the very presence of the colonial state and metropolitan capital blocked their further development as a class. Collaboration and opposition arose from within the same emerging class. Administrators were increasingly aware of the potential threat they posed, and the 'progressive' Africans they had sought to encourage were increasingly seen as 'irresponsible agitators' inciting the masses to opposition.

The basis for mass opposition emerged from the crises of the capitalist world system which began to transform the linkages of colony and metropole. Already during the Depression of the 1930s and the Second World War there was increasing intervention by colonial administrations to increase commodity production and attempts by both Britain and France to tie colonial output and trade more directly to metropolitan interests.[97] After 1945, however, such efforts became continuous, systematic and focused on the needs of metropolitan capitalism in an era of post-war recovery and expansion. This is what Low and Lonsdale have aptly called the 'second colonial occupation'[98] – a massive expansion of state intervention and pressure on indigenous African societies to accelerate the penetration and development of capitalist social forces. As Cooper points out: 'This time, the transformation that took place did not entail the imposition of capitalist work discipline – which itself had not often gone very far – but large-scale investment in raw materials production and a "fundamental upheaval in technology, organization of labour and relations of production", in short a widespread shift toward the production of relative surplus value.'[99] It involved for both Britain and France the commitment of unprecedented amounts of metropolitan public capital for colonial development through the Colonial Development and Welfare Acts, the Colonial Development Corporation and the Fonds d'investissement et du développement economique et social des territoires d'Outre Mer (FIDES).[100] As earlier practices of colonial fiscal self-sufficiency were abandoned, grants were accompanied by increasingly centralized metropolitan planning and direction.

The era of colonial development brought with it not only a massive expansion of the scale and complexity of the bureaucratic apparatus of the colonial state, but also a profound shift in the internal centres of state power. Throughout French and British Africa new institutions and policies managed the development effort: rural development programmes, commodity marketing boards, investment incentive schemes for metropolitan and international industrial capital, wage and labour stabilization policies, and expanded investment in social and economic infrastructure.[101] The colonial state was increasingly dominated by its role as an instrument of metropolitan accumulation. The technical and specialist agencies of the state proliferated rapidly and increasingly assumed control of activities previously largely carried out, if at all, by the prefectural apparatus. Among the peasantry 'the agricultural extension agent replaced the district officer as the embodiment of colonial authoritarianism'; while elsewhere 'most strikingly in British Africa, labour departments began to move towards decasualizing and stabilizing labour forces in key sectors', often in the face of opposition from rural administrators and established employers.[102]

As the power of the specialist agencies and central governments grew, the discretion of the field administrators and their ability to adapt policy and to mobilize resources for local accommodation and collaboration declined, and they were increasingly confined to their primary control functions. As their reports show, the prefects became obsessed with the techniques of control and employed coercive sanctions with increasing frequency and vigour.[103]

The accelerated development of capitalist commodity and production relations promoted by the specialized state agencies of development and economic management, and the increasing repressiveness of the prefectural apparatus, served not only to stimulate rising levels of conflict and class struggle – between metropolitan interests and African peasants, proletarians and the emergent bourgeois, and among the developing indigenous classes themselves – but also to focus these conflicts directly on the state.[104] As post-war development brought rising conflict and official coercion in response, the political and ideological fabric of domination began to crumble. The containment of African political forces at local administrative levels disappeared as they coalesced on a colony-wide basis in 'nationalist' organizations that brought the struggle to the very centre of the colonial state.

It is from this struggle that the logic of decolonization emerged. By the 1950s the colonial state itself, or more precisely, its agencies of political control centred on the prefectural apparatus, had become the central focus of conflict, and proved increasingly incapable of maintaining or restoring the earlier patterns of domination and collaboration. Indeed, rather than instruments of order and control, they became a source of disruption and conflict. In effect, a contradiction emerged between the further advance of capitalist development, both metropolitan and indigenous, and a colonial domination threatened and undermined by it.[105] Colonialism, in the paternalistic authoritarianism of the prefects and the intensely personal vested interests in the relationships they established with Africans in the countryside, was increasingly a problem rather than a solution for metropolitan interests. Accommodation of the emergent indigenous bourgeoisie leading the nationalist organizations was impossible without destroying the prefects' tenaciously guarded positions.

The political focus of decolonization was a restructuring of the state forms of domination and collaboration. The repression of African nationalism was replaced by attempts to fine a new *modus vivendi* at the highest levels of the local state. For metropolitan capital and state authorities it was apparent that it was less important who controlled the state in a colony, than whether they were capable of providing the basic conditions of order and stability conducive to expansion and accumulation. Once the decision to withdraw from direct political control was taken, metropolitan states left the colonies as soon as they could identify and negotiate an arrangement with an indigenous class that appeared capable of maintaining stable political and economic control of the territory.[106] Metropolitan and indigenous capital shared a common interest in the displacement of the constricting presence of the colonial control apparatus. Decolonization, as Delavignette put it, 'elle a dictée par l'argent'.[107]

Notes

1. I would like to thank the Department of Political Studies, the School of Graduate Studies and the Advisory Research Committee of Queen's University, Kingston, Ontario, for grants that made the research for this paper possible, and Guy Beaulieu for his invaluable assistance in compiling and indexing the material on which it is based. Special thanks are also due to John Lonsdale and Martin Klein for their very helpful criticism and suggestions on the first draft of this paper. This is a revised version of a paper presented to the First International Conference on the

167

Comparative, Historical and Critical Analysis of Bureaucracy, Gottlieb Duttweiler Institut, Zurich, Switzerland, 4–8 October 1982.

2. Mahmoud Mamdani, *Politics and Class Formation in Uganda* (London, 1976), pp. 142–3.

3. Geoffrey Kay, *The Political Economy of Colonialism in Ghana* (London, 1972), p. 9.

4. For a fuller exposition of the 'historical derivationist' approach to the theory of the state which is the basis of the present analysis of the colonial state see B.J. Berman, 'Class struggle and the origins of the relative autonomy of the capitalist state' (paper presented to the Annual Meeting of the American Political Science Association, New York, September 1981); Bob Jessop, 'Recent theories of the capitalist state', *Cambridge Journal of Economics* 1(4) (1977), John Holloway & Sol Picciotto, 'Capital, crisis and the state', *Capital and Class* 2 (1977) and Holloway & Picciotto (eds), *State and Capital: A Marxist Debate* (London, 1978), especially the introduction by the editors and the essay by Joachim Hirsch; Philip Corrigan *et al.*, 'The state as a relation of production' in Corrigan (ed.), *Capitalism, State Formation and Marxist Theory* (London, 1980). This general approach differs from the so-called 'capital logic' theory of the state which is an approach based on the 'pure' capitalist mode of production, from which it derives the *logical* necessity of the state as an 'ideal collective capitalist' and reduces history to an effect of the logical self-realization of capital. (Jessop, 'Recent theories' p. 364; Berman, 'Class struggle', pp. 12–15.)

5. Ellen Meiksins Wood, 'The separation of the economic and the political in capitalism', *New Left Review* 127 (May–June 1981), pp. 77, 78.

6. Eugeny Pashukanis, *Law and Marxism: A General Theory* (London, 1978; first pub. 1923), p. 139. More recently Nicos Poulantzas has pointed out that, 'What is involved here is not a real externality, such as would exist if the state intervened in the economy only from the outside. The separation is nothing other than the capitalist form of the presence of the political in the constitution and reproduction of the relations of production' (*State, Power, Socialism*, (London, 1978) pp. 18–19).

7. James O'Connor, *The Fiscal Crisis of the State* (New York, 1973), p. 6. This accounts for the often ambivalent and tense relations between businessmen and state officials, the continual necessity for sectors of capital to organize politically and attempt to maintain direct access to and influence over the state authorities, and the inevitable clashes between them which help to sustain, often, the apparent autonomy and neutrality of the state.

8. Corrigan *et al.*, 'The state as a relation of production', pp. 12, 19.

9. John Holloway, 'State as class practice', in P. Zaremka (ed.), *Research in Political Economy*, Vol. 3 (1980), p. 17.

10. Corrigan *et al.*, 'The state', p. 12.

11. Erik Olin Wright, *Class, Crisis and the State* (London, 1978) pp. 212–13.

12. The implicit criticism of 'bureaucratic and organization theory' contained in the perspective employed here is of the narrow focus and ahistorical character of its conceptual apparatus. Bourgeois organizational analysis, despite some notable exceptions, is relatively preoccupied with the analysis of 'through-puts', especially those which constitute, from the perspective of the higher authorities, 'obstacles' to 'efficient' operation, of organizations whose historical origins and development, basic structure and position within larger economic and political structures are ignored or taken as givens (see P. Goldman, 'Sociologists and the study of bureaucracy: a critique of ideology and practice', *The Insurgent Sociologist* 8(1), Winter 1978). However, as I hope this chapter suggests, when the state bureaucracy is viewed within the wider social context in which it operates and in relation to the social forces that shape it and are, in turn, shaped by it, bureaucratic analysis takes on a more compelling significance.

13. And, in fact, later additions to the state in the form of 'democratic' legislatures and

executives mostly disappeared in much of Africa within the first decade after independence, leaving the state bureaucratic apparatus as the enduring political legacy of colonialism. This, if nothing else, lends a continuing contemporary relevance to the study of the colonial state.

14. For a fuller exposition of the concept of articulation and the controversy surrounding it see Aidan Foster-Carter, 'The modes of production controversy', *New Left Review* 107 (1978); and Chapter 8, above.

15. The generalizations presented here are not intended to apply to the white-dominated societies of Southern Rhodesia and South Africa which are properly viewed as settler states, a related but quite distinct order of experience.

16. For an outstanding synthesis of contemporary research and analysis of the two phases of the scramble see J.M. Lonsdale, 'Conclusion: The European scramble and conquest in Africa history', in Roland Oliver (ed.), *Cambridge History of Africa*, Vol. 6 (Cambridge, 1985).

17. From a now voluminous literature see, for example, Jean Suret-Canale, *Afrique noire*, Vol. II, *L'ere coloniale* and Vol. III, *De la decolonisation à l'indépendance* (Paris, 1964 and 1972); E.A. Brett, *Colonialism and Underdevelopment in East Africa* (New York, 1973); A.G. Hopkins, *An Economic History of West Africa* (London, 1973); R. Howard, *Colonialism and Underdevelopment in Ghana* (London, 1978); R. van Zwanenberg with A. King, *An Economic History of Kenya and Uganda* (London, 1975); S. Amin & C. Coquery-Vidrovitch, *Histoire économique du Congo 1880–1968* (Dakar, 1970); R. Wolff, *The Economics of Colonialism: Britain and Kenya, 1870–1930* (New Haven, Conn. 1974); and J. Iliffe, *A Modern History of Tanganyika* (Cambridge, 1979).

18. All French colonies, for example, absorbed only 4 per cent of total metropolitan foreign investment in 1914, and the bulk of this went to the colonies in North Africa. The proportion of investment going to the colonies did not increase substantially until the 1930s (C. Coquery-Vidrovitch, 'De l'impérialisme ancien a l'impérialisme moderne: l'avatar coloniale', in A. Abdel-Malek (ed.), *Sociologie de l'impérialisme* (Paris, 1971), p. 106.

19. Hopkins, *An Economic History*, pp. 191–2. The bulk of private investment was concentrated in banking and commerce. Before 1945 the minute investment in industry, less than 10 per cènt of the total in French colonies, was devoted largely to essential first-stage processing of primary commodities to ready them for export, such as cotton ginneries. Broader industrialization was actively opposed by metropolitan interests fearful of the loss of local colonial markets and competition at home from low-wage production in the colonies, and by colonial authorities fearful of the creation of a permanent proletariat. Nevertheless, in a few colonies such as Kenya with larger European settler and other immigrant communities, industrial investment by local and metropolitan firms to supply the internal market did begin to appear in the interwar period. For contrasting accounts of the constraints on, and the development of, local industry see E.A. Brett, *Colonialism and Underdevelopment*, Ch. 9, and Nicola Swainson, *The Development of Corporate Capitalism in Kenya, 1978–1977* (London, 1980), Chs 1 and 2.

20. In British colonies such as Nigeria and the Gold Coast trade was dominated by a Unilever subsidiary, the United Africa Company, the Bank of British West Africa, and the Elder, Dempster Shipping Line; while in French West Africa the Banque de l'Afrique Occidentale dominated finance and the 'big three' trading companies, including again parts of the UAC, controlled two-thirds to three-quarters of overseas trade (see Suret-Canale, *Afrique Noire*, II, pp. 205–36; Hopkins, *Economic History*, Ch. 6; and Howard, *Colonialism and Underdevelopment*, Ch. 4).

21. The entry of the companies seeking monopoly concessions depended on a balance of political pressures in the metropoles. The concession seekers won access to French Equatorial Africa, but were blocked in French West Africa by the opposition of

already entrenched merchant capital. White settlers established themselves in Kenya and Tanganyika through strong pressures on initially reluctant and even hostile colonial officials. (I. Wallerstein, 'The three stages of African involvement in the world economy', in P. Gutkind & I. Wallerstein (eds), *The Political Economy of Contemporary Africa* (Beverly Hills, 1976) pp. 41-4.)

22. The profits of the large trading companies in French West Africa, for example, averaged over 20 per cent per annum. Even in the depths of the Depression of the 1930s the CFAO managed to pay dividends, while in more 'normal' years its profits rarely fell below 25 per cent (Sheldon Gellar, 'Structural changes and colonial dependency: Senegal 1885-1945', *Sage Research Papers in the Social Sciences*, Studies in Comparative Modernization Series, no. 5; Beverly Hills, 1976. p. 65).

23. For a similar analysis see Lionel Cliffe, 'Rural class formation in East Africa', *Journal of Peasant Studies* (Jan. 1977); and 'Rural political economy of Africa' in P.C.W. Gutkind and I. Wallerstein (eds), *The Political Economy of Contemporary Africa* (Beverly Hills, 1976).

24. In Tanganyika and Kenya the German and British administrations encouraged East Asian merchants to spread their activities into up-country areas where local Africans could develop a taste for cheap imported manufactures and become familiar with money. In the Gold Coast the development of the colony into the world's largest producer of cocoa was based on the initiative of African farmers while the colonial government was more concerned with servicing the needs of British mining capital. (Andrew Coulson, *Tanzania: A Political Economy*, Oxford, 1982, pp. 39-40, 60-61; Kay: *Political Economy of Colonialism*, Introduction.)

25. The rapidity of the development of a cash nexus is indicated in the experience of the Songea region of Tanganyika. When the German administration first imposed a hut tax of 3 rupees in 1899 it collected only 1,641 rupees in cash, the equivalent of 706 in kind and 21,209 in labour service from 7,000 men. By 1903 the tax collection returned 38,045 rupees in cash (Coulson, *Tanzania*, p. 35).

26. Forced labour for public and private projects was introduced throughout French Africa. In the form of compulsory production of cash crops it was employed to introduce groundnuts in Upper Volta and cotton in the Ivory Coast, and as a form of taxation in the *champs du commandant* that were widespread in both AOF and AEF. (Suret-Canale, *Afrique noire*, II, pp. 288-98.)

27. Lonsdale, 'Conclusion: the European scramble'. This attitude among administrators reflected, as Frederick Cooper notes, 'the deeply held belief in late nineteenth century ideology that work had to be directed from above and working classes vigilantly watched.' Cooper, 'Africa and the world economy', *African Studies Review* 24(2/3) (1981), p. 32.

28. Robert Delavignette, *Freedom and Authority in French West Africa* (London, 1950), p. 113. The use of forced labour for private companies was particularly marked in the concessionary economies of French Equatorial Africa. During the 1920s as many as 40 per cent of the male population between 20-40 years old was recruited for work in the forestry and mining consessions. The mortality rate among conscripted migrant workers was often very high. In one three-year period, of 1,000 men recruited from a single sub-division in Gabon, 182 died and a further 395 failed to return home. (Suret-Canale, *Afrique noire*, II, p. 320-1, 310-27.)

29. The system of labour recruitment and control in Kenya was probably the harshest of any British colony in West or East Africa. It was based on a Native Registration Ordinance that forced all adult African men between 15 and 40 years old to register with the administration and carry an identity card (*kipande*) that included space for employers to record the duration of employment, type of work and wages received. See Chapter 5, above.

30. The differences in the degree of coercion applied under these laws reflected the

differences in the degree to which various colonies relied on African wage labour or peasant commodity production. For example, charges and convictions of Africans in British colonies for violations of the Masters and Servants (or similar) ordinances: varied considerably; see, for example, the figures for 1929 cited in Chapter 5, above, n. 49.

31. Coulson, *Tanzania*, p. 48.
32. B. Bowles, 'Colonial control and cooperatives in Tanganyika, 1945–1952' (unpublished manuscript, 1979, pp. 14–15; quoted in Coulson, *Tanzania*, p. 69).
33. Jonathan Barker, 'Stability and stagnation: the state in Senegal', *Canadian Journal of African Studies*, 11(1) (1977), pp. 27–8; Suret-Canale, *Afrique noire*, II, pp. 299–310; and Gellar: 'Structural changes and colonial dependency', pp. 62–3.
34. Henri Cosnier: *L'ouest africain francqis* (Paris, 1921, p. 241; quoted in Suret-Canale, *Afrique noire*, II, p. 302).
35. D.M.P. McCarthy: 'Organizing underdevelopment from the inside: the bureaucratic economy in Tanganyika, 1919–1940', *International Journal of African Historical Studies*, 10(4) (1977), p. 585.
36. Suret-Canale, *Afrique noire*, pp. 39–40, 244.
37. Bill Warren, *Imperialism: Pioneer of Capitalism* (London, 1980), p. 126.
38. This instrumental inspiration for colonial health and education policies was nowhere more clearly expressed than in the words of Albert Sarrault, one of France's most energetic ministers of the colonies and architect of the post-First World War 'mise en valeur' programmes for colonial development:

> L'instruction, en effet, a d'abord pour resultat d'améliorer la valeur de la production colonial en multipliant, dans la foule des travailleurs indigènes, la qualité des intelligences et le nombre des capacités . . .
> [While medical services served] la nécessité, en un mot, de conserver et d'augmenter le capital humain pour pouvoir faire travailler et fructifier le capital argent. (*La mise en valeur des colonies francqises*; Paris, 1923, p. 95.)

39. Delavignette, *Freedom and Authority*, pp. 21–2.
40. John Lonsdale, 'States and social processes in Africa: a historiographical survey', *African Studies Review* 24(2/3) (1981), esp. pp. 181–4.
41. H. Bernstein, 'Capital and peasantry in the epoch of imperialism, (Economic Research Bureau, University of Dar es Salaam, Occ. Paper 77.2, Nov. 1977), pp. 10–14.
42. Beverly Grier, 'Underdevelopment, modes of production, and the state in colonial Ghana', *African Studies Review* 24(1) (1981), pp. 22, 33–4.
43. Peter Gutkind, *The Emergent African Urban Proletariat* (Occasional Paper Series, No. 8; Centre for Developing Area Studies, McGill University, Montreal, 1974), pp. 37–49.
44. Cooper, 'Africa and the world economy', pp. 40, 35; see also Lonsdale: 'States and social processes', *passim*; and John Tosh, 'The cash crop revolution in tropical Africa: an agricultural reappraisal', *African Affairs* 79(314) (1980).
45. Bernstein, following C. Meillassoux (*Femmes, greniers et capitaux* (Paris, 1975) notes:

> This exploitation undermined production in two ways: (a) by the withdrawal of productive labour; and (b) by substituting in the sphere of necessary consumption, commodities for use values previously produced within the domestic community or acquired through simple exchange. Once established, this process is irreversible and effects the degradation of the conditions of existence of the domestic community, not only through the transfer of value but through the erosion of an entire culture of production.
>
> The contradictions of this mode as super-exploitation are realized through a dialect of destruction and preservation effects . . . sooner or later the latter will prevail so that articulation has a transitional character not only theoretically but

historically . . . the reproduction capacities of the domestic community are run down through the regular course of its articulation with the capitalist mode. ('Capital and peasantry', p. 15.)

46. Suret-Canale, *Afrique noire*, II, pp. 369-84; Gellar: 'Structural changes', pp. 60-4; McCarthy, 'Organizing underdevelopment', p. 597; Coulson, *Tanzania*, p. 48. and B.J. Berman, *Control and Crisis in Colonial Kenya* (London, 1990), Chs 5 and 7.

47. P.P. Rey, *Les alliances des classes* (Paris, 1973), pp. 70-1; and also Aidan Foster-Carter, 'The modes of production controversy', *New Left Review* 107 (1978), pp. 64-7.

48. See, for example, Kay, *Political Economy of Colonialism*; Gellar, 'Structural changes'; Barker, 'Stability and stagnation'; Coulson, *Tanzania*. The most thorough study of class formation in colonial Africa is Gavin Kitching, *Class and Economic Change in Kenya: The Formation of an African Petite Bourgeoisie* (New Haven, 1980).

49. Geoffrey Kay, *Development and Underdevelopment: A Marxist Analysis* (London, 1975), pp. 95, 104-5. See also Warren, *Imperialism*, Ch. 6; Lonsdale: 'States', and Coquery-Vidrovitch, 'De l'impérialisme ancien', *passim*.

50. Nigeria had one British administrative officer for every 100,000 Africans, Uganda one for every 49,000, while Kenya, the most tightly administered British colony, had roughly one administrative officer per 22,000 people or an administrative cadre of 145 in 1921 (by 1939 this had declined to 114). (R.L. Buell, *The Native Problem in Africa*, Vol. 1; New York, 1928, p. 361; Berman, *Control and Crisis*, Ch. 3; Gellar: 'Structural changes', p. 30; Suret-Canale, *Afrique noire*, I, p. 392.) The normal garrison of the three British colonies of East Africa together amounted to only three to four battalions of the King's African Rifles, while all of British Africa contained about 15,000 troops – the equivalent of a single army division. The post-First World War military forces of French Africa were reduced from 63,000 in 1920 to 52,000 in 1922, of whom almost half were usually posted outside of the colonies in other parts of the empire. Most of the troops consisted of young men conscripted for three years' service (Suret-Canale, *Afrique noire*, I, p. 425-32). The equipment of these forces consisted largely of the cast-offs of the metropolitan armies.

51. Cooper, 'Africa and the world economy', p. 34.

52. D.A. Low and J.M. Lonsdale, 'Introduction: towards the new order', in D.A. Low & Alison Smith (eds) *History of East Africa*, Vol. III (Oxford, 1976). Lonsdale: 'Conclusion'.

53. D.A. Low, *Lion Rampant: Essays in the Study of British Imperialism* (London, 1973), Ch. 2.

54. Robert Heussler, *The British in Northern Nigeria* (London, 1968), p. 7.

55. Conflicting tendencies towards the centralization of control and the decentralization of discretion have long been recognized as a characteristic of bureaucracy in general and of organizations with dispersed field staffs in particular, with subordinate officials seeking to increase their sphere of autonomous action and limit their responsibility to their superiors. This results in the interpretation and modification of policies and orders by subordinates so that actual practice reflects a variety of purposes and interests in addition, and sometimes antithetic, to the intentions of higher authorities. See for example Michel Crozier, *The Bureaucratic Phenomenon* (Chicago, 1964), p. 156; and Anthony Downs, *Inside Bureaucracy* (Boston, 1967), pp. 133-6.

56. M. Semakula Kiwanuka, 'Colonial policies and administrations in Africa: the myths of the contrasts', *African Historical Studies* 3(2) (1970), p. 300.

57. J.M. Lee, *Colonial Development and Good Government* (Oxford, 1967), p. 12.

58. Margery Perham, 'Introduction' to V. Harlow *et al.* (eds), *History of East Africa*, Vol. II (London, 1965), p. xxxii.

59. William Cohen, *Rulers of Empire: The French Colonial Service in Africa* (Stanford, 1971), pp. 59-65, 71, 79.

60. Gellar, 'Structural changes', p. 21.
61. Hubert Deschamps, *Les Méthodes et les doctrines coloniales de la France* (Paris, 1953), p. 173.
62. Ibid., p. 214. See also Martin Klein, 'Chiefship in Sine-Saloum (Senegal), 1887–1914', in V. Turner (ed.), *Colonialism in Africa, 1870–1960*. Vol. 3, *Profiles of Change* (Cambridge, 1971), pp. 70–1.
63. See, for example, G.H. Mungeam, *British Rule in Kenya, 1895–1912* (Oxford, 1966); and A.S. Kanya-Forstner, *The Conquest of the Western Sudan: A Study in French Military Imperialism* (Cambridge, 1969).
64. Berman, *Control and Crisis*, Ch. 4; Suret-Canale, *Afrique noire*, II, pp. 117–18, 432–41; Albert Duchene, *Histoire des finances coloniales de la France* (Paris, 1938) Chs XVI and XX.
65. In Tanganyika the Secretary for Native Affairs complained in 1933 that 'House Tax, municipal tax, slaughter fees, royalties on forest produce, cesses, licence fees, and so on make up a formidable list . . . all these things reduce the volume of trade and increase the number of officials; indeed we seem . . . to be getting into the frame of mind that if anyone anywhere is making a profit we should tax and regulate him, and enact legislation about him' (quoted in McCarthy, 'Organizing underdevelopment', p. 590).
    Public revenue for colonies heavily dependent on export production was linked to the level of commodity prices in the metropolitan and world markets. Colonies such as Nigeria and Kenya accumulated budgetary surpluses when prices were buoyant circa 1923–28 and ran deficits when prices plunged in the late 1920s and early 1930s. (Michael Crowder, *West Africa Under Colonial Rule*, London, 1968, appendix G; R.L. West, 'Sources of aggregative fluctuations in the market sector of an underdeveloped economy, a case study: Kenya Colony and Protectorate 1923–39', PhD thesis, Yale University, 1956, Appendix, Table 2). In effect, colonies exercised budgetary restraint in 'good' years to build surpluses to ease the even more severe constraints of anticipated 'bad' years and avoid, if possible, the Treasury supervision from the metropole loathed by the local administrations. In French Africa local colonial governments consistently sought to build up their *Caisse de reserve* from budgetary surpluses. A backward labour reserve colony such as Chad, where minimal development was undertaken by the state, had budgetary surpluses for every year but one between 1906 and 1925. After the First World War, its substantial *caisse* was actually regularly raided by the Federation government of AEF. In 1923 the Federation appropriated the entire reserve of 3.4 million francs while 'l'administration locale se'en plait amèrement'. (Raymond Gervais, 'La plus riche des colonies pauvres; la politique monetaire et fiscal de la France au Tchad, 1900-1920', *Canadian Journal of African Studies* 16(1) (1982), pp. 101, 105; Suret-Canale, *Afrique noire*, II, p. 436.)
66. Hut and poll taxes provided 23–40 per cent of state revenue in Tanganyika from 1924–38; 14.5–24.3 per cent in Senegal, 1925–36; 54–70 per cent in Guinée, 1925–36; and no less than 70–80 per cent in Chad, 1906–25. (McCarthy: 'Organizing underdevelopment', p. 585; Suret-Canale, *Afrique noire*, II, p. 436; Gervais, 'La plus riche des colonies pauvres', p. 101.)
67. Quoted in William Cohen, 'A century of modern administration: from Faidherbe to Senghor', *Civilizations* 20 (1970), p. 41; and quoted in Berman, *Control and Crisis*, pp. 99–100.
68. From 1919 to 1948 the recruitment of British colonial administrators was largely controlled by Sir Ralph Furse, the appointments secretary at the Colonial Office. A graduate of Eton and Oxford, a former cavalry officer during the First World War and a man of 'country' interests, Furse was himself a perfect example of the type of man sought for colonial administration, and an open and unashamed advocate of the ersatz 'aristocratic' ideology of the British dominant class. His beliefs and

methods are detailed in his memoirs, *Aucuparius: Recollections of a Recruiting Officer* (London, 1962), while the system of recruitment and development of the colonial administrative service is analysed in Robert Heussler, *Yesterday's Rulers: The Making of the British Colonial Service* (London, 1963). On French administrators, see Cohen, *Rulers of Empire*, especially Chs III–VI. He notes that by the 1930s colonial administrators were basically similar in education and social background to the higher civil service in metropolitan France.

69. Interview quoted in Berman, *Control and Crisis*, p. 80.
70. *Ibid.*, p. 67; Delavignette, *Freedom and Authority*, p. 12. (This book was based on a series of lectures given at the Ecole Coloniale in 1946 and first published in French as *Service africain*.)
71. Heussler, *The British in Northern Nigeria*, p. 95.
72. Heussler notes that the control of information by the field administration has meant that the reality of power in colonial administration is not reflected in official documents, especially annual reports, gazettes and minutes of conferences, which all show exaggerated deference to official hierarchy and give an impression of strict adherence to the wishes of the higher authorities (*Ibid.*, pp. 85–6). This has important implications for the methods of studying colonial bureaucracies. For a more extensive analysis of the communications process in colonial states and a study of its consequences in one colony, see Berman, *Control and Crisis*, Chs 3, 5 and 7.
73. Quoted in Berman, *Control and Crisis*, p. 205.
74. Lonsdale: 'Conclusion'.
75. Robert Heussler, 'British Rule in Africa' in P. Gifford & R.W. Lewis, *France and Britain in Africa* (New Haven, 1971), p. 578.
76. Quoted in Cohen, *Rulers of Empire*, p. 106.
77. This was the ideology of a supposedly stable, hierarchic society in which rulers and ruled were tied by mutual obligations. There was much in it that recalled in highly idealized form the traditional relations of lord and peasant in the European countryside, especially among British officials, and reflects the type of aristocratic anti-capitalist and anti-industrial reaction that Barrington Moore has called 'catonism', although in the colonies it was voiced by thoroughly middle-class officials in a state bureaucracy. (Barrington Moore, *Social Origins of Dictatorship and Democracy*, Boston, 1967, pp. 491–6.) It is ironic that such romantic anti-capitalist and authoritarian attitudes were exercised in the service of capitalist imperialism, especially in light of the contempt in which commerce and its practitioners ('box wallahs') were held by colonial administrators and soldiers. These attitudes do have some relation, however, to the willingness of bush administrators to restrain the excesses of European capital and reluctance to destroy the supposed 'organic community' of traditional African societies. (See also Berman, *Control and Crisis*, and Martin Klein, *Islam and Imperialism in Senegal: Sine-Saloum, 1847–1914*, Stanford, 1968).
78. Quoted in Ronald Robinson, 'European imperialism and indigenous reactions in British West Africa 1880–1914', in H.L. Wesseling (ed.), *Expansion and Reaction: Essays on European Expansion and Reactions in Asia and Africa* (Leiden, 1978), pp. 159–60.
79. Delavignette, *Freedom and Authority*, p. 73.
80. Heussler, *The British in Northern Nigeria*, p. 29.
81. Coulson, *Tanzania*, pp. 96–7. Even in Northern Nigeria Sir Donald Cameron, one of Lugard's most devoted disciples, noted when he returned as governor of Nigeria in the 1930s that indirect rule was 'a situation, in his own words of "make believe", in which administrators did as they liked regardless of policy. Northern Emirates and their Native Authorities, he thought, were British creatures, artificially founded and zealously protected from outside influences' (Heussler, *The British in Northern Nigeria*, p. 66.)

82. Delavignette, *Freedom and Authority*, p. 80. See also Klein, *Islam and Imperialism*, pp. 63-9.

83. The relationship between state employment and class formation is explored in Gavin Kitching, *Class and Economic Change in Kenya*, Chs 9, 13.

84. Gellar, 'Structural changes', pp. 43-4; Berman, *Control and Crisis*, Ch. 5.

85. Coulson, *Tanzania*, p. 69; Barker, 'Stability and stagnation', pp. 27-8; Kitching, *Class and Economic Change*, Ch 7.

86. Lonsdale: 'States' pp. 193-4.

87. A fascinating example of the contradictory pressures managed by the prefects is given in Robert Delavignette's account of a year in the life of a commandant in the Soudan in the late 1930s (*Les paysans noir*, Paris, 1946). The administrator's chief task is to increase peanut production for a new peanut-oil plant in the area (which, although Delavignette does not indicate this, is owned by a subsidiary of Unilever). His administrative standing with his superiors depends on his success. He does so by encouraging peanut production by peasant families rather than on the lands of the local *dioulas* (landlords), promising them enrichment and a better future if they take the 'chance' being offered them. Having tied his personal authority and prestige to this promised material reward, he must then negotiate a 'fair' price from the factory that will enable the peasants to pay their taxes and provide them with enough of an incentive to keep producing. In addition, to ensure the reproduction of the peasant households, he also negotiates with the factory to temper its demand for the cash crop so that local food production will not suffer.

88. Ronald Robinson, 'Non-European foundations of European imperialism: sketch for a theory of collaboration', in R. Owen & B. Sutcliffe (eds), *Studies in the Theory of Imperialism* (London, 1972), p. 136.

89. Barker, 'Stability and stagnation', p. 33; McCarthy, 'Organizing underdevelopment', p. 583.

90. T.H.R. Cashmore, 'Studies in district administration in the East Africa Protectorate 1895-1918', Ph. D. thesis, Cambridge University, 1965, P. 55.

91. Interview quoted in Berman, *Control and Crisis*, p. 207, and similarly in Heussler, *The British in Northern Nigeria*, p. 104.

92. Cohen, *Rulers of Empire*, Appendix III, p. 217.

93. Cohen, 'A century', p. 43; Suret-Canale, *Afrique noire*, II, p. 395.

94. Hailey was a former high official of the Indian Civil Service and during the 1930s and 1940s was one of the principal advisers to the Colonial Office on political and administrative matters. He is quoted in Ralph Austen, *Northwest Tanzania Under German and British Rule* (New Haven, 1968), pp. 214-15; Cohen, *Rulers of Empire*, p. 120.

95. Cooper, 'Africa and the world economy', p. 16.

96. The classic example is that of the 'warrant chiefs' in Eastern Nigeria whose actions were deeply involved in provoking the Aba disturbances. See Harry Gailey, *The Road to Aba* (London, 1971); and also Berman, *Control and Crisis*, Ch 5; Gellar, 'Structural changes', p. 34; Suret-Canale, *Afrique noire*, II, pp. 406-12.

97. During the Depression the first Colonial Development and Welfare Act in Britain was to supply £1 million a year for colonial development projects to help ease British employment problems, but the effort had little metropolitan effect and much of the money was never spent. France was more successful with colonial trade policies that captured a larger proportion of colonial exports and imports for metropolitan capital. During the Second World War, however, while the fall and occupation of France stalled further colonial development for several years, the British grasped virtually total control of colonial commodity production through a system of marketing boards that sold on forward contracts directly to departments of the metropolitan state. After the war this system of 'bulk-buying' was maintained into the 1950s. See David

Meredith, 'The British government and colonial economic policy', *Economic History Review*, 28(3) (1975). Charlotte Leubescher, *Bulk-Buying From the Colonies* (London, 1956), and Catherine Coquery-Vidrovitch, 'Mutation de l'impérialisme français dans les années 30', *African Economic History* 4 (1977).

98. Low & Lonsdale, 'Introduction: towards the new order', pp. 12–16.

99. Cooper, 'Africa and the world economy', p. 34.

100. The scale of investments can be seen, for example, in the fact that FIDES and the related CCFOM (Caisse Centrale de la France d'Outre-mer) committed 210 billion (1956) francs to AOF in the period 1947–56, while in the entire period 1903–46 only 90 billion (in constant francs) had been invested. See Coquery-Vidrovich, 'L'avatar', and Suret-Canale, *Afrique noire*, III, pp. 92–128.

101. *Ibid.*, Berman, *Control and Crisis*, Ch 6.

102. Cooper, 'Africa and the world economy', pp. 36, 42. For a study of this process in Kenya, see Berman, *Control and Crisis*, Ch 9.

103. *Ibid.*, Chs 7 and 8.

104. The impact of state intervention in this regard was very similar to that noted in metropolitan society. See Stuart Hall *et al.*, *Policing the Crisis* (London, 1978), p. 214.

105. Coquery-Vidrovitch, 'L'avatar', pp. 112–13.

106. John J. Grotpeter and Warren Weinstein, *The Pattern of African Decolonization: A New Interpretation* (Eastern African Studies Program, X, Syracuse University, 1973).

107. Quoted in Coquery-Vidrovitch, 'L'avatar', pp. 112–13.

Part IV

Pasts & Futures

Eight

Up From Structuralism

BRUCE BERMAN

Dependency theory and the temptations of structuralism

The attractions of dependency theory in the 1965–80 period for the study of colonialism in Africa seem increasingly clear today. It provided both an apparently incisive analysis and a sharp critique of the mechanisms and effects of imperialism that produced the 'distorted' condition of underdevelopment. This was, moreover, depicted as part of a self-reproducing global system in which the perverse underdevelopment of the periphery was the necessary mirror image of the genuine capitalist development at the centre.[1] The analysis could also be readily and quickly supported with easily available empirical data. Since the determining causal factors were seen to be located in the metropolitan centres of the global system, detailed information about the internal social and economic history of a colony was not initially required, and was, in any case, unavailable for any African colony before the 1970s. All that was needed was data that showed the results of imperial domination in the distorted structure of the colony as a dependent supplier of primary products to the metropole and purchaser of manufactures from it. This was available in published time series of trade data, along with some data on metropolitan investment in the colony, and maps to show the way railways and road development were routed to drain the primary commodities from producing areas to coastal ports for export.

The dependency model also neatly linked conditions before and after independence through what Gunder Frank called 'continuity in change',

179

i.e., the persistence of the relations of dependency and self-reproducing underdevelopment within the apparently changed forms brought by flag independence.[2] Thus colonialism and neocolonialism were considered explicable within the same theoretical paradigm.

The colonial state appeared to be the obvious agent of metropolitan capital in establishing and maintaining the structures of dependence. It was an externally imposed apparatus of domination acting upon and orchestrating the exploitation of Africans in unequivocal fashion. Since the structure of the colonial state apparatus was determined by metropolitan capital, whose interests it served, rather than by indigenous social forces, it was 'overdeveloped' in relation to the latter.[3] The class character of this state was unambiguous: it was the instrument of the metropolitan bourgeoisie.

Structuralist Marxism provided a theoretical structure for the analysis of the colonial (and postcolonial) state that was comfortably congruent with the premises of dependency theory. It also emphasized self-reproducing and self-maintaining systems, with the state serving as the 'factor of cohesion between the levels of a social formation . . . and as the regulatory factor of its global equilibrium as a system.'[4] The relationship between the state and capital was given in the nature of the system itself. The state acted to organize the unity of capital in a dominant, hegemonic 'power bloc'. Even more important was the fact that the presence and participation of the bourgeoisie in the state apparatus was seen to be theoretically unnecessary, so that there was no difficulty in explaining the colonial state as serving an absentee ruling class:

> the state is therefore always and tautologically the representative of the dominant class, whether or not the political or ideological representatives of this class predominate in political or ideological conflicts and irrespective of whether this class has any kind of representation at the level of the state. At this level of analysis, therefore, the state is the 'unambiguous political power of the dominant class or fractions'; since it is the power of the structure to ensure its own reproduction.[5]

The combination of dependency theory and structuralism saw colonialism from a distance, through the reverse end of a telescope, treating Africans as a relatively undifferentiated mass who were exploited, impoverished and impotent victims; dominated classes rather than agents of their own history. Indeed, human agency and subjectivity more generally were a matter at best of secondary importance in theories focused on the logic of self-reproducing systems guided by the their own internal laws. Metropolitan capital and the state tended also to be treated as relatively undifferentiated and playing structurally determined roles. This produced a history of colonialism that was largely retrospective in method and, as Kitching puts it, heavily 'front-loaded toward the present', i.e., it takes contemporary conditions and searches in the past for their origins and treats the more recent events of colonialism as of increasingly greater significance the closer we come to the present.[6]

The paradigmatic application of dependency theory to Kenya is contained in Leys' celebrated 1975 monograph *Underdevelopment in Kenya*. The core argument of that study has recently been succinctly summarized by Kitching:

> the central assumption upon which that argument rested was that the prime movers of *all* events and phenomena of any significance in the African political economy of Kenya had always been essentially *external* to that political economy. That is, to put it somewhat crudely, anything of note which had happened to Africans had always been *done* to *them* from outside, at first by white settlers and the colonial state – Leys' original account . . . simply treats the latter as the agency of the former – later by multinational capital and a few rich African 'compradors' and 'politicians' who were seen, unproblematically, as the agents or accomplices of multinational capital.
>
> . . . Leys' '1975' view was that the predominant consequence of the impact of colonialism and neocolonialism upon Kenya had been the continuing exploitation and suppression of the bulk of its African population. The aim of the whole analysis is to show that behind the apparent discontinuities of later Kenyan history . . . there lay a much more profound continuity. This continuity consisted in the poverty of the bulk of the country's African people and a structurally unchanged pattern of exploitation, inequality and drain of resources to the exterior . . . [7]

No sooner, however, did the dependency model begin to be employed as the basis for research, than research on colonialism in Africa began rapidly to accumulate anomalous and ambiguous situations that it could not adequately explain. This was particularly true of the veritable flood of research on the political economy of colonial Kenya. Brett's notable comparative analysis of Kenya, Uganda and Tanganyika, while remaining within the dependency framework, noted the considerable variation in internal structures of the three colonies. Dependency theory could record but not accord significance to such variations, since the result of colonialism, whatever the particular pattern of internal structure, was considered essentially the same: underdevelopment and the blockage of 'true' capitalist development and industrialization. Brett also noted the frequent conflicts between metropolitan and local capital, particularly the Kenya settlers, while Emmanuel stressed this as a general feature of settler colonialism. Which one, then, was the dominant sector of capital whose interests were served by colonialism; and if the interests of settlers were in conflict with those of metropolitan capital what did this imply about the position and significance of the settlers in colonial society? To make matters even more complex, Redley's doctoral thesis analysed the internal differentiation and cleavages within the white community in Kenya. What, then, was the settler interest? Dependency theory remained echoingly silent about such questions of structural variation and internal conflict.[8]

An even greater challenge was posed by the rapid accumulation of evidence concerning many parts of colonial Africa pointing to active internal social differentiation that had produced what looked very much like social classes and real, albeit relatively limited, accumulations of capital, sometimes based on indigenous precolonial patterns of trade, production and the distribution of wealth. For Kenya, the fine-grained analyses of dairy and wattle production in Central Province by Cowen and his conceptualization of the process of 'straddling' whereby wage employment for the colonial state, white settlers, and merchant capital was used as the basis for investment and accumulation in the African reserves; along with the work of Njonjo, Forbes Munro, Hay, Stichter and Cooper on the development of commodity production, trade and wage labour; the exemplary summary and synthesis of rural change and differentiation by Kitching; and Swainson's study of the parallel development of indigenous, metropolitan and foreign capital all documented a real, although incomplete and contradictory, process of class formation and capitalist development.[9]

After 1975 the weight of research followed the logic of these studies and increasingly shifted to the analysis of internal processes of change under colonialism, especially class formation and changing forms of production and labour. This change of focus further undermined dependency theory with its 'unidimensional "closure" of historical processes which follow from its highly "externalist" and overdetermining conception of colonialism and imperialism.'[10] The rigid determinism of dependency theory and its consequent inability to deal with the complexity, ambiguity and lack of neatness of real historical experience, especially within colonial Africa, has been its undoing. In short, dependency theory proved incapable of explaining variation or change, except to deny them significance and insist that the system continued to operate as before – not an analysis of history but its denial. It was the grip of the rigid teological and tautological 'system' that was loosened by Warren's attack, which insisted that colonialism laid the foundation for capitalist development and that the features of colonialism that produced aspects of 'underdevelopment' were matters of deliberate policy and not inexorable systemic logic.[11]

There has been a development, therefore, not only towards more Marxist approaches to the political economy of colonialism, i.e., analyses focused on internal structures of production, class formation and conflict, but also towards less deterministic modes of historical analysis that are capable of dealing with variation and contingency as central aspects of African experience. The challenge is to understand the intersection of global, metropolitan and indigenous social forces on the terrain of colonialism and give adequate weight to the importance of human agency – of men and women, especially Africans, as voluntary agents, to paraphrase Thompson, of their own involuntary determinations.[12] The domination of the forces of imperialism, their ability to reshape the structures of African societies, has not been as great, while the ability of Africans to resist or turn those forces to their own advantage has not been as small as the unyielding carapace of 'laws of development' or 'underdevelopment' demands.[13]

The task of theory has increasingly become not the development of deterministic models of unchanging universals, but rather the constant refinement of nuanced and subtle analyses of historical processes in which global and local social forces interact to produce contingent and often idiosyncratic trajectories of change. This is an endless process, politically as well as intellectually, and expresses the inevitable and essential dialectic of thought and reality. Such non-deterministic analysis of history cannot be written backwards or retrospectively, but only, as Tilly tells us, projectively, by beginning 'with a particular historical condition and search[ing] forward to the alternative outcomes of that condition, with a specification of the paths leading to each of the outcomes.'[14] It also requires giving full weight to the subjective experience and intentionality of historical actors. This does not mean replacing determinism with an equally arid instrumentalism, but rather giving theoretical recognition to the reflection of objective structural forces in subjective experience, as well as to the reciprocal influence of human will on those structures, while at the same time allowing for the impact of accident, failure and unforeseen and unintended consequences. Historical actors can then be rescued from the status of automaton agents to which dependency theory and structuralism had reduced them, and understood as people like ourselves living in an imperfectly understood present and struggling each day towards a partially conceived and intended, but ultimately uncertain, future.

The movement towards a less deterministic historiography has produced a rich and growing harvest in African social and economic history that has substantially changed our understanding of the diverse patterns of production, labour, class formation and conflict in rural societies during the colonial period.[15] Unfortunately, similar movement in the analysis of the state has been slower to appear and it largely remains in the grip of the structuralist model. This is partly the result of the fact that the structuralist model is a Marxist approach separable from dependency theory as such, and partly because most of the various Marxist approaches to the theory of the state share an essentially functionalist logic, i.e., they begin with the question: what is the role of the state in, or what contribution does it make to, the maintenance of the capitalist system? It has thus been difficult to escape from the model of a deterministic, teleological system. Even the German 'capital logic' approach sees the state as based primarily on the 'needs of capital' and 'reduces history to an effect of the logical self-realization of capital.'[16]

These characteristics have made it difficult to develop an approach to the state that can deal with such matters as internal differentiation, contradiction and conflict within the state apparatus and its complex relations with class forces, especially its critical linkages with and responsiveness to internal class formation. If the relationship between state and capital is structurally determined, the existence of a dominant or hegemonic class or 'fraction of capital' can be simply assumed; this assumption has led to much fruitless argument over who or what it might be in particular contexts. This formulation also takes as unproblematic givens both the basis of the power of such a dominant class and the conditions of its effective exercise. Such issues are virtually impossible to sort out because of the difficulty of obtaining adequate empirical evidence, and also because of the usual vagueness in defining what constitutes domination or hegemony: does it mean the interests (howsoever defined) of the particular fraction prevail within the state 90 per cent, 66.6 per cent or 51 per cent of the time? In any case, simply asking this question makes it difficult to understand how the colonial state was linked to internal class formation and capitalist development, and how the colonial state often found itself in conflict with elements of metropolitan capital. The epithets that British colonial administrators and businessmen applied to each other, 'box wallahs' and the 'heaven born', were, after all, not intended as compliments.

Structuralist approaches to the state have particular difficulty in dealing with the subjective, cognitive dimensions of the state. For example, studies of colonial administration and policy have revealed repeatedly that colonial officials frequently had little conception of capital or its interests beyond those of particular individuals and groups operating in their area of responsibility, and conceived such matters through extremely simplistic and ambiguous concepts such as 'trade', 'progress', 'welfare', etc. How they could then 'serve the interests of capital' was problematic and contingent on all of the attendant possibilities of misperception, amateurish incompetence and unforeseen and unintended consequences.[17] The efficient economic management of a colony in the interests of metropolitan capital cannot be taken for granted, but this is just what structuralist analyses do when they assume that the state serves the interests of capital 'by reason of the system itself'.

Up From Structuralism

For similar reasons, structuralist approaches to the state have little capacity to analyse actual processes of policy formation and implementation within the apparatus of the state, since the outcome is largely assumed in advance. The protagonists in the 'Kenya debate' have been largely unable to move beyond shared structuralist assumptions about the state and have been mired in arid arguments over which 'fraction of capital' dominated which portions of the state.[18] It is significant that no major study of the development of the state in Kenya after independence in relation to capitalist development and class politics has been produced by writers working within dependency theory or Marxism.

Finally, structuralist analyses of the state have little capacity to deal with class struggle, although they often talk a good deal about it. This emphasis turns out to be an appeal to a *deus ex machina* to overcome the static, ahistorical and reductionist character of the analysis of the state. Class struggle becomes the metaphysical principle that is inserted to provide a dynamic for capitalism, given the failure to link the state to its contradictions and developmental tendencies. Furthermore, structuralist analysis is especially prone to the 'water over the dam' approach to the role of class struggle, i.e. if the state is assumed to act effectively as the 'factor of cohesion' ensuring the reproduction of capitalism, class struggle is unproblematic and only has a significant effect in the 'last instance' of revolution. How the point is reached at which class struggle overtops the walls of so powerful an apparatus of control remains a moot point. Furthermore, the structuralist model cannot really consider, let alone explain, the possible effects of class struggle throughout the historical development of capitalism and the state, whether a revolution occurs or not. And, as we all know, such revolutions have seldom occurred. Other than the 'interests of capital', however, and by whoever conceived, what factors are we left with to explain the development of the frequently less-than-imposing and rather rag-tag edifice of the colonial state?

From systemic categories to historical processes: the colonial state as the product/determinant of contradiction and struggle

We came to our joint concern with the colonial state through earlier research on, respectively, the bureaucratic apparatus of provincial administration, and the development of African political organization and activity in Western Kenya.[19] This resulted in the development of intimate knowledge of portions of the surviving historical record of the colonial period in Kenya in the form of official and private documents, and the oral testimony and recollections of European and African participants. From these we derived a shared sense of the frequent

185

confusion, uncertainty, and ignorance of the historical actors rather than any commanding, deliberate and omniscient confidence. At the same time, we could retrospectively reconstruct more accurately than they could themselves at the time the structural circumstances and consequences of their actions. These considerations brought us directly to the dilemma of the relationship of structural forces and subjective human agency, and we have consistently sought to bring these levels of reality together rather than select one or the other as the locus of historical 'truth'. In particular, we reject and have tried to avoid the unfortunate trap of structuralist theories of reducing humans to mere 'bearers' of objective structural forces, what one might style the 'head porter theory of history'.

The previously published and unpublished essays reproduced earlier in this book record instead our efforts since 1976 to develop not only an analysis of the development of the colonial state in Kenya, but also a conceptual and methodological base for the study of colonial rule elsewhere in Africa that projectively locates historical actors within structural contexts that they at best partly understood and that were affected by their actions in ways never entirely foreseen or intended. We have groped our way towards an approach free of the limitations of dependency theory and the structuralist analysis of the state that were our initial starting points. Some of the earlier essays seem from our present vantage point to be rather too structuralist and mechanical in their formulation of the state, particularly with regard to the key issue of articulation. Nevertheless, we have a sense of a cumulative advance towards a more powerful and more nuanced approach, and it seems appropriate at this point to extract and summarize its main elements.

Our view of the colonial state in Africa continues to share with dependency theory and structuralist Marxism the initial premise that the state was the central agency of European intervention transforming African societies and forging their structural linkage with metropolitan capital. Beyond this point, however, we reject simplistic deterministic connections of state and capital and the reduction of African societies to the status of passive receptors of external forces. Instead, we see the colonial state not as a self-reproducing system controlling and maintaining a drain of surplus to the metropole, but rather as the central structural focus of a complex *process* of political and economic domination marked by continual contradiction and struggle.

Rather than constituting a systemically unified whole, the structural forms of the colonial state reproduced the conflicts of colonial society both by providing the institutions in which such conflicts were joined and by those institutions themselves becoming the objects of confrontation. We share, with such writers as Cooper and Berry, a strong sense of the importance of African resistance and the limits of the European ability to overcome it fully with the meagre resources of most colonial states.[20] African compliance with European orders – whether for taxes, labour or the production of cash crops – always remained to some degree problematic and subject to African manipulation and initiative in ways neither anticipated nor desired by colonial officials or metropolitan businessmen. The history of institutional innovation and reconstruction, of the groping and often confused formulation and reformulation of policy, and of the succession of administrative circulars and ordinances records, indeed provides a veritable archaeological chronicle of, the travails of the European colonial project in Africa.

Once introduced into Africa the institutional and ideological forms of the colonial state became part of diverse internal processes of capitalist development within African societies, interacting with the precapitalist institutions of those societies in what Corrigan and Sayre aptly call the 'dialectic of constraint and construction'. Historical capitalisms, they note, 'are actively constructed through the transformation of pre-existing social forms. This historical legacy both constrains and provides the [only] resources for capitalist construction, "in-forming" it, giving it its particular shape and weight . . . The logical incongruities, in short, must serve as the starting point for reconstructing the history of capitalist civilization in England – or anywhere else, since in the real world all cases are in their own ways "peculiar". They should not be dismissed as a set of irritating disturbances to be put on one side.'[21] To extend the point, the role of theory in the study of the colonial state is to provide a basis for explaining the intricacies and contradictions of the varied and partly wilful, partly involuntary processes of capitalist construction in colonial Africa; and not to seek a level of abstract generalization that turns bumpy and twisted tracks into identical smooth motorways to the present.

We have come, therefore, to the realization that there really is no 'theory of the colonial state' to be constructed, and that such an abstract entity cannot and should not be the object of the study of the colonial state in Africa. Along with much of the post-structuralist Marxist analysis of the state in advanced capitalist societies, we 'challenge the idea of a universal theory of the State and replace that notion with the call for specific historical analyses within a set of universalistic "rules" about the relation between State and society . . . theories of the State can only be seen in terms of their specific historical applicability, totally contrary to either Althusserian structuralism or Leninist instrumentalism.'[22] We thus focus on a set of relationships between common or universal social forces of the state and capital whose character and interactions vary in different historical contexts, rather than on quixotic efforts to find a common sequence of development or universal outcome in the institutional forms and practices of the state. As a result, we cannot and do not claim that the pattern of development of the colonial state that we have delineated in Kenya will be found elsewhere in colonial Africa. Rather, we believe that the theoretical conceptualization of the social forces of colonialism and their interrelations that we have developed (see Chapters 8 and 9), when combined with the projective method of historical reconstruction, can be successfully applied to the explanation of the development of the state and capital in any specific colony.

Recent attempts at developing non-structuralist theorizations of the state have certainly proved helpful, although they are limited in their utility by an understandable preoccupation with analysing the state in contemporary advanced capitalist societies. At the highest level of abstraction our approach combines elements of what Carnoy has called the 'logic of capital' and the 'class struggle' theories (what we have elsewhere described as a 'historical derivationist' approach). We share with them the premises that 'the contradictions of capitalist development, following universal historical tendencies (derived from Marx's *Capital*), shape the capitalist State and its contradictions', and, in particular, the state is 'a product of the fundamental characteristic of capitalist society – class struggle – and [is] therefore a class state, but one that necessarily incorporates working-class demands. The reproduction of class relations is therefore conditioned by the *internalized* contestation of power in the state apparatuses.'[23] We also share the specific conceptualization of the 'relative autonomy of the state' that flows from these premises. We believe this is essential for understanding the development of the state and its role in the development of capitalism. As Carnoy puts it:

> It is only through such a theory that we can understand how the State can appear – indeed must appear – to be above class struggle, yet be a class State . . . Relative autonomy means that in order to represent class interests – that is, to be legitimate in the context of class and group conflict – the State bureaucracy must appear to be autonomous from the dominant class. Contradictions . . . occur within the State apparatuses, and are the result of struggles in the State to mediate the inherent tensions between the necessary state functions of accumulation and legitimation.[24]

However, if such abstract formulations are to be useful for historical analysis, we must translate them into the specificity of place and time by designating the particular local form and content of the dynamic conflict- and tension-ridden relationships they describe. With these general conceptual and methodological points in mind, our work has focused on four major issues: 1) the process of articulation that shaped the objectives of the colonial state and determined the particular character of primitive accumulation in Africa; 2) the process of political

domination and control by the colonial state and its relationship to the
co-operation of and collaboration with segments of indigenous African
societies; 3) the efforts of the colonial state to regulate the relations of
production and class struggle between labour and capital; and 4) the
relationship between the colonial state and patterns of class formation
in African societies.

THE PROCESS OF ARTICULATION

The development of a non-structuralist concept of articulation seems to
us to be the key to the construction of a more adequate theory of the
state in colonial Africa. This concept is descriptive of the tasks undertaken by the colonial state and the consequences of its efforts to collect
tax, stimulate trade and commodity production, and cajole or force
Africans into wage labour. It cannot be assumed to take any particular
structural form or generate a characteristic 'successful' outcome. The
fault of the structuralist versions of articulation was their assumption that
precapitalist social forms persisted or were only partly modified because
this served the 'needs' of metropolitan capital, i.e. this was said to help
fulfil in some manner the systemic requirements of self-reproduction.
Such a formulation actually reproduces the 'externalist' orientation of
dependency theory, which assumes that all change within the periphery
originated from the introduction of external forces and that whatever occurred therefore 'served the interests' of metropolitan capital.
This version of articulation, whether it is taken to involve conscious
agency on the part of colonial officials and metropolitan businessmen, or
as describing the structurally determined necessity of an impersonal
system, is simply empirically wrong.

The concept of articulation cannot and should not be used as a way
of avoiding the difficult, painstaking but historiographically necessary
task of analysing as many as possible of the remarkably diverse outcomes
of the interaction of elements of developed European capitalism with
the varied and by no means moribund precapitalist societies of Africa.
Instead, articulation must be conceived of as an instrument for the
explanation of that process of interaction in all of its particularity. From
the beginning of our work we have defined articulation not as a structural
feature of a system, but rather as an open-ended process. This involved
three interacting sets of factors, the internal set of pre-existing social
forms that provided the context from within which Africans reacted to
European intrusions; and two external sets, the first consisting of the
structural forces of the world economy with which African societies now
became linked and the specific elements of metropolitan capital introduced into a colony as the agencies of that linkage, and the second
consisting of the political apparatus of the colonial state.

The most common outcome of articulation has been an unstable combination of capitalist and precapitalist elements, syncretic synthesis rather than transformation, producing the characteristic kaleidoscopic incongruities of juxtaposed social forms of contemporary Africa.[25] We have come increasingly to emphasize the contradictions and conflicts that are contained within the process of articulation and define its confused results. In particular, we stress the constraints on the ability of the colonial state and European capital to establish generalized commodity production and wage labour in Africa. These constraints emerged not only from African resistance to European impositions, but also from the ambiguous goals of European merchant capital, which wanted to extract surplus from African production but not compete with a class of African capitalists, and from colonial states that 'were uniformly hostile to African rural capitalism, seeing it as not only socially and politically dangerous, but as somehow improper for Africans.'[26] Furthermore, indigenous social forms provided the resources and opportunities for some segments of African societies to resist European impositions and for others to take initiatives in developing production and trade in ways neither desired nor permitted by colonial interests.[27]

What should be clear is that the process of articulation comprehends the particular form of primitive accumulation in Africa and differentiates it from the supposed modal experience of European societies. According to Burowoy:

> the colonial state was concerned not with production per se but with the orchestration of relations among modes of production in such a way as to secure the ascendancy of the capitalist mode. Once the dominance of the capitalist mode of production has been established and other modes subordinated to its requirements, the raison d'être of the colonial state disappears. A new form of state emerges, concerned with the expanded rather than the primitive accumulation of capital, with the extraction of relative surplus value from production rather than of specific surplus labour through exchange, and with the production of specific types of labour power rather than the generation of labour supplies. The granting of formal political independence is but a symbol of the transition from the colonial to the post-colonial state.[28]

This is surely too mechanical and generalized a formulation, Burowoy falling here into the kind of structuralist rigidity he otherwise avoids. The point is that primitive accumulation has occurred within the process of articulation very unevenly, not only across different regions, but also within particular African societies, and has continued to be so in the post-independence period.

It is the patchiness and overall incoherence of the process of capitalist development in Africa that is its most distinctive feature. Each African colony and each successor independent state displays the distinctive idiosyncracies of the particular syncretic combination of capitalist and precapitalist forms that is the continuing heritage of the process of articulation. And this will continue to be the case as far into the future as we can look. The universal domination of capitalism in Africa is far from secured. This is why it was possible in the early 1960s to start in the industrial district of Nairobi, where international capital was developing advanced capital-intensive forms of production based on a permanently proletarianized labour force and actively collaborating with Tom Mboya and the Kenya Federation of Labour in the creation of a stable and apolitical union movement, travel north through the Kikuyu districts, where some of the most advanced elements of agrarian capitalism in Africa were still contesting for dominance against a far larger mass of middle peasants struggling to hold on to their land and sustain themselves as small commodity producers, and end in the desert scrub near the border with Sudan, where pastoral Turkana remained largely isolated from the circuits of production and exchange to the south. A quarter of a century after independence the advance of rural capitalism in Kenya against a tenacious middle peasantry remains unresolved, with scholars such as Cowen arguing that the linkages of the peasantry with international capital and aid agencies have enabled them to sustain their resistance.[29] The future course and the particular social structural and cultural forms of capitalist development in Kenya, while they will certainly be significantly shaped by its distinctive earlier experience, remain to some degree open and contingent. There is no single 'logic of capital' that we can call upon to give a determinate outcome.[30]

DOMINATION, CO-OPTATION AND COLLABORATION

The analysis of articulation as a contradictory and conflict-laden process comprising diverse attempts to link metropolitan capital with African production and labour against varying combinations of African resistance and receptivity has shaped our understanding of the colonial state as an instrument of political control or domination. Here, too, we found we could not assume that we were dealing with a systemic condition whose occurrence became automatic with the formation of an administrative apparatus of colonial rule. Domination, in the sense of the routine and predictable obedience of Africans to the ordinances, policies and directives of colonial officials, was the outcome of a process of labyrinthine complexity and continual uncertainty precisely because it was so intimately connected with and reproduced the dilemmas of articulation. Ruling was a demanding business in colonial Africa. Somewhere, in any given colony at any particular time, effective control was being undermined, challenged or repaired.

The history of the institutional apparatus, ordinances, and policies of the colonial state provides us with a running record of the successive more and less successful attempts to provide a stable and orderly environment within which the process of articulating European capitalism with indigenous African societies could take place. The colonial state was thus substantially shaped by the requirements of developing trade, production and wage labour within the particular context of each colony; and, in turn, it substantially shaped the way in which the tasks of articulation were (partly) achieved.

The colonial state certainly managed articulation, but only with considerable difficulty. The central dilemma was the one we identified as being between legitimacy and accumulation; these contradictory requirements pervaded not only the relations between the colonial state and both African and European capital, but also the internal relations among different parts of the state apparatus. The contradictions of articulation thus provided the substantive content of the structural cleavage between field officers and the central administration, which is intrinsic to the prefectural apparatus, and of that between generalist political administrators and technical specialists that became such a ubiquitous feature of the last two decades of colonial rule.

Externally, the clashing requirements of effective stability and order on the one hand, and of accumulation on the other, found expression most importantly in the complex patterns of collaboration between Africans and the colonial state and in the state's increasingly direct attempts to regulate class and production relations.

What we have found is how pervasive and intricate were the ties of collaboration between Africans and Europeans behind the colonial state's facade of unchallenged control. In Kenya, as was shown in Chapters 2 and 3, close analysis of the colonial 'conquest' reveals a pattern of violent confrontation, negotiation, and alliance between Europeans and Africans. From the very beginning, elements of various African societies were willing to collaborate with Europeans for their own anticipated advantage both within their own communities or over neighbouring societies. And, as is now well understood, colonial rule could not have survived or functioned without the willing cooperation of thousands of African chiefs, headmen, police, soldiers, traders, clerks, teachers, and clergymen who staffed colonial institutions and provided the actual muscle for the enforcement of colonial edicts. A significant portion of the institutional engineering in colonial society, both within and outside the state apparatus, focused on formalizing and routinizing the recruitment, duties and remuneration of these African cadres, and of making available to them social and economic advantages that demonstrated the benefits of European rule and encouraged their loyalty. What we stress is that this permitted, indeed, encouraged what we have called the 'vulgarization' of state power, i.e., the ability of a growing minority of Africans to use colonial institutions to further their own interests.

Up From Structuralism

Domination, once we penetrate behind the facade so assiduously protected by colonial officials and rather gullibly accepted in structuralist analyses of the colonial state, turns out to be something far more interesting and ambiguous in its operations and consequences. At least some of the dominated were able to bargain for and manipulate the system to gain substantial benefits from the European agents of the metropole, even if these were strictly speaking 'against the rules', in return for their complicity in maintaining the apparatus of control.[31] At the same time, and this is the most provocative point, the active pursuit of the accumulation of power and wealth by this minority generated cleavages and struggles within the fabric of African societies that repeatedly undermined the order and control they were supposed to maintain. Moreover, as many of the more perceptive European officials feared, and as later history was to demonstrate, this body of collaborators could readily move to opposition when their individual interests and collective projects as an emergent class were no longer advanced but blocked by the white cadres at the top of the state apparatus.

THE REGULATION OF PRODUCTION RELATIONS AND CLASS STRUGGLE

The involvement of the colonial state with its African agents and subordinates and their ability to use that relationship for their own 'vulgar' purposes, implicated it in the labyrinths of indigenous politics (which few white officials understood) and made it an often unwitting partisan in local processes of class formation. This paradoxically parallelled the colonial state's increasing involvement in the regulation of relations of property, production and exchange between Africans and European capital. In both instances the state authorities found themselves caught in the contradiction of being able to advance most effectively the interests of metropolitan business and of their African collaborators and clients only if the state appeared to be not simply a neutral, disinterested arbiter of clashing interests, but the paternal protector of the weaker African interest. The tenuous legitimacy of the colonial state rested on its appearing omnipotent, disinterested, and benevolent as well.

No colonial administration began with a worked-out plan for the development of its administrative, legal and coercive apparatus, least of all for that part that dealt with the organization of relations of property, production and exchange. Initial, often naive, expectations that the establishment of effective control would provide a framework of stability and order within which markets for labour and commodities could organize themselves out of the interactions of willing buyers and sellers rapidly proved illusory. Africans showed endless resourcefulness in resisting, evading or manipulating the roles demanded of them in the manifestly lopsided colonial market structures. European capital, meanwhile, as we have shown for Kenya, could not force or coerce Africans into accepting those roles without threatening the very basis of the colonial political economy. And so, step by step, ordinance by ordinance, circular by circular, labour exchange by labour training scheme, marketing board by rural co-op, trade licence by agricultural credit programme, colonial administrations throughout Africa found themselves drawn, often reluctantly, into the ever more direct and detailed regulation of commodity production and exchange, labour recruitment and the relations of production. The resulting, often idiosyncratic, pattern of institutions and practices both reflected and gave shape and structural substance to the process of articulation in a colony.

What is especially apparent, moreover, is the constant pressure on the state authorities that emerged from the central contradictions of capitalism in the particular forms in which they developed in each society; and, for us, the striking degree to which the historical record in a colony such as Kenya shows that state officials were often conscious of the need to maintain the state's appearance of autonomy, neutrality and benevolence, and the limits this imposed on their ability to intervene on behalf of metropolitan interests. Also apparent are the consequences of their efforts in the varied and often idiosyncratic layers of institutional forms and practices that attempt to establish, sustain, regulate and, indeed, reproduce politically and juridically the desired social relations of production and exchange.[32]

Regulation of the social relations of production is also, ipso facto, regulation of the forms and occurrence of class struggle as well as the establishment of the conditions of accumulation. As the above paragraphs suggest, and earlier chapters have tried to demonstrate, the colonial state's response conflict and African resistance involved a good deal more than knee-jerk repression. On the one hand, it fell to the often hard-pressed local administrators to decide whether to employ the limited coercive resources at their disposal or seek some form of accommodation and compromise; and from their decisions emerged the diverse local 'concordats of coexistence' that shaped the particular modes of development in a colony. On the other hand, we found that in Kenya developing class struggles penetrated the very apparatus of the colonial state through the perennial 'protest voice' of colonial officials (see Chapters 4 and 5) defending the rights of underpaid peasant producers, displaced squatters, and abused and exploited labourers.

CLASS FORMATION WITH AND AGAINST THE STATE

The role of the colonial state in the processes of articulation, domination and collaboration, and in the regulation of production relations and conflict, exercised a decisive influence on the patterns of class formation in each colony. Out of these processes emerged particular combinations of opportunities and constraints that encouraged some Africans and forced many others to enter into new forms of labour, production and exchange.

For us, the most important set of constraints and opportunities surrounded the development of the white settler bourgeoisie and African petit-bourgeoisie of colonial Kenya. The saga of these two classes in Kenya contains both the most signal success and the most striking failure in the history of class formation in colonial Africa. Both the white settlers and the African petit-bourgeoisie were called into being by the colonial state. The former were believed to be the necessary basis for the economic development of the territory; the latter emerged less deliberately as the result of the creation of a group of indigenous collaborators essential for the maintenance of effective colonial control and out of the desire of the colonial authorities to encourage African loyalty and obedience by providing concrete material benefits from British rule. The structural position in the political economy and collective self-awareness of both groups was rooted in an intensely ambivalent relationship of opportunity/dependence and constraint/conflict with the colonial state that strikingly illustrates the difference between and dialectical relationship of class and state power.

The white settlers came to Kenya largely from the developed capitalist civilization of Britain and therefore had clear notions of property and production relations, and a strongly developed class, racial and national consciousness. Characterized by a striking combination of political and social organization and 'clout', and economic weakness and inexperience, they expected the state to serve their interests in a straightforward way and responded with frustrated rage when the state authorities showed resistance or reluctance to do so. The settlers existed in Kenya as a dominant class largely because of the actions of the colonial state. Most of the major institutional innovations and policy initiatives of the colonial state in Kenya up to the Second World War were intended to establish and maintain the conditions for accumulation of capital by the white settlers, including the recruitment and control of labour, the regulation of relations with metropolitan and international capital, and the protection of settler production from competition and from the ravages of the Great Depression. The settlers were the most important practitioners of the 'vulgarization' of state power for their own material interests, treating the state as an instrument of their aspirations.

At the same time, the reaction of the colonial authorities to settler demands and to the threat of being turned into a direct agent of their interests offers the clearest evidence for the importance of the relative autonomy of the state. If the settlers defined themselves through their demands upon the state, the collective self-awareness of the state officials depended heavily on resisting and setting limits to those demands in what they understood to be the interests of the Africans and in order to defend the legitimacy of colonial rule. Even the very repressiveness of the state in Kenya (as noted in Chapter 5) was often prompted by a desire to pre-empt more brutal and destabilizing action by the settlers. The concept of 'imperial trusteeship', an exclusive prerogative of the colonial bureaucracy that could not be divided or shared with the settlers, provided in the interwar decades the ideological focus for the defence of the autonomy of the state apparatus.

The supreme paradox of the settlers in Kenya was that their very success in 'vulgarizing' state power to serve their interests ultimately provided the economic and political grounds for their failure as a dominant class and (given the frantic clamour of their earlier political activity) their astonishingly quiet disappearance from Kenyan society within a generation after independence. By the post-1945 period, the economic viability of settler estate production rested, in good times as well as bad, on an elaborate apparatus of state and parastatal financial, research, extension, production and marketing institutions. This dependence upon the state fragmented the focus and driving force of settler politics into isolated constituencies of specialized producers and deprived them of autonomous external bases of power with which to resist the dramatic shifts of colonial policy in 1959–60. By that point, settler resistance was largely reduced to the serious but self-annihilating threat of running down and destroying their estates. In Kenya at least, the confounding of class power with state power ultimately destroyed the putative dominant class.

The settlers also failed miserably to establish cultural and ideological grounds for the political and moral hegemony vital for their survival as a dominant class and for the success of their political project of directly assuming control of the state from the Colonial Office-appointed bureaucracy. While Africans surely learnt a great deal from them about capitalist property and production, and settler efforts and those of the state on their behalf cleared away much of the indigenous institutional underbrush that could have impeded capitalist development, the greed, bigotry, and racism of so many settlers and their underlying, yet very real, fear of Africans generated hatred and contempt rather than moral leadership. Equally important, the inability of the settlers to see beyond their immediate material interests or their testy adversarial relationship with the colonial state, along with the intemperate vituperation of their political action, appears as early as the 1930s to have convinced much of the colonial bureaucracy in both Kenya and Britain, along with major segments of Parliament, that the settlers would never have the moral authority and ideological hemony to rule a stable Kenya on their own.

These negative political and ideological characteristics of the settler community also served to undermine the one deliberate effort of the colonial state to directly intervene in the development of a multiracial dominant class. The strategic vision of Governor Mitchell and other senior officials to breach the racial exclusivity of class formation and bring Africans into a new level of politico-economic collaboration in capitalist development, which nevertheless preserved a predominant white position, was never accepted by more than a small progressive minority within the European community, usually those with direct ties to British and international capital. Furthermore, the latter, in the shape of the corporations that invested in Kenya in growing numbers from the 1950s, quickly came to see the settlers as an obstacle to political stability and capitalist development rather than as a condition for it. By the end of that decade both the state authorities and metropolitan capital had begun to turn towards the African petit-bourgeoisie as the basis for a potentially viable dominant class.

The development and character of the African petit-bourgeoisie in Kenya, and elsewhere in colonial Africa, cannot be understood outside its deeply ambivalent relationship with the colonial state. This ambivalence, expressed in sharply contrasting and often alternating patterns of collaboration and conflict, encouragement and constraint, attraction and rejection, was felt both by Africans and the colonial authorities and was grounded in some of the most fundamental contradictions of colonialism. The African petit-bourgeoisie consisted of varying and overlapping combinations of the African agents of the colonial state, merchants, artisans, wealthy commodity producers and elements of traditional ruling classes. All enjoyed some degree of wealth, status and power significantly above that of the masses and derived from their association with the political and economic institutions of colonialism.

There is abundant evidence in our own work and elsewhere that the colonial authorities regarded the African petit-bourgeosie as the essential grassroots instrument of political control and the active agents of social and economic progress, encouraging their participation in commodity production and trade both to reward their loyalty and demonstrate the material benefits of colonialism. As an emerging class, however, these groups represented an indigenous development of capitalism that potentially challenged metropolitan capital, and, in the particular circumstances of Kenya, white settler capital; and also a potential dominant class challenging the authority of the colonial state and exerting its power over the rest of the population. There is also abundant evidence of the colonial authorities' sensitivity to this threat in their common stereotypes of abusive chiefs, grasping politicians, and exploitative merchants and their frequent interventions to curb what was seen as the abuse of power, corruption, greed and exploitation of the poorer elements of the population.

The signals sent to the African petit-bourgeoisie were thus a confused mixture of encouragement and constraint, praise and condemnation. The disparate elements of this class comprised groups with quite different positions within the partial and syncretic transformations of African societies. In Kenya they derived a degree of coherence and unity from the phenomenon of 'straddling', which saw involvement in two or more spheres within a family or even the career of a single individual. Even more important, however, to the self-awareness and political cohesion of these elements as a class was the dialectic of collaboration and struggle with the colonial state. On the one hand, the African petit-bourgeoisie sought the vulgarization of state power in many forms through the formation of new organizations and solidarities to take advantage of the opportunities for wealth and power the state could offer. This constant formulation of new constituencies of interest probed and tested the limits of collaboration with the colonial state apparatus. On the other hand, however, the increasingly frequent conflicts with the colonial state provided an experience of frustration and struggle that served to crystallize and mobilize a community of class interest and its organized political and economic expression.

Beyond the limits of structuralism: culture, ideology and historical experience

We have become increasingly aware as our research has developed that the process of class formation and the syncretic synthesis of capitalist and precapitalist forms that characterized the process of articulation were intimately related to internal struggles over class and to the cultural reconstruction of concepts of community, identity, citizenship and status that it is increasingly apparent took place within many African societies. The institutions of property and power formally depicted in the work of 20th-century social anthropologists *c.* 1930–60 do not represent the forms of primordial 'tradition', but rather diachronic snapshots of a changing reality already significantly changed by colonial intrusion and African response. Class formation within African societies increasingly appears to have been to a large degree an often sharply contested process of restructuring inherited patterns of inequality already present in precolonial institutions. In Kenya, and particularly among the Kikuyu, the struggles over class engendered by the emergence of a petit-bourgeoisie were expressed within conflicts over lineage and clan boundaries, forms of rights to land and social dependence, and the conflicting claims and opportunities of successive generations maturing under colonial domination. The outcome of these struggles over social boundaries and statuses had not only important economic, political, spatial and temporal implications for the Kikuyu, but also critical cultural and ideological ones.

In his analysis of Kikuyu political ideas and their relation to the internal struggles that shaped the specific form of what we call 'Mau Mau' (see Chapter 7), John Lonsdale has shown that ethnic consciousness is not primordial 'tribalism', but rather 'a form of political association, supported by the contested cultural conventions that surround the performance of civilizing labour . . . and is socially and intellectually created and is, therefore, subject to continual redefinition by changing political coalitions within and between ethnic groups.' Ethnicity and class are not mutually exclusive processes and identities, the latter overwhelming and extinguishing the former, but intimately related phenomena whose protean forms are constantly being revised and fought over in the continuing and unfinished encounter of capitalism with African societies.[33] The notions of 'Kikuyuness' that cognitively framed Kikuyu social and political discourse by the 1950s were a conjunctural outcome of both the particularities of Kikuyu incorporation into the colonial economy and state and their distinctive responses grounded not only in the pre-existing forms and internal contradictions of their institutions, but also in the powerful structures of meaning embedded in their language and culture. Differential access to new sources of wealth and power derived from collaboration with the colonial state, and participation in commodity production and wage labour, provided both material resources and new sources of impoverishment; the ideological reinterpretation of 'Kikuyuness' and its key values provided the idiom of internal conflicts as well as the wider basis of consciousness and solidarity in the escalating conflicts with the colonial authorities. Ultimately, the internal and external levels of gender, ethnicity and class formation, within Kikuyu society and in its relation to wider colonial society and the state in Kenya, were mutually reinforcing.

If we are to take seriously some of the methodological and theoretical points made earlier in this chapter about the importance of not writing history backwards and that historical experience has to grapple with specific forms of capitalism and colonialism, then we must deal not only with the actions of particular groups of actors, but also with the cognitive cultural and ideological contexts within which their actions were conceived that form the vital link between social structure and human agency. Questions of subjectivity and the diversities of meaning cannot be ignored. This is as necessary for the Kikuyu considered in Chapter 7 as it is for the British administrators studied in Chapter 6. It is at this point, however, that we run up against the limits of Western theories of development – whether liberal modernization theory or Marxism –

which are grounded in the conception of a secular nation-state, whether capitalist or socialist, as the singular and inevitable destination of a universal human history. As Clifford has recently pointed out:

> whenever marginal peoples come into a historical or ethnographic space that has been defined by the Western imagination . . . their distinct histories quickly vanish. Swept up in a destiny dominated by the capitalist West and by various technologically advanced socialisms, these suddenly 'backward' peoples no longer invent local futures. What is different about them remains tied to their traditional pasts, inherited structures that either resist or yield to the new but cannot produce it.[34]

The history of Kenya, most dramatically in the case of 'Mau Mau', demonstrates that we cannot assume that African societies have entered on a linear process of development that will make them cultural as well as structural facsimiles of Western industrial societies, or that Africans will inevitably become the secular nationalists or class-conscious capitalists and proletarians predicted in theory. There is no one-to-one correlation that can be assumed between the development of capitalism and the state and the forms of culture and ideology, between identity and consciousness. The history of the Kikuyu, or of other African peoples, did not end with the beginning of colonialism, nor did they finally then enter into 'real human' history. The persistence of a distinctive Kikuyu history constitutes another of 'an unresolved set of challenges to Western images of modernity'[35]. This is, of course, easy enough to say, but hard to pursue in the practice of research. One of the unacknowledged (and unacknowledgeable) benefits of modernization theory and Marxism was that they made it unnecessary for scholars to plunge very deeply into the apparently impenetrable thickets of African culture, language and symbol, save as these constituted archaic relics that were 'obstacles to development' or led to 'false consciousness', and also thereby effectively marginalized in African studies the work of anthropologists who had first blazed the trail. If, however, we want to understand what Africans have actually made out of capitalisms, classes and states, rather than agonizing over why they have not followed the path of the mythical universal history of modernity, or laying the blame wholly at the feet of external Western agents of colonialism and imperialism, then it is in precisely that direction that the future path of research must lead. This is not to say that the theoretical approaches to capital and the state explored and revised in this book should ultimately be rejected, but rather that they are not in themselves sufficient to deal with problems of identity and meaning through which universal social forces are shaped and reshaped into persistently diverse trajectories of change. The explanation of such differences remains the most compelling analytic problem.

Notes

1. Ann Phillips, 'The concept of development', *Review of African Political Economy* 8 (1977) pp. 7-20.
2. Andre Gunder Frank, 'The development of underdevelopment', in A. Cockcroft and D. Johnson (eds), *Dependence and Underdevelopment* (New York, 1972).
3. H. Alavi, 'The state in post-colonial societies: Pakistan and Bangladesh', *New Left Review* 74 (1972); and J. Saul, 'The state in post-colonial societies: Tanzania', R. Miliband and J. Saville, (eds), *Socialist Register 1974* (London, 1974).
4. Nicos Poulantzas, *Political Power and Social Classes* (London, 1973), pp. 44-5.
5. Simon Clarke, 'Marxism, sociology and Poulantzas' theory of the state', *Capital and Class* 2 (1977), p. 18. (The internal quote is from Poulantzas, *Political Power*, p. 274).
6. Gavin Kitching, 'Politics, methods, and evidence in the "Kenya debate" ', in H. Bernstein and B. Campbell (eds), *Contradictions of Accumulation in Africa* (London & Beverly Hills, 1985), pp. 119-20.
7. *Ibid.* and Colin Leys, *Underdevelopment in Kenya*, (London, 1975).
8. E.A. Brett, *Colonialism and Underdevelopment in East Africa* (New York, 1973): Arghiri Emmanuel, 'White settler colonialism and the myth of investment imperialism', *New Left Review* 73 (1972); M.G. Redley, 'The politics of a predicament: white settlers and politics in Kenya, 1918-1940', Ph.D. thesis, Cambridge University, 1976.
9. M.P. Cowen, 'Differentiation in a Kenya location', East African Universities Social Science Conference, Nairobi, 1972; *idem*, 'Wattle production in the Central Province: capital and household commodity production, 1903-1964', Conference on the Political Economy of Colonial Kenya, Cambridge, 1975; *idem*, 'Capital and peasant households', unpublished ms. 1976; A. Njonjo, 'The Africanization of the White Highlands: a study in agrarian class struggles in Kenya, 1950-1974', Ph.D. dissertation, Princeton University, 1977; J. Forbes Munro, *Colonial Rule and the Kamba: Social Change in the Kenya Highlands, 1889-1939* (Oxford, 1975); Sharon Stichter, *Migrant Labour in Kenya: Capitalism and African Response, 1895-1975*, (Harlow, 1982); Margaret Jean Hay, 'Local trade and ethnicity in western Kenya', *African Economic History Review* 2(1) (1975); Frederick Cooper, *From Slaves to Squatters: Plantation Labour and Agriculture in Zanzibar and Coastal Kenya, 1890-1925* (New Haven, Conn., 1980); *idem*, *On the African Waterfront: Urban Disorder and the Transformation of Work in Colonial Mombasa* (New Haven, Conn., 1987); Gavin Kitching, *Class and Economic Change in Kenya: the Making of an African Petit Bourgeoisie* (New Haven, Conn., 1980); Nicola Swainson, *The Development of Corporate Capitalism in Kenya* (London, 1980).
10. Kitching, 'Politics, methods and evidence', p. 121.
11. Bill Warren, *Imperialism: Pioneer of Capitalism* (London, 1980), Ch. 6.
12. E.P. Thompson, *The Poverty of Theory* (London, 1978), p. 280.
13. The development of these themes has been well portrayed in several of the synthetic essays sponsored by the African Studies Association in the United States, especially Frederick Cooper, 'Africa in the world economy', *African Studies Review* 24(2/3) (1981) and Sarah Berry, 'The food crisis and agrarian change in Africa: a review essay', *African Studies Review* 27(2) (1984).
14. Charles Tilly, 'Reflections on the history of European state-making', in C. Tilly (ed.), *The Formation of National States in Western Europe* (Princeton, 1975), p. 14.
15. See the references in Chapter 7 above, especially n. 17.
16. Bob Jessop, 'Recent theories of the capitalist state', *Cambridge Journal of Economics* 1(4) (1977), p. 364; and also B.J. Berman, 'Class struggle and the origins of the relative autonomy of the capitalist state', paper presented at the American Political Science Association, New York, Sept. 1981.
17. A chance meeting with Trevor Gardner, former Minister of Finance of Northern

Rhodesia and later Treasurer of Cambridge University, revealed that financial policy and administration in most British colonies remained in the amateurish hands of seconded administrative officers until the 1950s, when professionally staffed ministries of finance were finally set up. The lead role in setting the standards for this development was Sir Ernest Vasey, Member and then Minister of Finance in Kenya from 1952 to 1959.

18. Kitching, 'Politics, methods and evidence'.
19. B.J. Berman, 'Administration and politics in colonial Kenya', Ph.D. Thesis, Yale University, 1974; J.M. Lonsdale, 'Politics in Western Kenya', Ph.D. thesis, University of Cambridge, 1965.
20. Cooper, 'Africa in the world economy', Berry, 'The food crisis'.
21. Philip Corrigan and Derek Sayre, *The Great Arch: English State Formation as Cultural Revolution* (Oxford, 1985), pp. 189–90.
22. Martin Carnoy, *The State and Political Theory*, (Princeton, 1984), p. 255.
23. *Ibid.*, p. 251 and also Chs. 5, 6 and 8.
24. Carnoy, *States and Political Theory*, p. 254.
25. This is explored further in J.M. Lonsdale, 'States and social processes in Africa', *African Studies Review* 24(2/3) (1981). See also John Iliffe, *The Emergence of African Capitalism*, (Minneapolis, 1982), pp. 35–8; and John Lonsdale, 'The European scramble and conquest in African history', in R. Oliver and G. Sanderson (eds), *The Cambridge History of Africa, Vol. 6*, (Cambridge, 1985).
26. Iliffe, *Emergence of African Capitalism*, p. 37.
27. As in the case of Ghanaian cocoa producers analysed by Geoffrey Kay in the 'Introduction' to his *The Political Economy of Colonialism in Ghana* (Cambridge, 1972).
28. Michael Burowoy, *The Politics of Production* (London, 1985), pp. 214–15.
29. Michael Cowen, 'Commodity production in Kenya's central province', in Judith Heyer *et al.*, *Rural Development in Tropical Africa*, (London, 1981). Other scholars have argued for the growing power and dominance of African capitalism after the defeat of Mau Mau and stressed its vigorous advance into new sectors including the former European estates of the 'White Highlands', as well as urban commerce and industry. See, for example, Apollo Njonjo, 'The Africanization of the "White Highlands": a study in agrarian class struggles in Kenya, 1950–1974', Ph.D. dissertation, Princeton University, 1977; and Colin Leys, 'Development strategy in Kenya since 1971', *Canadian Journal of African Studies* 13(2) (1979). See also the perceptive comments on the issue in Iliffe, *Emergence of African Capitalism*, pp. 39–42.
30. Kitching, 'Politics, methods and evidence', p. 139.
31. For an example of this in combination with a highly symbolic assertion of the facade of imperial omnipotence, see John Lonsdale, 'State and peasantry in colonial Africa', in R. Samuel (ed.), *People's History and Socialist Theory* (London, 1981), pp. 113–14.
32. Our understanding here owes much to the important analysis in Ellen Meiksins Wood, 'The separation of the economic and the political in capitalism', *New Left Review* 127 (1981).
33. Or, indeed, in ostensibly modern industrial societies, as the revival of virulent ethnic conflicts, apparently unsubdued by decades of secular communisn, in an unintended outcome of perestroika and glasnost in the Soviet Union should remind us. The interaction of class and ethnic or national identity and the enduring embrace of the latter in the face of the secular materialism of liberalism or Marxism is brilliantly explored in Ben Anderson, *Imagined Communities: Reflections on the Origin and Spread of Nationalism* (London, 1983).
34. James Clifford, *The Predicament of Culture* (Cambridge, Mass., 1988), p. 5.
35. *Ibid.*, p. 7.

Nine

African Pasts in Africa's Future

JOHN LONSDALE

> *Leave the dead*
> *Some room to dance.*
> Wole Soyinka[1]

> *Why is history subversive? Human beings make history by their actions on nature and on themselves. History is therefore about human struggle: first with nature as the material source of the wealth they create – food, clothing and shelter; and secondly, struggle with other humans over the control of that wealth . . . But it is precisely because history is the result of struggle and tells of change that it is perceived as a threat by all the ruling strata in all the oppressive exploitative systems.*

> Ngugi wa Thiong'o[2]

> *The BaKongo, of course, are not unaware of history; they simply deplore it. Any informant, asked to describe his own origin, quotes tradition; asked to describe the origin of his competitors, he recites history.*

> Wyatt MacGaffey[3]

The future is treacherous territory for historians.[4] It is also their continually imagined ideal. They may not admit it, even to themselves, but historians cannot help but judge the human successes and failures that they find in their re-creation of the past other than by the light of their own hopes and fears for the future. Effective political actors in the everyday world of the present require a complementary feat of the imagination. They can most easily recognize and work for a desired future when they have imagined it, and are then able to portray it to a wider public as a project that builds on the triumphs of a living past or avenges its defeats. The historical imagination can also 'seize hold of a memory as it flashes up at a moment of danger',[5] and help to ignite creative political passion in even the bleakest of situations. Few people would question that Africa is now passing through a moment of societal trial and danger. Too many of the continent's systems of government repress rather than foster the free institutions of civil society; too many of its peoples see their ruling authorities as evils to be evaded rather than as potential instruments of the public good. Whether an English historical imagination is able, or has the right, to envisage an appropriately alternative African future or to seize hold of the memories that may now be flashing up in African minds must be more open to doubt. Unlike Africa's own historians, Western Africanists do not 'have to put up with the consequences and the setbacks' of African history, 'in the most intimate and personal manner',[6] sometimes so intimate as to endanger the local scholar's freedom and even survival.[7] But African historians are themselves asking the questions to which this essay is addressed. What follows is a personal view, but it owes much to the ideas of my African colleagues.

Why should Africans read history and what African histories should they read? My answers to these questions are those that one would give anywhere else in the world, if with added urgency. My initial assumptions, from which all else follows, are that free political argument is essential to the formulation of alternative societal futures and that without such argument there is no sure means of mobilizing active consent to present authority. But political argument demands self-awareness in its protagonists, a public acceptance of the moral autonomy of political actors and, perhaps above all, a usable political language. By that I mean a commonly understood set of symbols that sum up, by allegory, myth and metaphor, the core values that ought to, but seldom do, govern the always disputable relationships between individuals and any society in their provision for the future, which is implicit in the way in which they reproduce the present out of the past. A political language unites people over what to argue about; it provides the images on which they can base their ideologies. Ideologies mobilize political support around social division but can be used in attempts to suppress debate. They can only enlarge understanding or fire enthusiasm if they accentuate, recreate or manipulate the common symbols of the language.

African Pasts in Africa's Future

Agreement on symbolic values is thus a necessary precondition for constructive debate about the distribution of their societal costs and benefits. Unless they share a political language, people can pursue their conflicting interests only by coercion or evasion – both denials of the possibility of a shared and productive, if still disputed, future.

A common political language and its inventive usage by the divided members of a political community can be produced in only one way, by historical process. Historical awareness is the only form of self-knowledge there is. But history is also open to constant reinterpretation, in what seems to be a universal quest for useful precedent.[8] History is therefore an anvil of identity that is vulnerable to distortion by any monopolists of power. In Ngugi's words, tyrants, whether colonial regimes or their successors, 'are terrified at the sound of the wheels of history . . . So they try to *rewrite* history, make up official *history*; if they can put cottonwool in their ears and in those of the population, maybe *they* and *the people* will not hear the *real* call of history, will not hear the *real* lessons of history', which teach of struggle and change.[9] It has to be said that radical history of the sort produced by Ngugi runs exactly the same risk,[10] but for the moment much of Africa's written history has indeed taken the part of its rulers rather than that of its people. That is rapidly ceasing to be the case; there is already, as this chapter tries to show, a vigorous alternative historiography (which should properly be called 'radical' were that not now a discredited term) that illuminates past African constructions of varied political languages of debate. These can well be seen as subversive of tyranny, but for that very reason might also prove to be supportive of responsible government.

Part of the danger in Africa's present moment lies in the restrictions imposed on Africans in their efforts to formulate alternative futures, thanks to the constraints that are often placed on their reformulations of history, the cotton wool stuffed in their ears. It is characteristic that where the future remains most stridently in question, in South Africa, there also past history is both most vigorously disputed and, until very recently, most rigorously suppressed. Times of ideological conflict create a 'massive thirst for history'[11] and, as a result, the contending schools of South African history are the liveliest in the continent.[12] We should not be surprised that those who have thought hardest about the future of black South African education should see History as the first element of the curriculum to demand reform.[13] And, with Ngugi, we should be still less surprised that the body concerned, the National Education Crisis Committee, was among the organizations to be banned early in 1988; *their* history was bound to be subversive.

It was bound to be subversive of white South Africa's definition of its own legitimacy, its 'hegemonic project',[14] for South Africa is a peculiar illustration of the historic flaw that lies at the heart of almost all African countries – the fact that they are very recent conquest states. South Africa is peculiar in that its official political language has some symbolic resonance in the memory of a large minority of its population, those white immigrants, Boer and Briton, on whose violently contradictory behalf the land was conquered. This does not mean that South Africa's political language is philosophically coherent, far from it. It is a discordant mixture of British legalistic liberalism, Afrikaner organic nationalism (itself a recent political construct)[15] and the practical suppression of the rights of the country's black nations, let alone its black citizens. But the political languages of other African countries are not merely just as incoherent as South Africa's; they have yet to evoke much symbolic resonance from within their civil societies. Apart from the cases of Ethiopia and the Islamic states of northern Africa, their official political languages have no historical links with the core values of their component nationalities. Instead, their state institutions straddle the historical divide between the stark discontinuity of alien conquest, with its imported civilizing mission or hegemonic project, and the continuities in the history of their conquered peoples, each with their own civilizing mission.[16] These submerged continuities exist because conquest could never be total. Its expensively imported violence had to be paid for by the economic returns on local political alliance;[17] it certainly changed, but could not remove, the grounds of cultural, social and political struggle that, such is human nature, will always draw for inspiration upon locally recreated ethnic pasts.

The question then is, given this discrepancy between the brief history of imposed African states and the long history of the formation of Africa's peoples, whether one can pursue any deep historical enquiry 'without touching the very foundations of the fragile legitimacy of the State itself',[18] even of those states that cannot properly be numbered among Ngugi's tyrannies. The number of historians among Africa's intellectual exiles testifies to the seriousness of the question. Joseph Ki-Zerbo, a member of the steering committee of the UNESCO *General History of Africa* and editor of its first volume, has declared from his Senegalese exile that Africa is 'gradually being reduced to silence'. In earlier times, he believes, it was possible for court historians to recall past achievements in order to admonish Africa's rulers; but nowadays too many regimes take after 'the thirteenth-century West African emperor, Soumaoro Kante who, according to legend, ordered those wishing to criticise him to voice their thoughts into a gourd which would then be sealed, thereby imprisoning their opinion!'[19]

More recently, Ghana's head of state, Jerry Rawlings, has condemned his country's intellectuals for adopting that same 'culture of silence' towards his own policies; but when Professor Adu Boahen, another editor of the *General History*, invoked past rulers of Ghana so as to admonish its present one, his voice was smothered by censorship.[20] With these experiences of two of its editors in mind, one can begin to catch the Delphic message expressed by the former president of UNESCO's drafting committee, Bethwell Ogot, when he hoped that his colleagues' efforts would have 'great topical significance. By showing the true face of Africa, the *History* could, in an era absorbed in economic and technical struggles, offer a particular conception of human values.'[21]

The question needs to be unpacked into its separate parts if it is to be properly grasped. First, must the historian's search for human values – the core of any effective political language – necessarily subvert African states? After all, they are the only institutions currently capable of resolving the conflicts between people locally, and between local people and the outside world, however much some of them seem bent on doing the reverse. Or do African states stand, rather, to gain from the sort of history to which, I have suggested, African historians are even now turning as their next intellectual challenge? Conversely, do Africa's domesticated conquest states really have no option but to try to construct their legitimacy out of the ideological cotton wool that suffocates self-interested consent and evokes, instead, the societal evasion and cynicism that in recent years seems to have been at least as important a cause of economic collapse as the external inequalities of the world economy? To unpack the question in this particular way is of course to answer it. If Africa is to have any sort of future then it has to have a different past, however much it may seem to subvert the present.

Four areas of historical enquiry suggest themselves in response to these questions, four sources for the development of Africa's political languages: the state, 'custom', ethnicity and religion. They are not only closely related to each other but also concerned with the issue of social inequality. All these fields are being reinterpreted in ways that speak directly to Africa's present moment of danger. Africa's alternative histories are full of relevance to Africa's future, if only they are rediscovered. It is difficult to say how far these new approaches are a response by historians to the challenge of the present, how far simply the pursuit of the logic of historical enquiry, in which successive explanatory frameworks prompt further sets of questions. Given the nature of historical enquiry, part intellectual and part moral, such a duality is inevitable. But perhaps one thing certain can be said of almost all historians nowadays, whatever our field of enquiry: that one of our central concerns is to escape the abstract tyranny of grand theory, so leaving real people now dead some room to dance.

There is no doubt that the first phase of professional African history in the 1950s and 1960s was a liberating enterprise.[22] It was 'history for self-government'.[23] But the 'king and trumpet' or 'kin and colonization' perspectives of the time were soon seen to be intellectually barren, not least because they mirrored too closely contemporary hopes – all too soon dashed – for the 'progress' that would be achieved by the consensual mobilization of popular energies in the new states of postcolonial Africa.[24] 'Lost in the maze of purple and gold',[25] our historiography expected too much of African states in the future and examined too little of their failings in the past. Those weaknesses are now better understood, and there is not now the same pressure for evolutionary emulation that then demanded that the most significant African history should be concerned with its early kingdoms and empires. In the economic field, it is now clear, African kingdoms were more often predatory than productive,[26] not least because in the land-rich and labour-scarce conditions of precolonial Africa the supply costs of labour for purposes of dynastic profit and power were inordinately high; peasants were too independent to be exploited and the alternative, slavery, needed military establishments that placed a ruinously high value on their own political privileges.[27] Further, when they faced the European scramble in the late 19th century, kingdoms generally put up a brittle and short-lived show of resistance, by comparison with peoples who were not burdened with dynasties and palaces. In their death throes kingdoms broke up along their internal fault lines – through the defection of subject provinces, the flight of slaves and quarrels between princes. The divisions within stateless peoples were, by contrast, less easily discerned by the white invaders, and their common, if internally competitive, productive interests could more easily be pursued into the colonial period, by a canny combination of evading administrative demands and seizing expanded market opportunities.[28]

The social history of colonial states has scarcely begun to be studied with the rigour that their records allow,[29] but in the context of a concern with the construction of political languages it is clear that their conquest of the terms of political debate was not only incomplete but also productive of disorder rather than order. The days are long past when they could be seen as neutral if unwitting conduits of societal 'modernization'.[30] Their official languages were both literally and symbolically alien, and even on their own imported terms they lacked all consistency, especially in the years after the Second World War. They increasingly paid lip service to representative democracy at the centre but continued to rely at bottom on approximations to hereditary chiefship; meritocratic criteria in the civil service ran up against the exclusions of racial discrimination; rational bureaucratic forms masked a reliance upon the religious supports of classical African, Islamic and Christian cosmologies.[31] The great gulf between African civil society and the alien administrative structure encouraged amoral ingenuities in those who sought inclusion within the patronage of power.[32] The saddest comment on the incoherence of the political language of late colonialism is the fate of the post-colonial project that followed most closely the logic of only one of its several strands. Tanzanian socialism failed not least because Nyerere gambled on the mobilizing power of the bureaucratic Fabianism that had inspired the British Colonial Office after the Second World War. But it was not this coherent strand of *ideology* that had preserved some order during decolonization, rather, it was the devolution of power to a nationalist party that hoisted on to its bandwagon all the jostling interests and symbols of Tanganyika's fragmented civil society. The actual, divided, *practice* of British rule had left Nyerere with peoples whose political thought, very much their own creation in changing times, was inherently hostile to the presidential Fabianism.[33]

Nothing in the historiography so far discussed suggests that the remembered past of African states, whether kingdoms or colonies, can foster a language of productive argument about the future. And when one turns to the question of 'custom', the next field of enquiry, it could be said that their histories have in fact been used to discourage debate. But anthropologists and historians have for some time been questioning the role of custom in the ideological presence of the past. It is now clear that the idea of African custom and tradition arose mainly as a means to hallow official histories or, better, officials' history. Our early consensual models of African kingship or chieftaincy were handed down to us by colonial officials who wanted to establish both political alliances with the then lords of the land and the legitimacy of their own rule. Rule through chiefs was defensible so long as they could be seen as the natural leaders of communal societies untroubled by a plurality of political ideologies, for whom consensus was an inherited state of mind rather than an ideological weapon of social conflict. But the African history that was so construed was, in effect, a denial of history, an attempt to suppress contemporary debate. The formal ideology of custom exalted authority through its insistence that African societies had none of that historical complexity and inequality that would render political argument essential to their stability. Custom was formalized in the turbulent early colonial years, when the powers of chiefs and heads of households were threatened by the new freedoms opened up to women and young men through the enlargement of the labour and produce markets, the abolition of slavery, and official restrictions on the political use of witchcraft accusations. Colonial conquest had helped in the narrow *building* of African power, by its offers of alliance with European violence; but the colonial pax and markets also allowed the spreading *vulgarization* of power, in the emergence of new occupational and religious associations, traders, workers and teachers, both Islamic and Christian.[34] In rapidly changing times the codification of customary law was a weapon of present social control rather than a summary of past history. The men who sought to create and exploit the new colonial order, both black and white, would have agreed with the BaKongo that history was deplorable, a complex political language of conflict that threatened present patriarchy with the revival of past vulgarity.[35]

The discourse of custom influenced both the structural-functional anthropologists of the time and African cultural nationalists, for whom it was important to show that all aspects of their society had in the past fitted together in due order.[36] The first leaders of independent Africa also turned to custom in their own search for authority. The myth of monarchical consensus and tribal reciprocity justified one-party rule and could show, for instance, that African socialism could be fostered by reform from above, without the need to be seized from below. As Nyerere put it, addressing both points: 'We, in Africa, have no more need of being "converted" to socialism than we have of being "taught" democracy. Both are rooted in our past – in the traditional society which produced us.'[37] Nkrumah agreed with Nyerere that there had been no classes in traditional African society. He allowed that colonialism might have introduced the corruption of capitalism but, nevertheless, he went on, 'because of the continuity of communalism with socialism, in communalistic societies, socialism is not a revolutionary creed, but a restatement in contemporary idiom of the principles underlying communalism.'[38] Nkrumah argued, further, in a doubtless unwitting echo of past colonial officials, that Africans had therefore had no ideological conflicts in the past nor any need for them in the future. The francophone philosopher Paulin Hountondji has convincingly condemned what he calls this 'unanimist illusion'; he believes that unless it is discarded, like Ngugi's cotton wool, there can be no 'liberation of political debate . . . able to be stated in terms of interests and conflicts of interests.'[39] And, to extend Hountondji's logic, we can say that without a liberation of debate, without an acceptance of political and institutional pluralism, there can be no effective critique of the factional politics of patronage and clientage. These may well nourish loyalties under the name of consensual custom, but they have also helped to starve African economies by their allocation of all-too scarce resources according to a political rather than productive logic. The politics of custom carries the seeds of its own destruction.[40]

But there are other versions of the past. Historians have provided a wealth of alternative images to the 'custom' in which precolonial history has been cocooned, should politicians dare to look for them. Even in the most powerful of Africa's old kingdoms people argued passionately about the sources and purposes of power. Perhaps that is why their kingdoms *were* powerful. Subjects espoused different theories of government.[41] Myths of genesis reflected on the duality of all power, its earthy brutality and divine authority.[42] Most African kingdoms were not only decentralized, they were built up on layers of power in which regional and occupational interests protected their own autonomies, so that court politics were also party politics. There was always conflict between centre and periphery, couched in a political language of rights and obligations. Rules of succession were generally loose enough to permit different criteria of eligibility and bases of consent. Royal rituals were shot through with the uneasy but essential dichotomy between the need to invest the monarchy with power while also protecting the people from the monarch's rages.[43]

All such history could be interpreted as subversion. The playwright Wole Soyinka saw the difficulty years ago. In his play *A Dance of the Forests*, commissioned to celebrate Nigeria's independence, his Council Orator, Adenebi, hoped to summon up 'the scattered sons of our proud ancestors. The builders of empires . . . Let them assemble round the totem of the nation and we will drink from their resurrected glory.' The historians of alternative pasts might well, as in this play, be blamed for inviting the wrong guests to the feast instead, 'slaves and lackeys. They have only come to undermine our strength. To preach to us how ignoble we are. They are disgruntled creatures who have come to accuse their superiors as if this were a court of law . . . We asked for statesmen and we were sent executioners.'[44] But I have just argued that by their reliance on a self-interested version of the past, the 'customary' ideology that suppresses what could otherwise be history's pluralist political language, many African statesmen have turned out to be their own executioners. Moreover, custom does not only imprison political debate, it is just as incoherent as the languages of colonial rule, for which it provided only a part of the vocabulary.

For while custom purports to respect the political language of Africa's 'tribes', the ethnicity that is custom's carrier is also seen as the bugbear of contemporary Africa.[45] Thus history is plundered for its symbols of authority yet feared for its divisive fascination with the corporate embodiments of those same symbols, in an era when the unification of societies within the state boundaries established from white conquest is the chief aim of 'nation-building'. But tribes divide what custom is said to unite only when one adopts ahistorical assumptions, only if historians allow ethnicity, as well as custom, to be captured by the politicians. I will argue, further, that a fresh approach to the internal moral perplexities of modern tribe formation presents historians with an opportunity to discuss how a political language of plural debate, over issues that include gender and class conflict, has been produced by Africans in our own day.

Earlier, I contrasted the discontinuities of European conquest with 'the continuities in the history of their conquered peoples'. But it is important not to be misunderstood; the continuities of history are built out of Ngugi's struggle and change. It is now generally accepted that self-aware tribalism is as much the product of social and political change in the modern era as of precolonial history.[46] In earlier times, Africa's political geography was a maze of internal frontiers of colonization, with political communities forming and reforming, all racked by the tensions between the ideological reciprocities of kinship and the realities of the social and economic inequality that distinguished civilizing 'first-comers' from later arrivals, client or captive. The dynamics of internal division gave rise both to fresh bids for frontier autonomy and to cross-cultural alliances that defended ethnic authority against such external subversion. The idea of culturally closed, self-sufficient worlds of tribal descent has had to give way before the growing evidence of the role of the close-fisted 'big men' of colonizing settlements, who were always striving for a legitimate hegemony of societal justice that they never quite achieved. 'Kin' or 'lineage' were ideologies of authority that 'custom' later elaborated, not accurate descriptions of actual friendly societies.[47]

Much has now been written of how political tribes crystallized out of this fluid past in more recent times. Colonial officials imagined tribes and then penned them into districts. Missionaries formalized tribal languages and hallowed them in the Bible. Workers in towns looked for labour exchanges, housing associations, skill protection and job reservation and found that they too were inventing tribes. Peasants found themselves growing cash crops that opened up marketing chains and property relations different from those of neighbours who grew and sold other crops higher up the hills or farther down in the plains. Employers seized on stereotypes of tribal aptitude for different sorts of work, governments similarly had their own simplifying maps of martial and clerical tribes, and Africans adjusted their identities accordingly. Literacy put tribes into print as African intellectuals published improving stories of 'their people'.[48]

If an historical explanation of the growth of 'ethnic prejudice, rivalry and violence' is a 'prerequisite to gaining greater control over it',[49] then historians have done their bit to see that the misunderstandings of the past do not bedevil the future. But there are other aspects to the growth of ethnicity that warrant more research, if there is to be the further possibility that the creative use of the ethnic dialects of a political language may transmute the parochial divisions of tribalism into the universals of human existence. So far historians have focused principally on the question of how members of small-scale societies tried to explain their external relations in a widening and increasingly power-ridden world. Following the logic of historical enquiry – but also the search for a plural political language – it is time to investigate the 'interior architecture' of tribe formation, the construction of social and moral codes in a time of rapid change, with particular reference to the issues of gender and class.

When one asks the simple question, how children are taught to behave and what to expect from others, one invites the collapse of the equally simple model of patrilineal segmentation that structures our understanding of most African tribes. For those who gave younger generations their outlook on life were their mothers or grandmothers. Precisely because they were outsiders in the patriclan, these were able to give intuitive shape to the wider society that has become the 'tribe'. An entirely male logic of lineage relations would have fallen apart without the social wisdom and intellectual creativity of women.[50] Equally, the social impudence of women in the colonial era roused many men to redefine 'tribal' norms to secure a degree of female subordination for which there was often little precedent.[51] Conflict over gender is one example of the universal problems that historians can illuminate in the seemingly divisive pursuit of the dynamic formation of 'tribes'.

Class is another. If one asks what makes a proletarian – as distinct from a migrant worker – part of the answer must lie in the contested experience of wage labour, probably in town. But that is the second part. The first part of the answer must focus on the expropriation of the worker from his means of production, his land. To be dispossessed of land rights, no matter how much these depend on clientage, is to be excluded from many of the rights of citizenship in rural society. It is scarcely surprising, then, that our social science is premised on the opposition between the two categories, tribe and class. Social change has been held to entail a growing consciousness of the latter, at the expense of the former. Much of our uneasiness about modern African tribalism has been due to our perhaps unconscious acceptance of the old colonial wisdom that tribe is a residual category, inhabited only by those very few who have not, through urban wage labour or Western education, suffered the creative pangs of 'detribalization'. From this it follows that political tribalism is created by a cynical manipulation of 'false consciousness'; workers are believed to be blinded to their true, class, interest by a political play on the cultural differences that peasants learn when they come to town and meet people whom they do not understand, but which are irrelevant to their class position.

But the conventional wisdoms of colonial rule and political science were little interested in class conflict. Conventional Marxisms are interested, but they can mislead. For people can enter into class struggle as much to *prevent* themselves from being treated as members of a separate social and moral category as to *defend* their economic interests in common with those who appear to the analyst to be their class colleagues. Much working-class activity in Africa, as elsewhere, has been invisible to students of strikes and trades unions; for workers have been concerned as much with rural social relations, in an effort to avoid *becoming* a proletarian, as with the second stage of class struggle, which seeks to use the power of *being* a proletarian. A beginning has been made in uncovering this invisible side of class struggle with the realization that migrant labour has often represented a double struggle against oppression both at home and in the workplace,[52] even if we need to know more about how workers reacted when growing concentrations of land-ownership and stricter employer disciplines squeezed their freedom of manoeuvre at both ends of their world. In general, however, it appears that workers have fought as much to protect their rights of membership in a 'tribe' – a community whose imagined value was enhanced by the threat of exclusion from it – as to create rights in the entirely new community of their class. Again, the universalities of class and the particularities of tribe are not opposed categories, they are intertwined.

Moreover, African middle classes emerged earlier than working classes, to face much the same problems of identity. The teachers, traders and commercial farmers of colonial Africa sought desperately *not* to allow their new beliefs and privileges to separate them from their social surroundings. Rather, they presented their new wealth and freedoms as the continuation in a new idiom of the civilized values of the colonizing frontier. They saw themselves as moral agents, creating not just wealth for themselves but an example of prosperous security for their people, in a hostile world in which colonial overrule took the place of the old enemy, nature, lurking in uncultivated forest or bush. 'Tribe' was the social crucible of a continuing moral debate about the relationship between individuals, community and the future, whether one was businessman or labourer.[53] African tribalism, in short, originated as much the same phenomenon as European nationalism. It had to face moral problems that territorial African nationalist movements were able to evade, thanks to the expanded opportunity they seemed to be able to promise for all by their invasion of the upper reaches of the conquest state.

Political tribalism exists; the problem is to transcend it. It is generally argued that since coerced assimilation has so often evoked ethnic revivals rather than built new nations, the only way forward is for neutral statesmen to avoid public debate on cultural issues.[54] It is difficult to see how such public avoidance can be prevented from sliding into state suppression of all argument about how small societies can hold large states to account. The new historiography of 'tribe' could provide a language, not for the avoidance of *cultural* issues but for the celebration of the central cultural *issue*, the universal problem at the heart of all our particularities, which is the relationship between the individual and society. Far from being the creature of civic irresponsibility, 'tribe' has been one of Africa's central metaphors of civic virtue.[55] The social separations and immoralities of gender conflict and class formation have given seemingly parochial tribes a poignant quality as bearers of an ecumenical language of political accountability. The language has been betrayed and manipulated no doubt, and tribes are also no doubt competitors for loyalty with the new states of Africa. But without doubt, too, they are also among the few historically resonant sources available for the construction of a language of debate about the future, if only the interior perplexities of 'tribe' were to assume the same degree of importance in the textbooks as their feared external rivalries. The familiar problems that people argue about are more important than the strange tongues in which they speak. The history of African political thought that would permit this transcendence of ethnic particularity by human universality has yet to be written, and the delicate statesmanship would still be needed, but it could be eloquent with a locally constructed political language rather than tongue-tied by the studious avoidance of one.[56] Another possible source of a common political language, rooted in all local historical soils, has a voluminous historiography. This is my fourth and final field of enquiry, that of religion.

Religion looks to be a yet more unpromising historical quarry than tribe in which to dig for a generalizing and productive political language of debate. After all, has not religion divided Africa, as it has divided most parts of the world, more bitterly than any other component of ethnicity? Nothing might seem better calculated to set political teeth on edge than the dozens of different forms of worship that structure the sacred geography of classical African religion within each modern state, or the wild suspicions and panics fostered by what has been called the sociology of witchcraft.[57] The historic conflict between the global religions of Islam and Christianity, too, has done much to inflame the zone of civil war that has at different times stretched across Africa from Nigeria in the west to Ethiopia in the east. Christianity's own divisions have provided the rival banners of civil war, as in precolonial Buganda, and the Christian map of Africa is dotted with thousands of parochial Zions that seem to belie its claim to treat all men as brothers. Worse even than these scandals of disunity, a devoutly believed version of Christian dogma has provided, and still provides for some South African whites, the moral basis for the oppressions of apartheid. But, and this is where the argument begins to turn, Christianity's doctrine of human equality has also helped to inspire the most steadfast opposition to the same regime. Moreover, while President Botha did not hesitate to ban any form of black political opposition, it was simply not possible for him to ban religious belief nor the churches that embody it, since the legitimacy of the South African state depended so heavily on its claim to defend its peoples from the ungodliness of communism. South Africa's churches have identified racial tyranny as sin, much as the Israelites

of old identified the bondage of Pharaoh's Egypt, and the state's eleva-
tion of law and order above obedience to God as blasphemy. Here is a
classic illustration of a political language in the making. The state could
not and cannot avoid using Christian symbols in its public ideology,
they are too deeply embedded in its yet-to-be discarded myth of Genesis-
in-Exodus, the Afrikaners' Great Trek. But on a different reading of the
language's central text, the Bible, these same symbols have been turned
against the state from below, by people who see in Exodus an image of
the future rather than the past.[58] Each side in the conflict understands
the other only too well; neither can disengage from the debate on moral
community.[59]

The relationship between church and state is still one of the staples
of the teaching of British or European history for precisely the reason
that their past conflicts have been the chief influence on the social construction of the political languages of Europe, both Western and Eastern,
since Marxism can well be understood as a Judaeo-Christian heresy. It
was often a bloody business, but the outcome has been that modern
European welfare states appear to be much like secular churches. African
history teaching ought also to give a central place to the relations between
religious and secular power, and for the same reason. It was observed
of Sayyid al-Hassan al-Mirghani, for instance, head of the Khatmiyya
brotherhood in the Sudan in the chaotic 1860s, that he was 'too intelli-
gent to change the moral and constant power he now enjoys, for the
temporal and ephemeral power that was his for the taking' during the
then crisis of Egyptian authority; he preferred to stand apart, as one of
those 'prophets, venerated and feared, who when governments totter in
the throes of revolution, are there to throw themselves between the com-
batants, to quieten for the salvation of society the passions and hate that
are let loose.'[60] This universal tension between the constant and the
ephemeral, between ends and means, between society and the state, has
been as critical an element in the history of Africa as anywhere else in
the world. Islamic rigour stiffened commercial ambition in achieving the
great renovations of statehood in 19th-century West Africa; Christianity
caused colonialism's officials to question its means and helped African
nationalists to transcend its ends. In their modern mass movements both
have become authentic expressions of African religious sensibility. Even
classical African religion, which has generally been understood to be not
so much the moral basis of 'customary authority' but virtually insepar-
able from it, we now know to have been as often critically distant from,
as well as critically supportive of, temporal power as other religious
traditions have been.[61] The Mbona cult of central Africa is a particularly clear example of this general characteristic, with its inherent
tension or 'dual tradition' between a routine association with social
hierarchy and periodic outpourings of spirit-possessed egalitarianism. In

Mbona religious practice, as perhaps in all religions, there was a triangular competition between chiefs and people for the ambiguous moral messages delivered by the medium, the officer of the cult.[62] Similar dynamics gave spirit mediums a central role in the Zimbabwean war of independence, just as Kongo Christianity became a means of liberation for former slaves.[63]

These general arguments in favour of a greater awareness of religious history can be illustrated by a brief look at Kenya, to return from the general to the specific history with which these essays have been principally concerned. In precolonial times the different peoples who have now become Kenyans seem to have had few prejudices against sharing their neighbours' names for and concepts of God, and cults of lesser spirits were just as ecumenical.[64] Nearly all tribal myths of origin, as a recent school history of Kenya points out on its first page, speculate on the relation between man's creation and God,[65] and in colonial times the first Christian converts in a number of Kenyan peoples seem to have assimilated the Exodus story to their local migration myths, so that many elderly informants will now answer 'Egypt' to the question 'where do your people come from?'[66] It is an unasked question how far this link between history and cosmology includes the belief that the present tribal lands were promised to a people whose sense of moral community was proved in the trials of migration and alien overrule. But echoes of an Exodus myth were undoubtedly heard by some members of Mau Mau in their fight for *ithaka na wiathi*, Land and Freedom, or 'land which gives one the capacity to act as a moral agent'.[67] The culture of modern Kenya is so soaked in Christianity that even the novelist Ngugi, who calls himself an atheist, has admitted that 'as a Kenyan African, I cannot escape from the Church. Its influence is all around me.'[68] Certainly, it is impossible fully to appreciate his writings without a grounding in the Bible, as all those young Kenyans who read his works as school literature texts must know.

The relations between church and state have occupied a central place in Kenya's modern political history. Goran Hyden has suggested that church organizations can act in Kenya, as in other countries, as a substitute for the as-yet incomplete penetration of capitalism, as a means to generalize political solidarities that are wider than the parochialisms of clan; in this way churches may 'facilitate governance' by bridging ethnic tensions.[69] One can see the logic of the argument, but the issue goes much deeper than this. It is more illuminating to compare Kenya's historical experience of Christianity with the triangular dynamics of the Mbona cult, with the churches providing a ground of moral and institutional competition between state and people.

Christianity both justified and undermined alien rule in colonial times. It was imported but very soon domesticated. Kenyatta's formulation of Kikuyu political thought was imbued with a 'Protestant ethic' that was as much indigenous as taught by the churches. The civilizing frontier mission of hacking material and moral culture from out of the wilderness of forest and bush became translated into the proper use of one's talents on behalf of a community now wider than the clan.[70] His successor, President Moi, has unashamedly based his own public doctrine on Christianity and his youthful experience as a mission-school teacher.[71] Kenya's churches, encouraged by such official endorsement of their doctrines and yet challenged to assert their own autonomy, have in recent years responded with increasingly clear statements of the qualifications that Christian allegiance places on the responsible citizen's obedience to the state. They were first moved to question the state's claims to total loyalty in the 1969 'oathing crisis', when Kikuyu ethnicity was mobilized to defend the government against the threat of radical opposition.[72] This experience of meeting a 'moment of truth', or *kairos*, gave the churches a confidence in their right, as one of the few critical institutions of civil society, not so much to facilitate governance as to liberate the vocabulary of Kenya's political language. Their journal, *Beyond*, was banned as a result early in 1988, for criticizing the ending of the secret ballot in the ruling party's primary elections. And there seems little doubt that this independence of the churches has encouraged the emergence of a folk Christianity no longer concerned exclusively with personal redemption but also with articulating a biblical theology of power; one of the most popular of contemporary hymns, *Mai ni maruru*, 'water is bitter', recalls the complaints of the Israelites when they found that freedom from Pharaoh meant hardship in the wilderness (Exodus 15:23).[73] In 1987 the Kenyan press was thronged with letters debating the nature of King Darius' tyranny in biblical Persia, following a bishop's sermon on Daniel in the lion's den.[74] A *national* language is being invented out of a religious idiom. While the state searches for legitimacy, church and people translate its symbols of hegemony into the demanding images of public accountability. Conversely, the religious pluralism of Kenya, as of most of sub-Saharan Africa, is perhaps as good a defence as any against clerical critiques of public morality turning into a censorious moral authoritarianism.

In conclusion, African history provides many bases for the construction of a political language in which it is both possible and permissible to debate Africa's future. Many precolonial kingdoms lived with constitutional oppositions that preserved order by parcelling out sovereignty. The image of 'custom' was later invented in circumstances that show its 'unanimist illusion' to be a rulers' ideology designed to circumscribe the legitimate limits of political languages that had previously been deplorably vulgar, telling of struggle and change. But in a world in which the multicultural state is the norm rather than the

African exception,[75] tribes are not only competitive constituencies but also internal arenas of conflict over the fundamental moral issues of gender and class; religion has always furnished a field for a transcendent critique of secular power.

Finally, historians must remember to leave the dead some room to dance. The 'human values' that states ought to protect and which would, in return, strengthen the sovereignty that comes from ruling by consent, can best be offered to a modern audience through studies of real people coping with daily problems in association with their neighbours. New departures in African history are beginning to do this, sounding out 'the silences in the old narratives'.[76] Ethnic history, for example, is being transformed by a new focus on regional ecological history; people could often not cope with ecological stress such as drought or epidemic except by a trans-ethnic cooperation that cultural boundaries regulated rather than obstructed.[77] At the other extreme, it has also proved possible to present a minute portrait of village life through all the radical changes of the past century.[78] The agrarian history of South Africa has begun to be seen through 'the lives of men and women who lived and worked and struggled', in the hope that 'rural South Africans will not be ignored or short-changed when power and wealth are fundamentally redistributed in a transformed society.'[79] A similar concern to rescue so-called dominated classes from 'the grinding and grating of so many abstracted categories against the processes of history' has inspired the exploration of 'the warm, vibrant and intensely human struggle of people to find a place of dignity and security' as townsmen in the capital city of South African capitalism, Johannesburg.[80] Africa's real heroic dead are the poor.[81] They were themselves heroic in their struggles to survive, they evoked heroic care at times from others in society. But it is vital to recognize, too, that the African past is, after all, another country and the land on which the dependent poor once lived is no longer freely available. In the more stringent country of the present the poor, a growing majority of Africa's people, will have to be able to use an ever more demanding language of public responsibility, local as well as global, if there is to be for them a recognizably human future.

Notes

1. Dirge-man in 'A Dance of the Forests', in *Five Plays* (London and Ibadan, 1964), p. 39.
2. Foreword to Maina wa Kinyatti (ed.), *Kenya's Freedom Struggle: The Dedan Kimathi Papers* (London, 1987), p. xiii.
3. *Custom and Government in the Lower Congo* (Berkeley, Cal., 1970), pp. 82-3.

4. I am indebted to the critical ideas offered not only at the Edinburgh 'African Futures' conference at which this paper was presented in December 1987 but also at seminars at the Universities of Aarhus, Copenhagen and Roskilde in early 1988, and especially to Bodil Folke Frederiksen who arranged my visit to Denmark, and to Preben Kaarsholm.

5. Elizabeth Gunner, 'Literature and Apartheid', in J. Lonsdale (ed.), *South Africa in Question* (London, 1988), p. 220, quoting Walter Benjamin.

6. Ndaywel e Nziem, 'African historians and Africanist historians' in Bogumil Jewsiewicki and David Newbury (eds), *African Historiographies: What History for Which Africa?* (Beverly Hills and London, 1986), p. 25.

7. B. Jewsiewicki, 'Introduction' to *ibid.*, p. 16.

8. J.F. Ade Ajayi and B. Ikara, 'Introduction' to their edited collection *Evolution of Political Culture in Nigeria* (Ibadan, 1985), p. 6.

9. Ngugi wa Thiong'o, 'Foreword' to Maina wa Kinyatti, *Kenya's Freedom Struggle*, p. xiii.

10. See pp. 297-8, below.

11. Richard Elphick, 'Historiography and the future of liberal values in South Africa' in J. Butler, R. Elphick and D. Welsh (eds), *Democratic Liberalism in South Africa, its History and Prospect* (Cape Town, 1987), p. 166.

12. For recent guides to South African historiography see, S. Marks, 'The historiography of South Africa: recent developments', in Jewsiewicki and Newbury (eds), *African Historiographies*, pp. 165-76; C.C. Saunders, *The Making of the South African Past* (Johannesburg, 1988); L. Thompson, *The Political Mythology of Apartheid* (New Haven, Conn., 1985).

13. Harold Wolpe, 'Educational resistance', in Lonsdale, *South Africa in Question*, p. 213.

14. To adopt the phrase of J-F. Bayart; see his *L'Etat au Cameroun* (Paris, 1985), *passim.* Revising this chapter for publication, in August 1991, it remains uncertain how far and in what ways white South Africa is prepared to abandon its project.

15. H. Giliomee, 'The beginnings of Afrikaner nationalism, 1870-1915', *South African Historical Journal* 19 (1987), pp. 115-42.

16. J. Lonsdale, 'Political accountability in African history', in P. Chabal (ed.), *Political Domination in Africa: Reflections on the Limits of Power* (Cambridge, 1986), pp. 126-57; and, for an example of an African civilizing mission, see the discussion of Kikuyu political thought in Chapter 12, below.

17. J. Lonsdale, 'The European scramble and conquest in African history' in R. Oliver and G.N. Sanderson (eds), *The Cambridge History of Africa 6: from 1870 to 1905* (Cambridge, 1985), pp. 680-766.

18. Jewsiewicki, 'Introduction' to Jewsiewicki and Newbury (eds), *African Historiographies*, p. 17.

19. Joseph Ki-Zerbo, 'Africa: silent continent?' *Index on Censorship* 15(2) (February 1986), pp. 16-18.

20. Cameron Duodu, 'Dateline West Africa', *The Observer* (London), 27 March 1988, p. 21.

21. B.A. Ogot, 'Description of the Project', in each volume of the UNESCO *General History of Africa*. For an amplification of Ogot's views see R.W. July, *An African Voice: The Role of the Humanities in African Independence* (Durham, NC., 1987), pp. 155-6.

22. T.O. Ranger, 'Towards a usable African past', in C. Fyfe (ed.), *African Studies since 1945: A Tribute to Basil Davidson* (London, 1976), pp. 17-30.

23. K.O. Dike's phrase as early as 1953; see, L. Kapteijns, *African Historiography Written by Africans* (Leiden, 1977), pp. 23-34, 80.

24. J. Lonsdale, 'States and social processes in Africa: a historiographical survey', *African Studies Review* 24(2/3) (1981), pp. 143, 148-51, 170-2.

25. Rola, the Courtesan, in Soyinka, 'A Dance of the Forests', p. 8; she is criticizing 'The accumulated heritage . . . Mali. Chaka. Songhai. Glory. Empires' extolled by

Adenebi the Council Orator. African playwrights and novelists saw through the pretensions of triumphalist national historiography rather sooner than historians did.

26. C. Coquery-Vidrovitch, 'Recherches sur un mode de production africain', *La Pensée* 144 (1969), pp. 61-78; *idem, Afrique noire: permanences et ruptures* (Paris, 1985), pp. 72, 76-8.

27. J. Goody, *Technology, Tradition and the State in Africa* (London, 1971).

28. J. Thornton, 'The State in African historiography', *Ufahamu* 4(2) (1973), pp. 113-26; Lonsdale, 'European scramble', pp. 731-49; and Chapters 2, 3 and 4, above.

29. Of the several exceptions to this generalization the most notable is J. Iliffe, *A Modern History of Tanganyika* (Cambridge, 1979).

30. As in J.S. Coleman, 'Nationalism in tropical Africa', *American Political Science Review* 48 (1954), pp. 404-26; see the extended critique of the myth of colonial modernization in Chapter 11, below.

31. R.C. Crook, 'Legitimacy, authority and the transfer of power in Ghana', *Political Studies* 35 (1987), pp. 552-72; K.E. Fields, *Revival and Rebellion in Colonial Central Africa* (Princeton, 1985).

32. P.P. Ekeh, 'Colonialism and the two publics in Africa: a theoretical statement', *Comparative Studies in Society and History* 17(1) (1975), pp. 91-112; J. Vansina, 'Mwasi's trials', *Daedalus* 111 (1982), pp. 49-70.

33. Iliffe, *Tanganyika*, pp. 567-76.

34. For this distinction see above, Chapter 2.

35. MacGaffey, *Custom and Government*; M. Chanock, *Law, Custom and Social Order: The Colonial Experience in Malawi and Zambia* (Cambridge, 1985); S.F. Moore, *Social Facts & Fabrications: 'Customary' Law on Kilimanjaro, 1880-1980* (Cambridge, 1986). For the authoritarian tendencies in the oral traditions on which 'custom' was based see J. Vansina, *Oral Tradition as History* (London, 1985), Ch. 4.

36. For a good example of this compulsion see J. Kenyatta, *Facing Mount Kenya* (London, 1938).

37. J.K. Nyerere, 'Ujamaa – the basis of African socialism' in his *Freedom and Unity: A Selection from Writings and Speeches 1952-65* (London, 1967), p. 170.

38. K. Nkrumah, *Conscienscism: Philosophy and Ideology for Decolonization and Development with Particular Reference to the African Revolution* (London, 1964), pp. 69, 74.

39. P. Hountondji, *African Philosophy, Myth and Reality* (London, 1983 [Paris, 1976]), p. 155.

40. Chris Allen, 'Staying put: handy hints for heads of state' (paper for the ASAUK symposium on Authority and Legitimacy in Africa, University of Stirling, 1986).

41. Contrary to M. Fortes and E.E. Evans-Pritchard, 'Introduction' to their *African Political Systems* (London, 1940), p. 13.

42. Luc de Heusch, *The Drunken King, or, The Origin of the State* (Bloomington, Ind., 1982 [Paris, 1972]).

43. From an enormous literature see especially, J.C. Miller, *Kings and Kinsmen: Early Mbundu States in Angola* (Oxford, 1976); J. Beattie, 'Checks on the abuse of political power in some African states; a preliminary framework for analysis', *Sociologus* 9 (1959), pp. 97-115; T.O. Beidelman, 'Swazi royal ritual', *Africa* 36(4) (1966), pp. 373-405.

44. Soyinka, *Five Plays*, pp. 32-3, 30.

45. E.A. Ayandele, 'Historians and the Future' in C. Fyfe (ed.), *African Futures* (Edinburgh, 1988), p. 22, n. 1.

46. For a case study, see Chapter 12, below.

47. I. Kopytoff (ed.), *The African Frontier: The Reproduction of Traditional African Societies* (Bloomington and Indianapolis, Ind., 1987).

48. Again, there is a vast literature. I have found especially helpful, Iliffe, *Tanganyika*, Ch. 10; T. Ranger, *The Invention of Tribalism in Zimbabwe* (Gweru, 1985); and J. Guy

& M. Thabane, 'Technology, ethnicity and ideology: Basotho miners and shaft sinking on the South African gold mines', *Journal of Southern African Studies* 14(2) (1988), pp. 257–78.

49. *Ibid.*, p. 259.
50. D.W. Cohen, 'Doing social history from Pim's doorway', Ch. 4 in O. Zunz (ed.), *Reliving the Past: The Worlds of Social History* (Chapel Hill, NC., 1985); the phrase 'interior architecture' is Cohen's. Also, C.M. Clark, 'Land and food, women and power, in nineteenth century Kikuyu', *Africa* 50(4) (1980), pp. 357–70.
51. L. White, 'A colonial state and an African petty bourgeoisie: prostitution, property and class struggle in Nairobi, 1936–1940', Ch. 5 in F. Cooper (ed.), *Struggle for the City: Migrant Labor, Capital and the State in Urban Africa* (Beverly Hills, Cal., 1983), esp. pp. 169, 177, 186–91.
52. F. Cooper, 'Africa and the world economy', *African Studies Review* 24(2/3) (1981), pp. 15–16, 40–45; P. Harries, 'Kinship, ideology and the nature of pre-colonial labour migration: labour migration from the Delagoa Bay hinterland to South Africa up to 1895', Ch. 5 in S. Marks & R. Rathbone (eds), *Industrialisation and Social Change in South Africa* (Harlow, 1982).
53. This discussion is based on my own research into the history of Kikuyu political thought, presented in Chapter 12, below, but my reading of other cases suggests that it is not far from being a general process.
54. C. Young, *The Politics of Cultural Pluralism* (Madison, Wis., 1976).
55. As Ekeh argued long ago in 'Colonialism and the two publics', with much but not all of the reasoning I have used here.
56. An excellent example of the consequences of cultural avoidance for the development of political values can be seen in the Resolutions of the national seminar on Nigeria's political culture in November 1981, in which 'moral regeneration' was to be sought principally by altering systems of government contracts and tightening up financial administration; there was scarcely a mention of rights, entitlements or the practices of political accountability: Ajayi & Ikara, *Evolution of Political Culture*, p. 214.
57. T. Callaghy, *Politics and Culture in Zaire* (Ann Arbor, Mich., University of Michigan Center for Political Studies, 1987).
58. The Kairos Theologians, *The Kairos Document: A Theological Comment on the Political Crisis in South Africa* (London, British Council of Churches, 1986 [Braamfontein: 1985]); M. Walzer, *Exodus and Revolution* (New York, 1985) – a reference I owe to Bruce Berman – has shown the pervasiveness of the Exodus theme in European revolutionary politics. This is equally true of Africa, as seen for instance in Albert Luthuli's echo of Moses in the title of his autobiography, *Let my People Go* (1962), even when the echo has come via India, as in Nelson Mandela's phrase 'no easy walk to freedom', which he borrowed from Nehru: *No Easy Walk to Freedom: Articles, Speeches and Trial Addresses of Nelson Mandela* (London, 1965), p. 31.
59. One of the most powerful South African political images in early 1988 must surely have been that of a protest march through Durban on Good Friday of people carrying crosses and with their mouths gagged. (Photograph in *The Independent* [London], 2 April 1988).
60. Consul Munzinger, quoted in M.W. Daly, *British Administration in the Northern Sudan 1917–1924* (Istanbul, 1980), p. 57. This might be a good description of the Eastern European and South African churches in the 1980s.
61. T.O. Ranger, 'Religious movements and politics in sub-Saharan Africa', *African Studies Review* 29(2) (1986).
62. J.M. Schoffeleers, 'Cult idioms and the dialectics of a region', Ch. 8 in R.P. Werbner (ed.), *Regional Cults* (London, 1977), pp. 219–39; *idem*, review of Jan Vansina's *Oral Tradition as History* in *Journal of Southern African Studies* 14(3) (1988), pp. 487–8. Schoffeleers' concept of a 'dual tradition' seems much like my 'political language'.

63. David Lan, *Guns and Rain: Guerillas and Spirit Mediums in Zimbabwe* (London, 1985); T. Ranger, *Peasant Consciousness and Guerrilla War in Zimbabwe* (London, 1985), pp. 184–216; W. MacGaffey, *Modern Kongo Prophets: Religion in a Plural Society* (Bloomington, Ind., 1983).

64. E.S. Atieno-Odhiambo, 'A note on the chronology of African traditional religion in western Kenya', *Journal of Eastern African Research and Development* 5(2) (1975), pp. 119–22.

65. M. Oludhe Macgoye, *The Story of Kenya: a Nation in the Making* (Nairobi, 1986), p. 1.

66. W.R. Ochieng', 'Misri legends in East African history', *East Africa Journal* 9(10) (October 1972), pp. 27–31.

67. See Chapter 12, below.

68. Ngugi wa Thiong'o, *Homecoming: Essays on African and Caribbean Literature, Culture and Politics* (London, 1972), p. 3; I am grateful to the Revd John Shabaya for pointing out this reference.

69. G. Hyden, *No Shortcuts to Progress: African Development Management in Perspective* (London, 1983), p. 118.

70. From among countless examples see his speech at a church conference in October 1976, quoted in S. Bottignole, *Kikuyu Traditional Culture and Christianity* (Nairobi, 1984), p. 18.

71. G.I. Godia, *Understanding Nyayo: Principles and Policies in Contemporary Kenya* (Nairobi, 1984).

72. J. Lonsdale, with S. Booth-Clibborn and A. Hake, 'The emerging pattern of Church and State co-operation in Kenya', in E. Fashole-Luke *et al.*, (eds), *Christianity in Independent Africa* (London, 1978), pp. 267–84.

73. A. Chepkwony, *The Role of Non-Governmental Organizations in Development: A Study of the National Council of Kenya 1963–1978* (University of Uppsala, Ph.D thesis: 1987), p. 156.

74. David M. Gitari, *Let the Bishop Speak* (Nairobi, 1988).

75. W.H. McNeill, *Polyethnicity and National Unity in World History* (Toronto, 1986).

76. B.A. Ogot, 'The silences in, old narratives, or, new trends in cultural history', *Journal of Eastern African Research & Development* 12 (1982), pp. 36–45.

77. R.D. Waller, 'Ecology, migration and expansion in East Africa', *African Affairs* 84(336) (1985), pp. 347–70; D. Johnson and D. Anderson (eds), *The Ecology of Survival: Case Studies from Northeast African History* (London, 1988).

78. L. White, *Magomero: Portrait of an African Village* (Cambridge, 1987).

79. W. Beinart and C. Bundy, *Hidden Struggles in Rural South Africa* (London, 1987), p. ix.

80. C. van Onselen, *Studies in the Social and Economic History of the Witwatersrand 1886–1914 1: New Babylon* (Harlow, 1982), p. xvi. I am indebted to B. Jewsiewicki, 'African historical studies: academic knowledge as "usable past", and radical scholarship' (ACLS/SSRC commissioned paper for the African Studies Association, Nov. 1987), pp. 18, 62 for reminding me of these last two references.

81. J. Iliffe, *The African Poor, A History* (Cambridge, 1987).

Index

Index

rise of, 294; settler (landed), 102, 135, 181, 188; state, 14, 78–9, 329
capitalism, capital investment, 86; colonial, 351; development, 150, 197; dominant, 131, 138; merchant, 131, 134–5, 150–1, 190; rural African, 190, 191, 352, 353, 359; settler (private), 5, 15, 81, 84, 89, 301; state, 142–3, 197
capitalist mode, 129, 190
capitalist system, world, 101, 144, 165, 184; producers, production, 135, 146, 147
Carothers, J.C., 274, 305 n.36, 333
Carrier Corps, 369; Kikuyu Mission Volunteers (KMV), 369–70
cash crops, resistance to planting, 150–1
'Catonism', 234
Chege wa Kiburu, 430
Cheney, C.R., 319
chiefs and headmen (see also collaborators), 2, 15, 21, 31, 86–7, 89, 93, 118, 137, 160, 165, 197, 229, 272, 278, 361, 362–3, 364–5, 366, 372–3, 420
Christianity, among Kikuyu, see under religion
Churchill, Winston, 33, 48, 111
Church Missionary Society (CMS), see under missionary societies
Church of Scotland Mission (CSM), see under missionary societies
circumcision (initiation), 340–1, 357 n.317; female (clitoridectomy), 340, 381, 388–90, 395; crisis over, 228, 241, 476 n.155, 388–95, 446; male, 327, 388, 414; guilds among Kikuyu
civilising mission: see ideology
clan (muhiriga) and subclan (mbari) among Kikuyu, 84, 326, 327, 335–6, 339–42, 349–50, 352, 354, 359, 360, 361, 366, 369, 370, 378, 394, 400–1, 413, 426, 437–8
clans, colonial use of, 330
Clarke, Simon, 180
Clayton, A., 83
class and classes (see also bourgeoisie), 33; formation (see also social differentiation), 1, 6, 33–4, 95, 134, 137, 140, 151, 161–2, 182–3, 194–98, 317, 351–2; dominant, 79, 80, 117, 180, 195, 196; multi-racial, 197; dominated, 103, 192–3; domination, 103, 142–3, 184, 191–3; inequality of, 351; struggle, 138, 166, 184–5, 188, 193–4, 277, 301–2, 350–2
classes, capitalist, 79; settler, 117, 150, 195–8; African middle class (accumulators), 151, 161, 193, 197, 214; African working, 137, 166, 213–4; 276, 277, 316–7, 352, 424; ruling, 34
cleanliness, 344
Clifford, James, 200
clitoridectomy, see under circumcision, female
cocoa, in Ghana (Gold Coast), 150
coercion (see also labour, coercion of), 147, extra-economic, 131, by the state, 135–6; local, 158, 166
Cohen, William, 164
Coleman, James, 281–2, 286
collaboration, collaborators (see also class formation): 7, 31–2, 81–2, 86, 89, 118, 137, 152, 160–1, 165, 191–3, 197, 199, 229, 272

Colonial Development and Welfare Acts, 242
Colonial Development Corporation, 166, 175–6 n.97
Colonial Office, 16, 32–3, 84, 111, 116, 153–4, 232, 236, 243, 436
colonial states, African, 102, 135, 140–75, 330
colonial rule, problems, of, 230, 324–5, 351
colonialism, in Africa, European, 4, 140, 144, 145; French: 6, 169 n.18, 145, 147
'community work', see under labour, forced
concessions, company, 146, 147; monopoly, 169–70 n.21
conquest, of Kenya: 13–44, 86; of Western Kenya: 45–73; of Africa generally, 322
control, stable political, 7, 93
Cooper, Frederick, 132, 133, 135, 150, 164, 165, 186
cooperative and provident societies, in British colonies, 148–9, 162; in French colonies, 148–9, 162
co-optation, 191–3
Corfield, Corfield Report (see also Mau Mau), 291
Corrigan, Philip, 142, 187
Crown Lands Ordinance 1915, 89, 115–6
Crush, Jonathan, 130
culture (see also nationalism), Kikuyu, 241
custom, political uses of

death, 14, 23, 86; from influenza, 105
decolonization, 166–7
Delavignette, Robert, 149, 157, 160, 167
Delamere, Lord (1870–1931), 34, 383, 384, 428
delinquency, see poverty
dependency theory (see also underdevelopment theory), 3, 7, 21, 129, 138, 179–85, 189
Deschamps, Hubert, 154, 159
'desertion', see under labour
development, capitalist, 86, 130, 176; concessionaire, 89–90; economic, 323–4; pre-capitalist, 129; indigenous, 167
Devonshire, Duke of (Secretary of State for the Colonies), 405–6
dini (see also religion), 397
dini ya Jesu Kristo, 444, 447
disease, 14, 23, 86; and malnutrition, 105, 151
domination, political, 164–5
Dorobo (hunters), 320
drought, 14, 23, 86

East African Protectorate, 16, 18, 68, 85
East African Revival movement, 445, 447
East African Rifles, 17
East African Trades Union Congress, see under trades union
economy, white export, 423; African, 64–5
Egypt, 45, 47
Eliot, Sir Charles (Commissioner 1900-1904), 34, 94
Embu (people and district), 19, 32, 347–8, 449
Emergency, state of, (see also Mau Mau), declared, 8; 227, 252–7, 290, 446, 452, 463
Engels, F., 276, 277
epidemics, 14, 23

Index

ethnicity, 199, 207–11, 303 n.10, 268–9, 277–8, 328–30, 350–3; construction of, 13, 38, 353–4, 360, 371, 404; inter-ethnic relations, 14, 25, 329; Kikuyu, 326–30, 336, 346–7, 392, 437; *karing'a*, 327, 336, 393, 397, 406; *kirore*, 384, 393, 397, 406; tribalism, 267–8, 277, 279, 315; tribalism as a metaphor, 330–2; tribal identity, 268, 353; of Mau Mau, 315–7; and politics, 327–30, 330–2; precolonial, 348
ethnographies, in Kenya, 320, 468 n.7
explorers, European, in Kenya, 319

Fabianism, 209
false consciousness (*see also* ideology *and* class conflict
famine, famines, 14, 23, 30, 342, 346, 349, 364, 372
Fazan, Sidney, 376
fiscal policies, for colonies, 155, 166
Fonds d'investissement et du developpement economique et social des territoires d'Outre Mer (FIDES), 166, 176 n.100
Foreign Office, 16, 32, 85
'formal subsumption of labour', 129
forms of production, pre-capitalist, 129; domestic, 131, indigenous, 145
Fort Hall (Murang'a) District, 251, 395, 421, 433
Fort Smith, 25, 26
Forty Group, *see under: anake a forti*
Frank, Gunder, 179–80
French Colonial Africa, 145, 146–7, 148–9, 151, 153, 154–6, 157, 159, 160–3, 164, 165, 166–8
frontiers: African hunting, 17; farming, 90; Kikuyu frontier, 85, 342; Swahili trading, 21, 22; settlers, 47
Furedi, Frank, 297–8, 302

Ganda, 67
Gatu, Domenic, 428, 436
'Gatundu affray', 444
gender (*see also* circumcision), and ethnicity, 213, 329, 340; and labour, 359; and land, 359; and Mau Mau, 456, 457; and morality, 316–7; and Nairobi; sexual morality and, 316–7, 325, 386, 414; relations, 6, 340, 386–7, 390–91, 457
Gem, 52, 55
generation sets *riika*, *iregi*, among Kikuyu, 326–7, 336; succession, handover (*ituika*, *ndamathia*), 344–6, 475 n.131; 360, 364, 367, 370–1, 373–6; generational conflict, 56; over labour; Mau Mau as *ituika*, 450–1
German East Africa, *see* Tanzania
Getutu, 64
Ghai, Y.P., 83
Ghana (Gold Coast), 146–7, 170 n.24, 427
Gikonyo, Muchohi, 436
Giriama, 94
Girouard, Sir Percy (governor 1909–12), 88, 156
Grant, Nellie, 460
Griffiths, James (Sec. of State for the Colonies), 251
Grigg, Sir Edward (governor 1925–30), 112
Grogan, Ewart, 106
guns, firepower, 57

Gurr, Ted, 229
Gusii, 20, 32, 48, 49, 50, 51, 53, 58, 60–61, 62, 64, 66

Hailey, Lord, 164
Hardinge, Sir Arthur (consul-general, commissioner 1895–1900), 19, 33
Hay, Margaret Jean, 182
hegemony, 205–6
Heussler, Robert, 152, 159, 233, 237
historical analysis, 7
historical methodology, 2–3
historiography, 315; Africa generally, 204–212; colonial Kenya, 82–4; of Kikuyu ethnography, 320; of Mau Mau, *see* Mau Mau; projective and retrospective
Hobley, Charles (Uganda and E.A. administration 1894–1921), 26, 30, 53, 54, 56, 57, 65, 67, 71
Hodgkin, Thomas, 277, 281
Hooper, Cyril, 454
Hooper, Canon Handley, 454
Hountondji, Paulin, 210
Hyden, Goran, 27

ideology: of colonial states ('civilising mission'), 95, 235, 238–9, 323, 354; dynastic theory among Kikuyu, 428, 459; of Christianity, 274, 414–6; 'free things'; landlord theory: *see* dynastic theory; of Kikuyu, 315–6, 334, 353–5, 361–3, 410, 438–42; of Mau Mau; of multiracialism, 272–3, 283, 424; of nationalism, 275–6; of settlers, 354; of dominationaccumulation, 80; segregationist, 95
Igbo (Nigeria), 277
Imperial British East African Company (IBEAC), 16, 18, 22, 53, 85
imperialism, 322–6
Indians (Asians), settlement, 34; traders, 37, 38, 64; troops, use of, 17, 30, 34, 71, 87, 88
'indirect rule', myth and reality, 160–1
initiation, (*see also* circumcision), 388–9
Islam, 22; Muslims (Kikuyu), 53, 390
ituika, *see*, generation succession
ivory hunting, 51, 58, 78; trading: 21, 22, 26, 66, 85

Jackson, Frederick (IBEACO 1889–94; Uganda and E.A. administration 1894–1911), 69
jiggers (sandfleas), 23, 25, 381
Johnston, Sir Harry, 66, 68

Kabetu wa Waweru, 14
Kabras, 56, 70
'Kaffir farming' *see* squatters
Kaggia, Bildad, 333, 430, 436, 451, 462
Kagumba, Muhoya, 434
Kahinga Wachanga, 458
Kahuhia (Murang'a), 388, 393, 395
Kakamega, 70
Kakelelelwa, 56, 62, 67
Kakungulu, 69
Kalenjin-speaking peoples, 20, 23, 29–30, 51, 52, 66

Index

Index

Index